PHYSICAL SIGNS

OF CHILD ABUSE

—A COLOUR ATLAS—

PHYSICAL SIGNS

OF CHILD ABUSE

—A COLOUR ATLAS—

CHRISTOPHER J HOBBS, BSC, MBBS, FRCP, DOBST RCOG

CONSULTANT COMMUNITY PAEDIATRICIAN

ST JAMES' UNIVERSITY HOSPITAL, LEEDS

SENIOR CLINICAL LECTURER, LEEDS UNIVERSITY

LEEDS, UK

AND

JANE M WYNNE, MB CHB, FRCP

CONSULTANT COMMUNITY PAEDIATRICIAN

UNITED LEEDS TEACHING HOSPITAL NHS TRUST, LEEDS

SENIOR CLINICAL LECTURER, LEEDS UNIVERSITY

LEEDS, UK

W B SAUNDERS COMPANY LIMITED

LONDON   PHILADELPHIA   TORONTO   SYDNEY   TOKYO

W.B. SAUNDERS COMPANY LTD

24–28 OVAL ROAD
LONDON NW1 7DX, UK

THE CURTIS CENTER
INDEPENDENCE SQUARE WEST
PHILADELPHIA, PA 19106–3399, USA

HARCOURT BRACE & COMPANY
55 HORNER AVENUE
TORONTO, ONTARIO M8Z 4X6, CANADA

HARCOURT BRACE & COMPANY, AUSTRALIA
30–52 SMIDMORE STREET
MARRICKVILLE, NSW 2204, AUSTRALIA

HARCOURT BRACE & COMPANY, JAPAN
ICHIBANCHO CENTRAL BUILDING, 22–1 ICHIBANCHO
CHIYODA-KU, TOKYO 102, JAPAN

BRITISH LIBRARY CATALOGUING IN PUBLICATION
DATA IS AVAILABLE

ISBN 0–7020–1778–7

THIS BOOK IS PRINTED ON ACID-FREE PAPER

DESIGNED BY DESIGN/SECTION, FROME, SOMERSET
TYPESET BY KEYSTROKE, JACARANDA LODGE, WOLVERHAMPTON
PRINTED IN GREAT BRITAIN BY BUTLER & TANNER LTD, FROME, SOMERSET, UK

Contents

Preface

This book provides a detailed account of the common physical signs seen in abused children. It is based on the authors' many years of working with abused children. The cases illustrated represent a unique way of recording some of that accumulated experience. In recent years, child abuse has become increasingly recognized as a major source of morbidity and mortality for children in countries of both the developed and developing world. A wealth of published material from a range of disciplines which care for children and families has described the theory and practice of child protection including prevention, investigation, management and treatment.

It is often said that one photograph can say as much as a thousand words. This is never more true than in those distressing and hidden areas of human experience where the reality may be worse than one can bare to imagine. People may be moved to express their care and concern for starving children in Africa when able to witness them through television coverage. So it is our hope that this atlas may enable a better understanding of the suffering of children in our society and thereby motivate people to increase efforts on their behalf. Whilst written primarily for professionals working in child protection, it is hoped that others concerned for children who are abused and neglected will also read it.

As an atlas it focuses on the visible clinical findings of abuse and unlike other publications covers all the major forms of abuse and neglect in a single volume.

For professionals to intervene confidently, they must be able to recognize the common physical signs including injuries, signs of neglect, emotional abuse and sexual abuse.

Each of the colour photographs is provided with a caption. In many cases this provides a brief thumbnail sketch of the history, a background and a description of the findings. The book is divided into four sections, techniques of examination and photography of children; and three broad areas of clinical importance: physical abuse, neglect and emotional abuse, and sexual abuse. The illustrations include: findings linked to abuse, normal findings, and findings due to other conditions which can be confused with abuse. The latter are of obvious

importance as incorrect diagnosis in this area of practice can have serious consequences for all concerned.

This book is useful as a reference and by nature of the accompanying text can also be read and studied alone. It can provide a useful addition to distance learning material as in the increasing numbers of child protection training packages now available.

The sections on physical abuse, and neglect and emotional abuse are of direct relevance and importance to all professionals who see children, including doctors, social workers, nurses and health visitors, police officers, nursery nurses and school teachers. The section on sexual abuse whilst principally addressed to doctors who examine children, contains material of which other professionals should be aware. As all the material in this book may help to clarify evidence in legal proceedings, solicitors, barristers and judges involved in childcare work will undoubtedly find it useful.

For the doctor, either in primary care, paediatrics, orthopaedics, plastic surgery, accident or emergency medicine, paediatric surgery, or other speciality that sees children, this book will be an invaluable resource when faced, for example, with a worrying injury or other unusual finding in a child. Departments such as these as well as the children's wards in hospitals will find a copy to hand useful.

Given the intensely emotional impact and distressing nature of the material in this book, its preparation was of necessity spread over many months and we are grateful to the publishers for their patience and understanding. David Atkins of W B Saunders in particular has been a great help with this project. The origins of this book lie in the discipline of our early mentor Dr Michael Buchanan who encouraged us to photograph all our cases, a practice which has continued. We would like to acknowledge those colleagues who have been generous in providing material and especially the doctors who work closely in the child protection teams in Leeds who are carrying on the tradition of photographing their cases. We are also very grateful to Mrs Judith Scott who typed the text and undid our many muddles.

Chapter 1

Methods of examination

The medical examination of the child who may have been abused

The paediatrician's role in the evaluation of abuse extends beyond the physical examination, and has been described in detail elsewhere (Hobbs et al., 1993; Hobbs and Wynne, 1993). The medical examination is part of a wider assessment which includes a social services and often a police investigation. It is important that the physical examination is seen in the context of this wider assessment and given appropriate weight. Certain injuries or conditions are almost always caused by abuse but the signs may be non-specific and interpretation is difficult.

Bamford and Roberts (1989) have suggested five main reasons why a child thought to have been sexually abused should be examined:
- to detect any traumatic or infective disorders which need treatment;
- to evaluate the nature of any abuse;
- to provide forensic evidence which may be helpful to the future protection of children;
- to reassure the child;
- to begin the process of recovery.

These reasons are relevant for the assessment of any child who may have been abused.

The timing of the medical examination depends entirely on the circumstances, and it should be remembered that healing takes place following genital and anal injury as following any other injury and undue delay may render the examination less informative.

Although forensically it would be very helpful if it were possible to accurately age injuries, this is not possible clinically, although there are some guidelines (Hobbs et al., 1993; Hobbs and Wynne, 1993; Royal College of Physicans, 1991).

Method of examination

Children should be examined by paediatricians in child-friendly accommodation. The examination includes a full physical examination and the examiner should describe the method used, for example when examining the anus 'left lateral for 30 seconds' or 'supine, labial separation'.

The child should be weighed and measured and these measurements plotted on a standard growth chart.

Description of the child and his injuries

- Physical state – describe hair, skin, nails, cleanliness, nutrition (height, weight, mid-upper arm circumference), head circumference.
- Describe the child's demeanour, behaviour during examination.
- State of clothing (if relevant).
- Physical examination, including teeth, eyes etc.
- Superficial injuries such as bruises, abrasions, scratches, bites, ligature marks – site, size, shape, colour, and where possible a view as to likely causation, e.g. a hand-slap.
- Burns and scalds – site, shape, thickness, healing and an assessment if possible based on the characteristics, e.g. scald or contact (cigarette, flame, friction).
- Fractures – bone, type of fracture (spiral, metaphyseal), periosteal new bone, signs of healing.
- Female genitalia – bruises, abrasions, reddening, swelling, labial fusion, configuration of hymen (crescentic, annular, notches, bumps, size of opening, tags, vascularity, scarring), posterior fourchette (abrasions, scars, friability), discharge, vesicles, warts.
- Male genitalia – bruises, abrasions, lacerations, burns, warts, discharge, etc.
- Anus and perianal region – bruises, abrasions, reddening, swelling, lacerations, burns, warts, vesicles, discharge, distended veins, reflex anal dilation, anal laxity, fissures, verge haematoma, visible rectal mucosa and stool.

Interpretation of the physical signs

Neglect

Neglected children may be inappropriately clad, in thin, torn, dirty clothes. They may be dirty and unkempt (note pallor, hair, nails, feet, infected skin, nappy rash) and smelly, i.e. their physical care is unacceptable. Developmental assessment may show global delay in the most severe cases or delay in the acquisition of language and social skills, these being skills which require adult attention in order for the child to learn.

Demeanour

Many children are understandably anxious about the examination but with reassurance are able to cooperate. Others are very passive or have a change in attitude when their genitalia are examined, e.g. become very fearful – both these behaviours are more common in sexually abused children.

Children, while playing in the clinic room, may show signs of emotional deprivation, e.g. are avoidant, socially unresponsive, overactive, indiscriminately friendly, aggressive or destructive.

Children who do not refer back to their carer but prefer to climb on the doctor's knee show emotionally deprived behaviour. Children who run out of the clinic, climb on the desk, kiss the doctor or who enjoy the attention of the examination demonstrate inappropriate behaviours.

Observation of the young child's play will allow an assessment of attention span and distractibility as well as demonstrating whether he has imaginative play and the development of internal language.

Growth

Standard methods are use to weigh and measure and the values plotted on growth charts. Single measurements are of less value than serial ones but show if the child is underweight for height, or has matched weight for height etc., but cannot inform as to growth pattern.

Patterns of growth (Hobbs et al., 1993)

- Falling centiles – the classic feature of failure to thrive shown when a child having grown along the 50th centile drops down to the 25th, 10th, or 3rd centile for example.
- Parallel poor centiles – many children who fail to thrive appear to go through a situation when their centile position falls and they then take a position of continuing to grow, sometimes rather erratically but overall parallel to the 3rd centile for both weight and height, with the height on a centile just above the weight.
- Height and weight markedly discrepant.
- Family pattern discrepant.
- Retrospective rise – seen by improvement in the child's centile position, i.e. catch-up growth after a period of poor growth.
- Saw-tooth pattern – refers to a pattern where the weight goes up and down, crossing and re-crossing centile positions, perhaps reflecting fluctuating standards of care.

Mid upper arm circumference (MUAC)

This measurement is useful in the assessment of nutrition. It may be used serially in the assessment or to help recognize small, well-nourished children from small children with poor nutrition.

An increase of 0.5–1.0 cm in MUAC as measured by the same examiner usually correlates with significant improvement in the child's nutritional state.

MUAC measurements from 12 to 60 months	
MUAC < 14 cm	Very likely to be significantly malnourished and needs full assessment
MUAC 14–15 cm	May be malnourished, especially if 48–60 months. Monitor growth
MUAC > 15 cm	Nutrition reasonable (NB at 72 months > 16 cm)

Physical injury

Bruises

Bruises are seen in 90% of abused children. Bruising occurs when blood vessels are damaged and blood seeps into the skin and subcutaneous tissues. Trauma is the cause of bleeding except in the case of severe bleeding disorder.

Patterns of inflicted bruises may be recognized:
- hand marks;
- marks of implements, e.g. strap, stick, buckle, flex;
- bruises from pushing, throwing, swinging against a hard object;
  - bites;
  - bizarre marks;
  - kicks.

Age of bruises (approximately)

Age	Colour
0–48 hours	Swollen, tender, red/purple
2–3 days	Purple/yellow
4–7 days	Yellow/brown
> 7 days	Brown/fading

Differential diagnosis of bruising:
- accidents;
- paint, ink;
- Mongolian blue spot;
- bleeding disorder (idiopathic thrombocytopenic purpura, haemophilia etc);
- capillary haemangioma;
- rarities, e.g. leukaemia.

Burns and scalds

Interpretation of thermal injury may be difficult, especially if presentation is delayed.

Patterns of injury:
- dip scald or forced immersion injury;
- splashed, thrown or pour scald injury;
- food burns;
- contact burns;
- cigarette burns;
- flame, caustic, radiant and electrical burns.

Differential diagnosis of burns:
- impetigo
- severe eczema or nappy rash;
- contact dermatitis;
- 'deprivation hands and feet' (acrocyanosis);
- cellulitis.

Characteristics of various types of thermal injury

Scald	Variable thickness between and within different lesions, tend to be deepest in centre. Dip, splash and pour patterns. Smooth edges. Peel and slough. Blisters. Moist lesions.
Contact burn	Shape conforms to object. Sharply delineated margins. Square and straight edges. Depth varies, usually uniform. Dry and scabbing.
Cigarette	Circular 0.5–1.0 cm. In abuse often full thickness, cratered, leaving circular, depressed, paper thin scar. In accident, superficial, eccentric, with tail from brushed contact.
Flame	Tissue charred. Hair singed.
Chemical	Scald like distribution, staining, may be deep with underlying tissue destruction.
Friction	Superficial over body points, nose, shoulder, forehead.

Hobbs et al., 1993.

Fractures

Fractures are caused by trauma, are painful, lead to loss of function in a limb and abusive skull fractures are often associated with head injury (concussion, contusion, subdural haematoma) and retinal haemorrhages. There is frequently swelling at the fracture site but there may be no superficial bruising.

The fractures may be single, multiple, recent or healing and certain fractures are unusual following ordinary accidents (rib, scapular, sternum, wide, complex skull fractures and multiple fractures)

There are also limb bone fractures which should always be investigated carefully as possible abusive fractures. These are:

- spiral/oblique or metaphyseal fractures of humerus;
- fractures of the shaft or metaphyseal fractures of femur (especially < 2 years).
- fractures of the shaft or metaphyseal fractures of tibia.

Radiographic changes in fracture healing

Sign	Time	Comments
Soft tissue haemorrhage and oedema	Immediate	
Resolution of soft tissue changes	2–21 days	Earlier in absence of bony injury, later severe fracture
Periosteal new bone formation	5–14 days	Earlier younger child, absent metaphyseal
Loss of definition of fracture line	10–21 days	
Obliteration of fracture line	10–21 days	
Consolidation and remodelling of callus	3–12 weeks	Earliest in the youngest, later in the older child
Remodelling of bone with reconstitution of the medullary cavity	3 months–2 years	Depends on the initial deformity and volume of callus formed

Chapman, 1993

Differential diagnosis of fractures:
- accident;
- abuse;
- birth injury;
- osteogenesis imperfecta;
- osteomyelitis;
- rickets;
- copper deficiency.

Intracranial injury

Injury to the brain is the commonest cause of death in child abuse, and the majority of deaths occur in the first year of life. Brain injury is very uncommon after minor falls and even falls down stairs are unlikely to result in skull fracture or cerebral contusion. The mechanism of abusive intracranial injury is usually shaking and an impact, i.e. the shaken impact syndrome. There may be an associated skull fracture.

Patterns of injury:
- scalp injury;
- skull fracture (wide, complex);
- subdural haematoma;
- retinal haemorrhages;
- cerebral contusion, oedema and haemorrhage.

Differential diagnosis (at presentation):
- accident;
- spontaneous intracerebral bleed, e.g. from an arterio-venous malformation or aneurysm;
- encephalitis;
- meningitis;
- 'near-miss cot death';
- toxic state;
- metabolic disorder.

Abdominal injury

Abdominal injury is usually seen in the context of other serious abuse and the injury may be recognized only as the child's condition deteriorates, with potentially serious consequences. On other occasions the child presents with an 'acute abdomen' and the diagnosis of a traumatic lesion is made during investigation of the disorder or at laporotomy. The injury is caused by a punch or a kick (compression) or a crushing injury or shaking.

Patterns of injury:
- perforation of gut – stomach, duodenum, duodenal-jejunal flexure;
- haemorrhage;
- laceration, contusion, haematoma – liver, duodenum, pancreas.

Sexual abuse

The signs seen in association with sexual abuse are

due to trauma, and any co-existing infection. Healing may be very rapid and signs will depend on the time since the last assault, the type of assault (rubbing, penetration etc.), the age of the child, the number of previous assaults and over what time scale. Use of lubricant may minimize injury, and use of finger, penis or implement cause differing signs (not necessarily distinguishable clinically).

Site	Lesion	Description	Cause
Labia majora	Erythema	Reddening of skin	Inflammatory response to trauma, infection, skin disorder
	Bruising	Red/purple/yellow	Trauma
	Vesicles	Vesicles	HSV-1 HSV-2
	Warts	Warts	Chickenpox
			Anogenital warts ? type
Vulvovaginitis	Erythema	Swelling, reddening, discharge	Non-specific – common in
	Oedema		child sexual abuse, STD
Labia minora, perihymenal area	Erythema	Reddening	Inflammatory response to
	Bruising	Red/purple	irritation, e.g. soap, infection,
	Oedema	Swelling	trauma
			Lichen sclerosis
	Abrasion/laceration	Loss of superficial layer mucous membrane	Trauma
	Labial adhesion	Agglutination of labia at posterior fourchette	Inflammation, e.g. nappy rash, child sexual abuse, infection damages tissues which then adhere
Posterior fourchette	Erythema	As labia minora	
	Oedema		
	Bruising		
	Laceration	Tear often vertical	Trauma
	Friability	Tissues easily bleed	Trauma
	Scarring	Altered vascularity	Trauma
		Thickened white irregular area	Distinguish from mid-line streak
Hymen	Erythema	As labia minora	Infection – swelling erythema
	Oedema		
	Abrasion		Trauma
	Bruising		Lichen sclerosis
	Dilated opening	Attenuation (loss of tissue)	Penetrating trauma
		Wider than normal	Stretched
	Deficit	Discontinuity in margin	Healed penetrative tear
	Tear	If recent bleeding	Penetrating trauma
		Incomplete or complete transection	

Site	Lesion	Description	Cause
Hymen	Bump	In margin of hymen	Healed tear, NB vaginal ridge*
	Shape of hymen	Posterior rim or crescentic	Normal variant
		Annular	Normal variant
		Septate	Normal variant
		Imperforate	Normal variant, rare
		Attenuated	As above
		Asymmetric	? due to earlier tear, e.g. 'V' shape
		Obliterated	Due to previous trauma
	Scar	White irregular thickened area	Trauma, rare
	Remnants	Incomplete hymen	Trauma with disruption of hymen
Vagina	Bruising/abrasion	Areas of reddening, loss of superficial mucous membrane	Penetrative trauma
	Dilated	Accommodates one or more digits†	Repeated penetration causes widening and dilatation with loss of rugae
	Loss of rugae	Flattening of rugae	
	Tear	Extending through hymen to posterior vaginal wall	Severe trauma, e.g. rape
	Scar	Posterior wall scar	May scar
Urethra	Erythema	Reddened swollen	Infection
	Oedema	periurethral tissues	Rubbing
	Bruising	Pouting or gaping urethra	Penetration
	Dilatation		
Perianally	Venous congestion	Purple discoloration, varies from discrete swelling to flat halo In arc ring single	Seen in association with anal abuse. NB examination technique 30 s left lateral
Configuration of anus	Funnelled	Deeply set fixed funnel shape	Seen in long-standing abuse in older children
	Shortening or eversion of canal	Anorectal junction with characteristic star-shaped folds approximated to anal orifice	Seen in 1–3 years in association with lax anal tone
External sphincter	Laxity	On parting buttocks anus gapes	Anus normally shut on inspection, sphincter may relax in 10–20 s
	Gaping	A widely gaping anus up to 2 cm may be seen soon after abuse	Within hours of abuse
	Twitchy	External sphincter contracts/relaxes every 2–5 s	Manipulation of anus, suppositories, digital penetration

Site	Lesion	Description	Cause
External and internal sphincter	'Reflex' anal dilatation	When buttocks parted both sphincters relax and central hole allows view to rectum 0.5–2.0 cm AP and vertically May open and shut Faeces may be visible	Passage of wind or stool Previous ano/rectal manipulation, enemas, instrumentation Inflammatory bowel disease Repeated anal penetration
Perianal skin	Erythema	Reddening	Inflammatory response to trauma Infection
	Thickened Pigmented Loss of folds	Thicker darkened skin

Thickening of folds Often pink shiny skin and loss of fold pattern | Non-specific response to trauma

Skin disorder with scratching, rubbing over long period |
	Scars	Fan-shaped linear heaped up skin, distorted folds	Uncommon, may result from fissures of any cause‡
	Warts Vesicles Thread-worm	Warts Vesicles Cotton-like associated with reddening itch, excoriation	As before
Anal margin	Oedema Bruising Haematoma Skin tag	'Tyre sign' Red/purple/yellow Discrete red swelling Mound of skin	Recent trauma Severe trauma Severe trauma Deep fissures may heal and leave tag May be congenital
	Fissure	Break in lining of anal canal extends from canal to anal verge/open lesion narrow wide/ superficial deep/acute chronic/ 1 or more	Due to stretching of anal margin as in severe constipation, anal abuse, Crohn's disease etc.
	Anal verge deficit	Indentation covered in skin	Is this an old injury/normal variant?

* A bump in the hymenal margin may be due to a vaginal ridge opposing the hymen posteriorly.

† Measurement of the hymenal margin in prepubertal girls is usually by use of a tape measure at the introitus. The dimensions increase with age but also with method of examination (labial separation/traction, knee–chest) and relaxation of the child. The dimensions of the hymenal opening are not apparent on inspection alone at puberty and beyond, as the effects of oestrogen are apparent and the hymen has redundant folds.

‡ Smooth wedge-like areas perianally at 6 and 12 o'clock are normal variants – scars are thicker and irregular.

Interpretation of the physical signs associated with sexual abuse

As in other forms of abuse there are certain patterns of injury and the examination is seen in the context of the history and other investigations. The physical findings may be consistent with abuse and are sometimes proof of abuse but this is uncommon. There may be no abnormality even if it is clear that abuse has occurred; this may be due to the type of abuse (fondling, oral sex) or healing may have occurred.

Sexually transmitted diseases (Royal College of Physicians, 1991) are sexually transmitted in children too but some infections, e.g. ano-genital warts, may be vertically transmitted. Gonorrhoea and trichomoniasis are infections highly correlated with abuse as are chlamydial infections but care must be taken with the microbiological investigations. Herpes and ano-genital warts are of concern and the question of sexual abuse must be discussed (American Academy of Pediatrics, 1991).

Forensic samples may establish the presence of semen, saliva and other body fluids on the child, his clothing or furniture (Royal College of Physicians, 1991).

The guidelines of the American Academy of Pediatrics (1991) and the Royal College of Physicians report (1991) list signs which are consistent with abuse.

An abbreviated list includes:
- the child's demeanour during the examination;
- any physical trauma but especially of the mouth, breasts, genitalia, perianal region, buttocks and anus;
- chafing, bruising or abrasions of inner thighs and genitalia;
- scarring, tears (when healed seen as notches, bumps, thickening), distortion of the hymen;
- decreased amount of hymenal tissue (attenuation, remnants);
- lacerations in hymen which may extend to the posterior vaginal wall;
- enlargement of hymenal opening;
- injury or scarring to posterior fourchette;
- bruising, skin changes perianally;
- dilated perianal veins;
- anal fissures;
- anal laxity;
- reflex anal dilatation;
- sexually transmitted disease;
- positive forensic tests.

References

American Academy of Pediatrics (Committee on Child Abuse and Neglect (1991) Guidelines for the evaluation of sexual abuse children. *Pediatrics* **87(2)**, 254–259.

Bamford F. and Roberts R. (1989) Child sexual abuse. In *ABC of Child Abuse* (Edited by R. Meadow). British Medical Journal, London.

Chapman S. (1993) Recent advances in the radiology of child abuse. In *Child Abuse (Clinical Paediatrics)* (Edited by C.J. Hobbs and J.M. Wynne). Baillière Tindall, London.

Hobbs C.J. and Wynne J.M. (1993) The evaluation of child sexual abuse. In *Child Abuse (Clinical Paediatrics)* (Edited by C.J. Hobbs and J.M. Wynne). Baillière Tindall, London.

Hobbs C.J., Hanks H.G.I. and Wynne J.M. (1993) *Child Abuse and Neglect: A Clinician's Handbook.* Churchill Livingstone, Edinburgh.

Royal College of Physicians (1991) *Physical Signs of Sexual Abuse in Childhood.* Royal College of Physicians, London.

Chapter 2

Photography in child abuse

Photography has an important role in the recognition, assessment and management of child abuse. Its proven use as a means to record crucial clinical findings provides the basis for this atlas.

The photograph is often the best means of recording visual aspects of the clinical situation and is particularly useful for the static signs which are observed in child abuse and neglect.

The video camera comes into its own in recording verbal and non-verbal information contained in interviews. Information relating to interactions and the patterns of relationships between children and adults can also be recorded and analysed.

The main functions of photography in child abuse are:

■ to document findings, particularly visible injuries;
■ to provide information for discussion with colleagues, courts, other professionals and those with responsibility for the child including parents;
■ for teaching and research purposes.

Photography may be used to record:

■ injuries, e.g. bruises, burns;
■ genital and anal signs (usually injury or infection);
■ aspects of growth and development;
■ the overall appearance, including demeanour, emotional signs and features associated with neglect.

The American Medical Association's diagnostic and treatment guidelines for the abused child recommend that all visible lesions should be photographed.

In practice it is helpful if the doctor masters basic photographic techniques particularly for those situations or occasions when professional medical photographic help is not available. The photographs in this atlas have been taken by both professional medical photographers and by physicians. In the case of colposcopic photographs, these have all been taken by the examining doctor.

Legal considerations

It is usual practice for consent to be sought for the taking of medical photographs. Informed consent indicates that it has been explained to the parents and child that the photographs are being taken and may be used for the following purposes:

■ as part of the medical record to provide as accurate a record as possible;
■ the photographs may be used anonymously in teaching;
■ if asked it is our policy to state that as with all medical records, they may be used as evidence in court if required or requested by the court.

If requested by another medical opinion involved in the case, the photographs are made available and may avoid the need for further examination of the child.

Photographs should not be copied without the expressed consent of the doctor who has responsibility for them. Photographs should always be returned on completion of the assessment and should not be used or borrowed without permission.

The court may require that the doctor confirms that the photographs are those of a particular child and by whom and when they were taken.

The photographs should be of a good technical standard and free of technical error. Prints are often presented in the form of a bound booklet available to each party in the case, and are used particularly in prosecution (criminal cases). An alternative method of presenting photographic information is to project slides in the courtroom for all relevant parties to see. This gives the advantage that the doctor can point out all the relevant findings and relate them to the medical report. If these slides have been shown to other medical experts in the case they will have had the opportunity to comment in advance.

Photographic technique

Taking adequate photographs requires:
- equipment – camera including lens;
- light source;
- film;
- basic knowledge of photographic composition;
- patience;
- professional laboratory services.

Equipment

Camera

All sorts of cameras will give a result in photographing abused children although quality will vary. These include 'point and shoot', instant or self-developing and 35 mm single lens reflex (SLR) cameras. The main requirements are:
- close up facility;
- sufficient resolution to appreciate detail;
- accurate colour rendition.

All the photographs in this atlas have been taken with 35 mm SLR cameras either attached directly to the colposcope or with an interchangeable lens attached. The principal advantage of the SLR, apart from the flexibility of the systems that have been developed around these cameras, is that the photographer is able to see precisely what is being photographed in the viewfinder. SLR cameras can be technically demanding in terms of adjustments and settings that need to be made but many of the newer generation of camera have a number of automatic facilities which virtually make them 'point and shoot' in operation. Many of the photographs in this atlas have been taken by examining doctors with a programmed SLR camera that also winds on the film after each exposure. Speed and lens aperture are automatically set and flash discharge fully controlled by electronic metering. All the photographer has to do is to point the camera, focus and shoot.

Lenses

The most useful lens for use with an SLR in this situation is a medium telephoto lens with close–up facility. This is also known as a macro lens and enables detailed photographs of small lesions such as burns or small bruises to be taken. The 105 mm focal length is ideal in many respects and a typical image size on the negative might be 50% of that in real life, or expressed in another way, a ratio of 1:2. This lens also gives a greater working distance and less distortion. It is possible to record genital and anal findings satisfactorily with this lens although the colposcope offers better magnification.

Light source

Whilst studio lighting provides the ideal set up, it is often more convenient for the child to be photographed in the ward or consulting room. Good lighting is essential for good photography and influences significantly the quality of the results. The most practical alternative to studio lighting is the electronic flash which may be camera mounted or hand held. Ring flash is ideal for close ups and for shadowless lighting in hollows, e.g. vaginal introitus. The colposcope has integral lighting and flash is not required.

Points when using flash:
- remove other bright light sources, e.g. theatre light, sunlight;
- ensure batteries are always in good condition – run down batteries give slow flash recycling times and bored children.

Film

The standard film used is the 35 mm colour slide film, also known as colour transparency or colour reversal film. Medium speed films are most useful (in this atlas ISO 100 is standard). Prints can be obtained from slide film if necessary. Slide copies can be made but with some reduction in quality and colour accuracy. Films should be stored in a refrigerator. Tungsten balanced film may be used for the colposcope. In this atlas a film rated at ISO 160T is used.

The colposcope

This is an instrument designed for examination of the cervix uteri. It is increasingly used for genital and anal examination in suspected child sexual abuse.

The instrument provides:
- a bright and variable cold light source;
- binocular magnification;
- integral photographic facility, with self-developing, 35 mm SLR or miniaturized video cameras available.

Advantages include:
- comfortable for child and examiner;
- good visualization of structures;
- non-intrusive photography;
- direct measurements, e.g. hymenal opening diameter;
- video facility allows transmission for 'out of room' observation in teaching including videotaped recording for playback.

Disadvantages include:
- expensive;
- relatively non-mobile;
- danger of over-interpretation of minor changes;
- may be seen as essential (examination cannot be done without it).

Photographic technique and composition

It is important that all visible injuries and other relevant findings be photographed for the individual child. The following practical points apply:

- requests to professional photographer must include details of every injury etc.;
- a physician should accompany and assist where possible;
- support is needed for the child as with any other procedure;
- include both close-up and more distant views to locate site of lesion;
- take more than one shot for each view;
- use a neutral and uncluttered background, e.g. green surgical towels;
- incorporation of a measure in the photograph is often recommended – our policy is to measure lesions and record on diagrams to simplify photography where there are multiple lesions;
- a facial view will assist in identification;
- a tested and reliable system for identification is required;
- always keep spare film and batteries with the camera.

Identification and labelling of photographs

For clinical and medico-legal reasons it is vital that photographs are correctly labelled. Minimum information should include full name and date when photograph was taken. There are various methods used singly or in combination which can assist this:

- use one roll of film per child;
- photograph a label or form with the child's name before taking the sequence;
- 'data back' imprint of date or other identifying information;
- record frame counter numbers and match to film;
- photograph a facial view;
- ensure that examining physician cuts and checks films.

Common errors in photography

- Blurred image – child moved or subject out of focus.
- Under- or overexposed – exposure compensation adjustment on camera may be moved accidentally. With fully automatic exposure control in many modern cameras exposure problems are few.
- Unidentifiable lesion – this may be a faint bruise which has been washed out by the electronic flash and skin reflection.
- Parts of the photograph are out of focus – a wide aperture has been used giving little depth of field. Use smaller aperture (higher f number).

References

Hobbs C.J., Hanks H.G.I. and Wynne J. M. (1933) Physical abuse. In *Child Abuse and Neglect: A Clinician's Handbook*, Chapter 4, p. 52. Churchill Livingstone, Edinburgh.

Ricci L.R. (1988) Medical forensic photography of the sexually abused child. *Child Abuse and Neglect*, **12**, 305–310.

Ricci L.R. (1991) Photographing the physically abused child: principles and practice. *Am. J. Dis. Child.*, **145**, 275–281.

SECTION 2

PHYSICAL ABUSE

Chapter 3

Bruises and soft tissue injuries

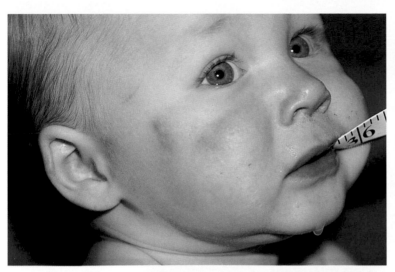

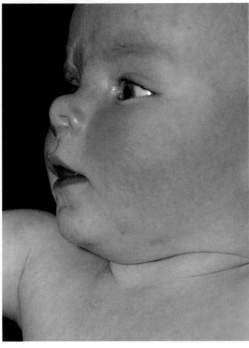

▲ 3.1 Male aged 5 months

Presented as having 'hit himself with a bottle'. Old, paired, irregular shaped bruises on the cheek, consistent with a pinch mark made by an adult, are shown.

▲ 3.2 Female aged 3 months

Presented as having 'rolled over in her cot against the bars'. Different coloured bruises on the cheek and lower jaw can be seen, due to fingertip bruising.

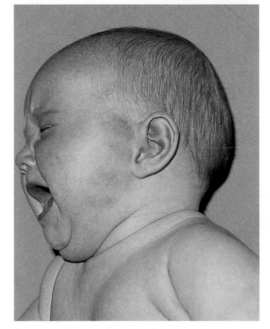

▲ 3.3 Male aged 5 months

His mother admitted to slapping him. Four linear bruises can be seen in front of and extending across the ear and cheek, consistent with an adult hand slap.

▶ 3.4 Male aged 9 months

He was supposed to have 'fallen off the settee'. Recent extensive bruising to the forehead, nose and left orbit is evident. This was caused by multiple adult hand slaps, with fingertips discernible on the left forehead.

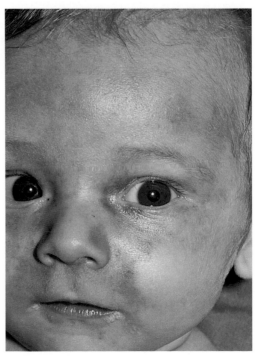

His father claimed to have tripped and fallen against a door jamb whilst holding him. Swelling of the orbit with bruising below the eye and a short abrasion can be seen. This was caused by being hit in the face with a clenched fist; the scratch is possibly due to a ring.

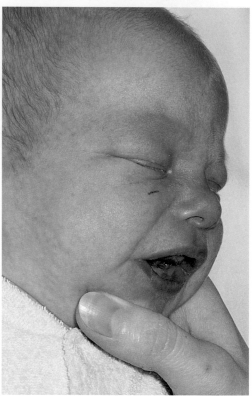

▶ 3.5 Female aged 8 months
She was claimed to have been 'choking on feeds'. Recent extensive bruising to the left side of the face is seen, with a characteristic hand mark seen as linear petechial bruises.

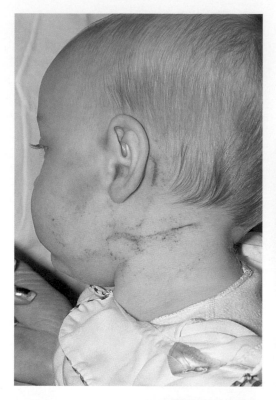

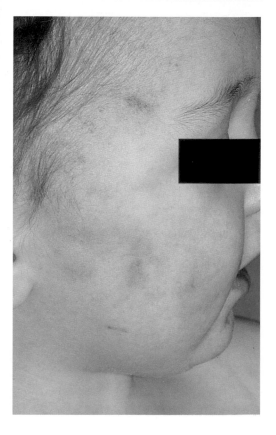

▲ 3.6 Female aged 3 years
She presented as having 'fallen downstairs'. Recent horizontal linear bruises extending across the cheek are consistent with an adult hand slap.

▶ 3.8 Male aged 4 years
No history available. Two generations of bruises can be seen: scattered petechial bruising in rough lines over the temple extending back into the hairline, and patchy old yellowing bruises over the cheek. These were due to two separate assaults. Probably hand marks are also evident.

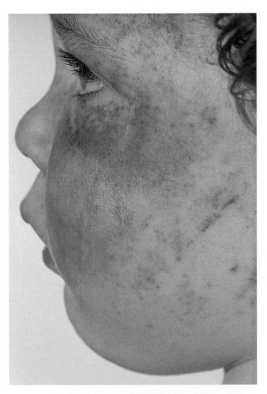

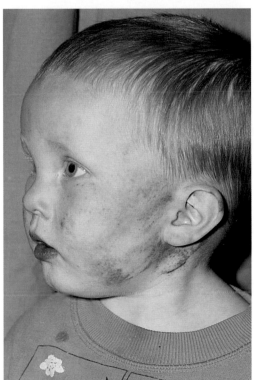

◄ 3.9 Male aged 2 years

He was left in the care of a babysitter. The babysitter, who was known to the social services having murdered her own child, claimed the child fell off the settee onto a carpeted floor. Extensive petechial bruising over the forehead, eyelids and cheek are seen, caused by repeated adult hand slaps.

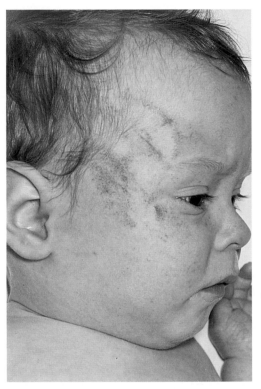

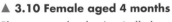

▲ 3.10 Female aged 4 months

She presented as having 'rolled over on toys on the floor'. Four linear red marks with scattered petechiae are seen on the right side of the face, consistent with an adult hand slap. Note also the anxious expression.

▲ 3.11 Male aged 3 years

He was assaulted by his mother's male partner. There is extensive recent diffuse and petechial bruising with swelling across the cheek, ear and behind the ear, caused by an adult hand slap.

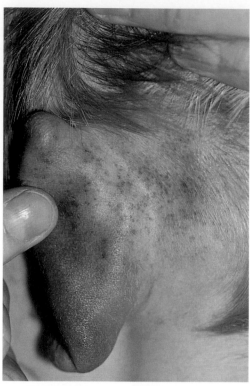
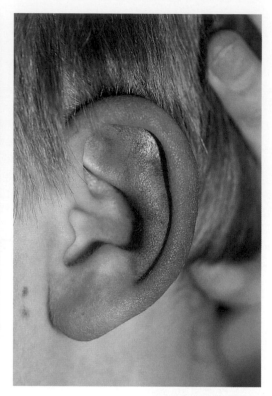

▲ 3.12, ▲ 3.13 Male aged 6 years

His school teacher noticed a 'rash' when the child complained of earache. Multiple petechial bruises of pinna and temporal area of skull are consistent with a hand slap by an adult.

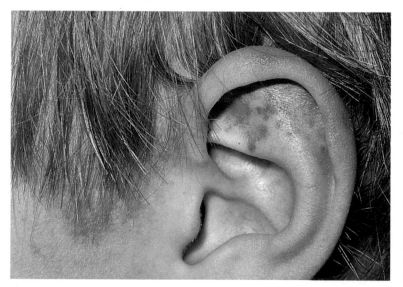

▲ 3.14 Male aged 8 years

He was beaten up by his mother's male partner. In addition to multiple bruises elsewhere, there is bruising of the upper rim and helix of the pinna, caused by a blow to the ear.

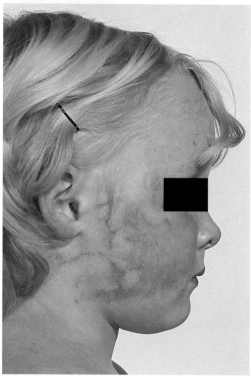

▲ 3.15 Female aged 6 years

Her mother had called the social services and told them that she had hit her daughter to punish her for wandering around the streets. There is extensive recent petechial bruising and swelling, with a prominent vertical and several horizontal lines extending across the cheek. These were caused by a hand slap, the vertical line representing the metacarpo–phalangeal joint.

▶ 3.16 Male aged 8 years

He was claimed to have been 'fighting with his brothers'. There is a swollen ageing bruise on the mid-forehead and recent bruising of both orbits inferiorly, which are unexplained.

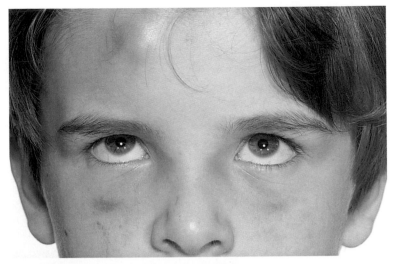

▼ 3.17 Male aged 5 years

He was admitted to hospital because of gastroenteritis, and found to have unexplained scalds in both groins and signs of anal abuse. The photograph shows bruising of the upper rim of the pinna, which is probably a pinch mark.

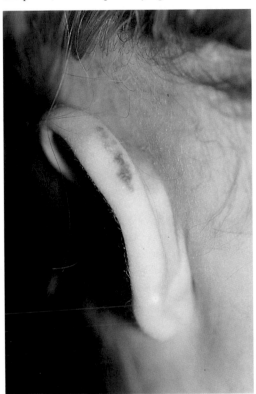

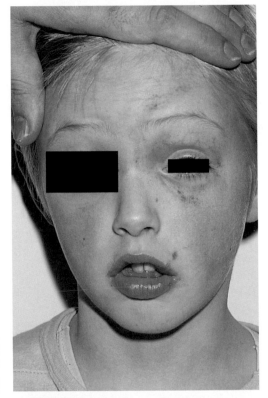

◀ 3.18 Male aged 13 years

He was assaulted by his father. There is petechial bruising above the left orbit and extending below the eye, and a swollen lower lip with a scratch mark. The injuries were caused by fist blows to the eye and mouth.

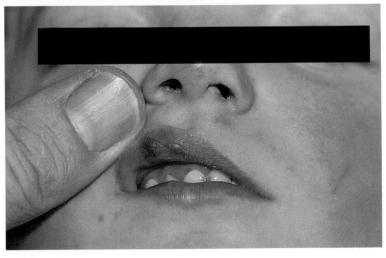

▶ 3.19 Female aged 4 years

She presented as neglected and sexually abused with an unexplained mouth injury. The photograph shows a swollen, bruised, abraided upper lip caused by an unexplained injury, probably a blow to the mouth.

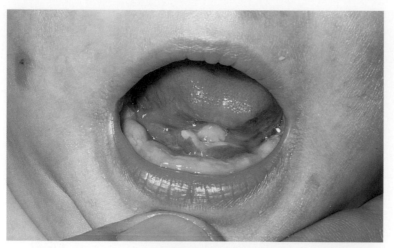

◀ **3.20 Male aged 5 months**
He was described as a miserable baby who would not take feeds properly. Extensive ulceration of the frenulum below the tongue can be seen. This is a healing injury; the mother later admitted to forcing a spoon into the infant's mouth.

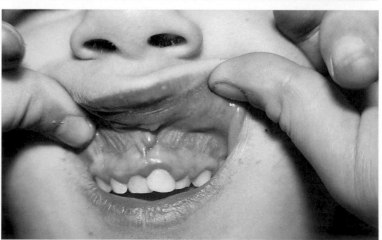

◀ **3.21 Male aged 10 months**
His mother mentioned bleeding from the mouth at a routine follow-up appointment in the neonatal clinic. There is a torn frenulum and swollen upper lip with tooth mark imprints, ulcerating and fresh bleeding. These were due to two mouth injuries, one probably inflicted by a bottle causing the torn frenulum, and the second a blow to the mouth.

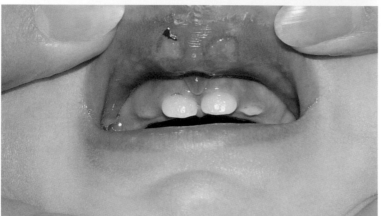

◀ **3.22 Male aged 2 months**
Presented at the hospital emergency department with unexplained bleeding from the mouth. Recent extensive injury to the inner aspect of the upper lip and frenulum is seen with bruising and bleeding. This is a feeding bottle injury.

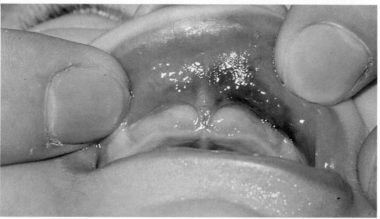

◀ **3.23 Male aged 5 years**
Presented with unexplained bruising (not described). An old, healed tear of the frenulum is seen, and the right central incisor is misaligned. This is an old mouth injury.

▶ **3.24 Male aged 7 months**

He presented with a fractured humerus. The photograph shows a healing tear of the frenulum. This is an old mouth injury, in conjunction with recent further injury.

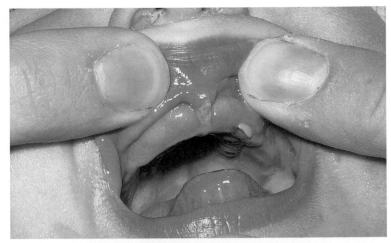

▶ **3.25 Female aged 3 months**

She presented unconscious in the hospital emergency department. A grossly swollen upper lip with recently torn frenulum is seen. There were also other serious injuries. These injuries were caused by a blow to the mouth, and other trauma.

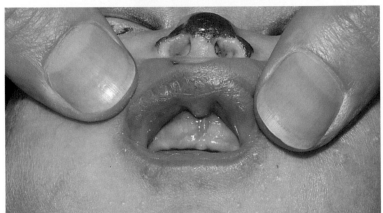

▶ **3.26 Female aged 18 months**

She attended at her doctor's surgery with a history of not using her right arm for 3 days. The photograph shows an old healed complete tear of the frenulum, caused by a blow to the mouth. In addition, failure to thrive and other multiple injuries including supracondylar fracture were seen.

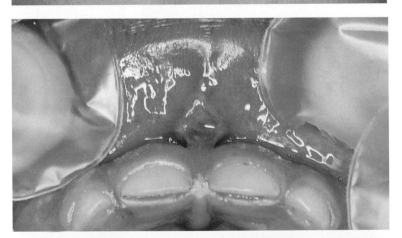

▶ **3.27 Female aged 2 years**

She presented as having 'fallen off a climbing frame in the park'. Recent bruising at the margin of the upper lip and gum, and a recently torn frenulum are seen. These constituted unexplained mouth injuries in a child who had been physically and sexually abused. The child had other multiple injuries (see Figs. 3.28 and 3.29).

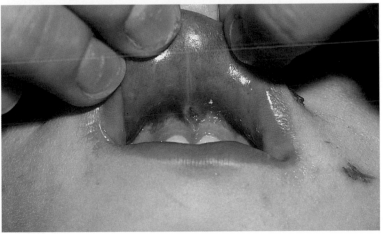

▶ 3.28 Female aged 2 years

The same child as in Fig. 3.27. This photograph shows irregularly shaped superficial lesions of the face showing early healing. They are probably finger scratch marks.

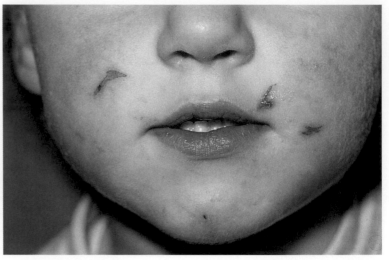

◀ 3.29 Female aged 2 years

The same child as in Figs 3.27 and 3.28. This photograph shows an area of diffuse old bruising with an overlying linear scratch. The injuries are unexplained.

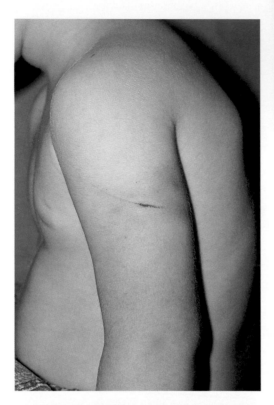

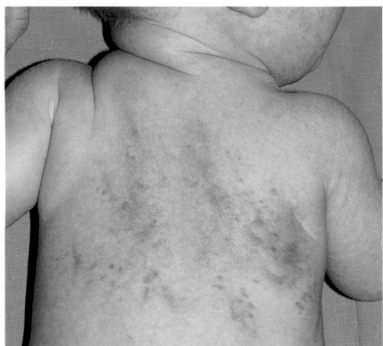

▲ 3.30 Female aged 4 months

Her doctor was called for a night visit because she was crying. Diffuse petechial bruising is seen over the entire upper back, caused by adult hand slaps through clothing.

◀ 3.31 Female aged 4 years

She had a previous 'accidental' laceration of the liver when she fell on a vegetable knife. At paediatric follow-up bruising was found. The photograph shows two circular old brown bruises, which are unexplained, and in an unusual site for accidental bruising. They are probably fingertip bruising.

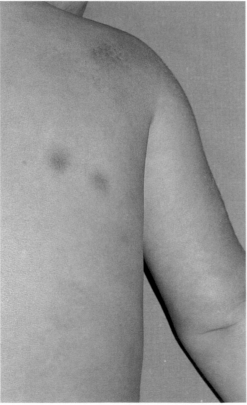

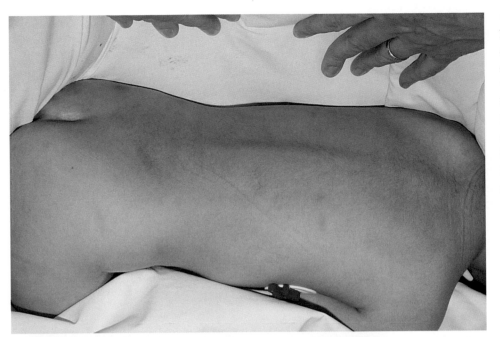

◄ 3.32 Male aged 2 years
Presented in the hospital emergency department with severe head injury, having 'fallen down stairs'. Multiple bruising of different ages can be seen across the back. The diagnosis is fingertip bruising, in association with severe head injury due to kicking, and anal abuse.

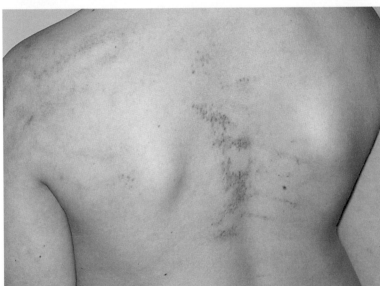

◄ 3.33 Male aged 12 years
He complained at school that his older brother had hit him. Recent extensive bruising over the upper half of the back can be seen, the configuration of bruising suggesting finger marks. This was due to multiple blows from an outstretched hand.

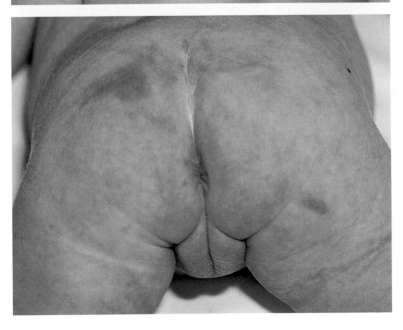

◄ 3.34 Female aged 3 weeks
The midwife noticed bruising at a routine follow-up. Recent, complex bruising of the buttocks can be seen, due to unexplained serious non-accidental injury.

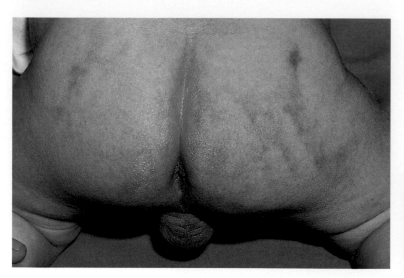

◀ **3.35 Male aged 2 weeks**
He was taken to the clinic by his mother because of his 'crying'. Recent linear bruising of both buttocks can be seen, probably caused by repeated blows from an outstretched hand.

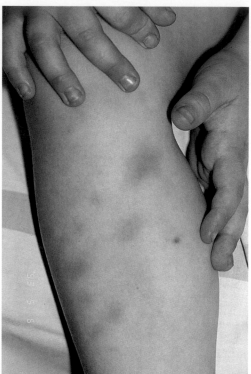

▶ **3.36 Male aged 4 years**
He was referred to the paediatrician by his doctor because of behaviour problems. The photograph shows a cluster of roughly circular bruises of similar age on the inner aspect of the lower leg. These are probably grip marks. The child later disclosed anal abuse.

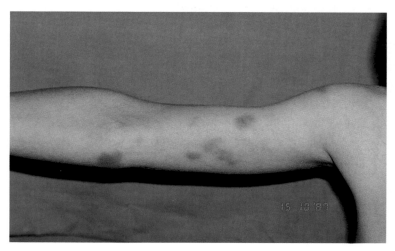

▲ **3.37 Male aged 6 years**
He was seen as a routine after his younger sister presented with neglected burns. Multiple bruising can be seen, of similar age but differing in size, over the shoulder and inner aspect of the upper arm and elbow. These are unexplained bruises in an unusual site, probably grip marks.

▶ **3.38 Male aged 5 years**
He had recently come to the UK from Hong Kong. His mother admitted disciplining her son by kicking him. The photograph shows multiple large irregular bruising, mainly on the outer aspect of the legs, of varying ages, consistent with kick marks.

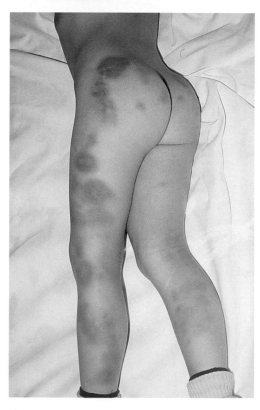

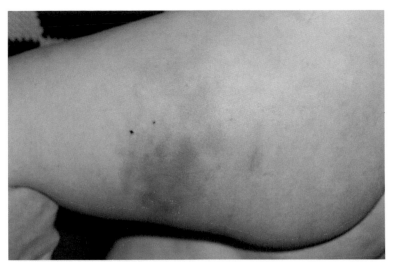

◀ 3.39 Male foster child aged 2 years

When seen to have bruising at his nursery, he said 'Daddy hit me'. There is diffuse complex ageing bruising on the outer aspect of the left upper thigh, consistent with being hit with a hard object, or kicked.

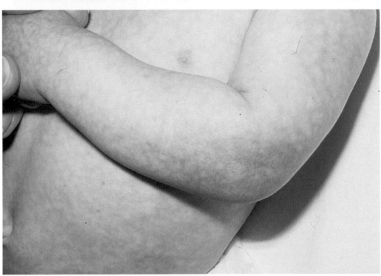

◀ 3.40 Male aged 6 months

He presented with facial bruising and the examining doctor noted a reluctance to move the left arm. A swollen left elbow can be seen, diagnosed as a pulled elbow in association with other non-accidental injury.

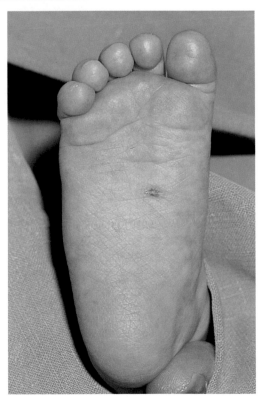

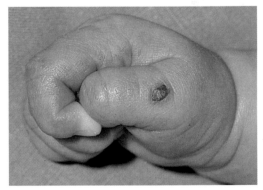

▲ 3.41 Female aged 4 weeks

She was born pre-term. The midwife on a home visit noticed unusual lesions on the hands and feet, 1 day after discharge from the neonatal unit. The photograph shows a superficial abrasion on the outer aspect of the thumb. This is an inflicted nail injury by an adult.

◀ 3.42 Female aged 4 weeks

The same child as in Fig. 3.41. This photograph shows an abrasion to the sole of foot, a nail injury inflicted by an adult.

▶ **3.43 Male aged 14 years**
He was assaulted by his father after he and a friend drank a bottle of his father's whisky. Scattered petechiae and linear marks round neck anteriorly are seen, caused by attempted strangulation with a hand around the neck.

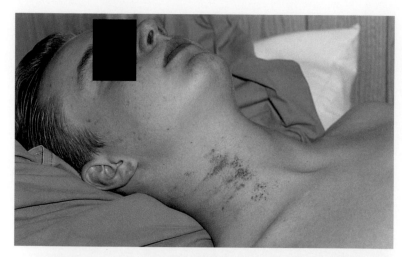

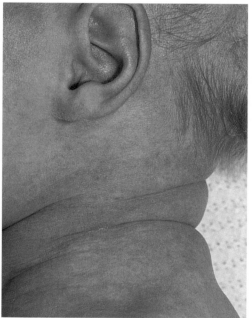

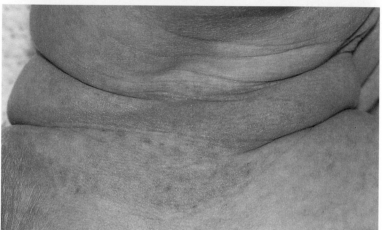

◀ **3.44, ▲ 3.45 Male aged 6 weeks**
His elderly primigravida mother was resident in a mother and babies home for assessment as to her mothering ability. When told the baby would be removed she took him to her room and strangled him. He was resuscitated by care staff. A faint petechial rash is seen around the neck.

▶ **3.46 Male aged 9 months**
It was claimed that he had fallen down uncarpeted stairs, and scratched himself on carpet tacks. The photograph shows parallel scratches over the shoulder and side. These are inflicted scratches, probably caused by a metal dog grooming comb.

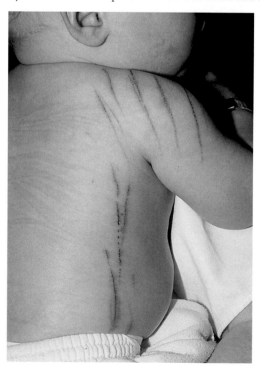

▶ 3.47 Male aged 9 months

The same child as in Fig. 3.46. This photograph shows small puncture marks in the scalp and a linear vertical bruise above the right eye. The marks fitted a carpet gripper rod. The bruise on the forehead is unexplained but consistent with a fall against a hard object.

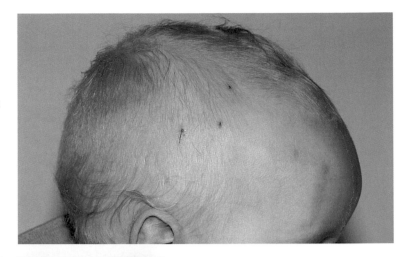

▲ 3.48 Female aged 4 weeks

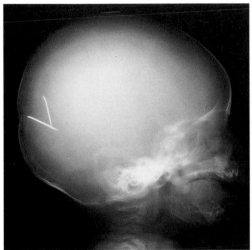

She died suddenly due to pneumonia. A skeletal survey was performed because of abuse in an elder sibling. The lateral skull X-ray shows fragments of three sewing needles, two posteriorly within the skull and one lying subcutaneously over the vertex. The needles were deliberately inserted by an adult. (Photograph supplied by Dr A. Habel.)

▶ 3.50 Male aged 2 years

He presented in the hospital emergency department with a severe head injury. The photograph shows a circular ring bruise with central bruising, and a cluster of adjacent bruising. The ring bruise was shown to fit precisely the shape of the base of a torch; the cluster of bruises is consistent with fingertips, i.e. grip marks.

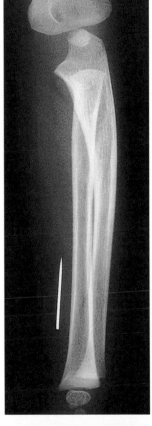

◀ 3.49 Female aged 18 months

A sibling of the child in Fig. 3.48. There was a previous history of failure to thrive and non-accidental injury, and she was examined following the death of her sibling. A needle is seen to be present intramuscularly in the forearm, inserted by an adult. (Photograph supplied by Dr A. Habel.)

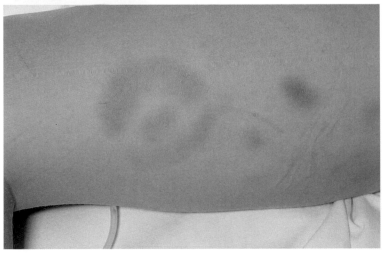

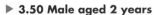

▼ 3.51 Male aged 2 years

He presented to the hospital emergency department with burns to his hands, feet, mouth and trunk and injury to both sides of his face. There are multiple superficial excoriations/lacerations, which extend from the angle of the mouth symmetrically on each side of the face towards the ear, and are at various stages of healing. The injury is consistent with some form of gag.

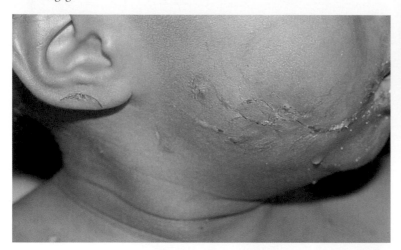

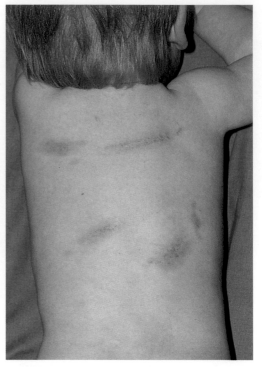

▲ 3.52 Male aged 18 months

Social worker was shown marks on a routine home visit. (The child had suffered previous neglect.) The mother claimed he had been hit with a fire engine by his 6-year-old sibling. There are several linear bruises with a central line of petechiae, horizontal, oblique and vertical, caused by repeated blows from an unidentified object.

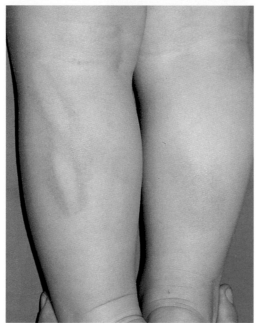

◀ 3.53 Male aged 15 months

He had repeated unexplained marks noticed in day nursery. The parents were both full-time students and complained that the child cried. Two similar shaped parallel red marks can be seen on the back of the lower leg, inflicted by an adult with some implement, it was later found to be a riding crop.

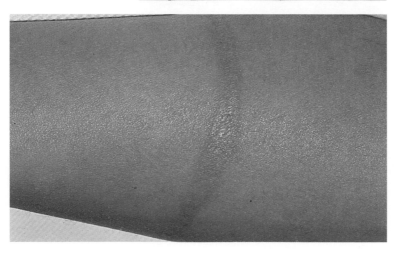

◀ 3.54 Female aged 3 years

She had unexplained marks noted at nursery school. There is a healed ligature mark around the leg.

▶ 3.55 Female aged 7 years

The child complained to her teacher that her mother had beaten her. She said that this was a punishment for losing her little brother in the park. Multiple linear petechial bruising can be seen. These are inflicted marks, consistent with beating with a stick.

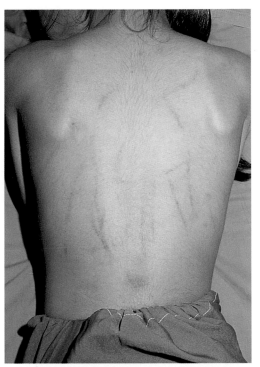

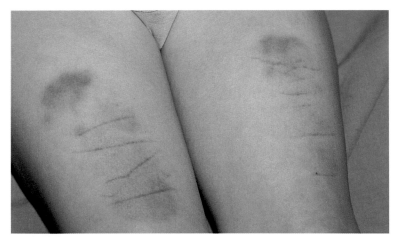

▲ 3.56 Female aged 8 years

Her school noted unusual marks. Her parents said she was injured while playing. The photograph shows old, symmetrical bruising and linear scratches to both anterior thighs, due to unexplained but non-accidental injury.

▶ 3.57 Male aged 3 years

Father said that he had hit the child across the face as he was choking on baked beans, thereby saving his life. Two parallel linear bruises, and two shorter red linear marks at right angles to the upper mark are seen, consistent with being hit across the face with a hand, and the shorter marks due to impact from a ring.

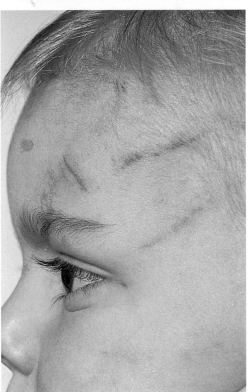

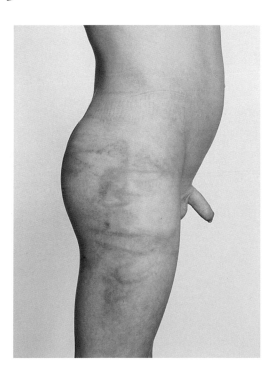

◀ 3.58 Male aged 9 years

His teacher noted extensive bruising during a sports lesson. There is extensive bruising on the outer aspect of the upper thigh and buttock, comprising loops, linear marks, and diffuse bruising of recent origin. This is inflicted bruising due to blows with a looped skipping rope.

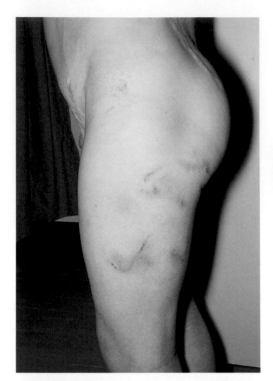

◄ **3.59 Male aged 6 years**

Mother found him lighting a fire in the middle of the sitting room floor and hit him with a belt. Multiple linear marks and abrasions to the outer aspect of the upper thigh are seen. These are not typical belt marks, but consistent with the history given. (Note: scarring due to surgery for ectopic vesicae.)

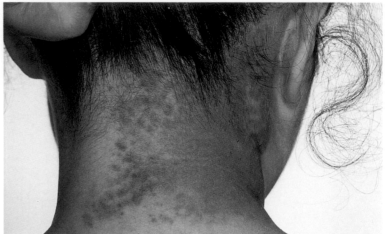

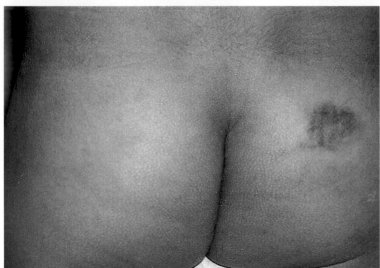

▲ **3.60 Female aged 11 years**

She complained of a sore neck at school. Later she said she had been hit by her mother with a slipper. There is an extensive confluent and textured bruise extending on the back and side of the neck extending into the hairline and ear consistent with multiple blows from a slipper.

◄ **3.61 Male aged 4 years**

He presented because of bruise seen at day nursery. The child had previous behaviour problems. The photograph shows one of several identical roughly circular bruises with linear marking, this one on the right buttock. The mother later admitted to hitting him with a golf club.

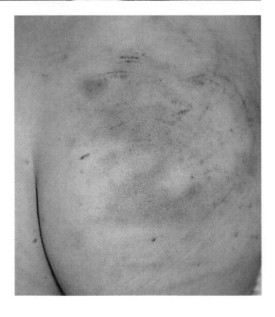

◄ **3.62 Male aged 8 years**

He had run away from home several times previously, and was punished by being put in a dog kennel. On this occasion when he was returned by the police he complained he had been beaten. An extensive complex area of recent and old bruising is evident over the right buttock. Loops and linear marks can be seen within the bruising. The injuries are consistent with repeated beatings, including the use of a belt.

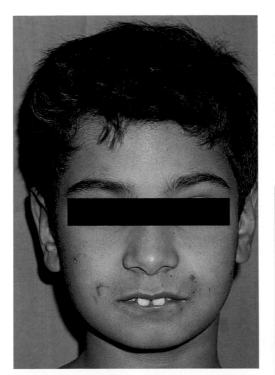

◀ **3.63 Male aged 12 years**

He had stolen money from a doctor's surgery where his mother was a cleaner. The mother admitted hitting him with a shoe, but had shared the money. There are multiple irregular lacerations on face, and a similar lesion was seen on the scalp, caused by repeated blows from the heel of a shoe.

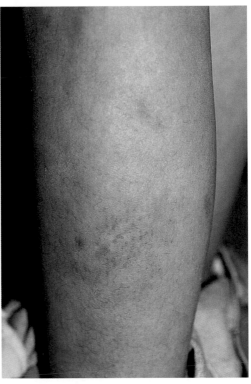

▲ **3.64 Male aged 13 years**

His parents admitted the injury as punishment for the boy spending housekeeping money on gambling machines in an amusement arcade. The photograph shows one of several identical marks on the body – linear bruise marks separated by a linear reddened mark. They are consistent with the history of beating with a stick.

▲ **3.65 Male aged 13 years**

He was belted by his father for playing truant. Parallel linear red marks across the upper back are consistent with belt marks.

▼ **3.66 Male aged 13 years**

The same child as in Fig. 3.65. This photograph shows a similar lesion on the forearm, i.e. a belt mark.

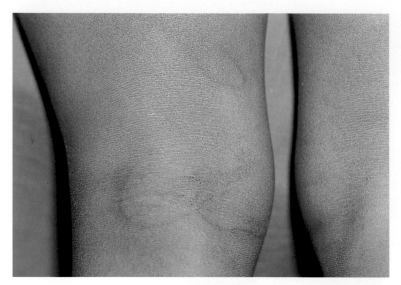

◀ 3.67 Male aged 6 years

Presented because of a history of bedwetting, when unusual marks were noted on the backs of the legs. Fine pigmented open-ended semicircular marks are seen on the back of the thigh and knee. These are healed loop marks – the mother admitted to previously hitting the boy with a looped electrical flex.

▼ 3.68 Female aged 6 weeks

A bite on her cheek was noticed by staff at a mother and baby home. The photograph shows a typical bite mark on the cheek, and a deep healing laceration in the pinna. Diagnosis is an adult bite on cheek, and the laceration in the ear is consistent with nail injury.

▶ 3.69 Male aged 9 months

Bruising was noted by staff at a child health clinic. A double elliptical yellowing bruise can be seen on the cheek, probably due to an adult bite.

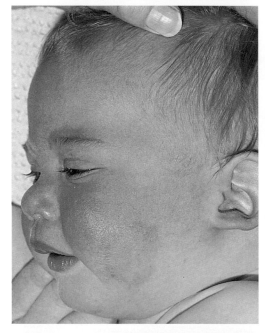

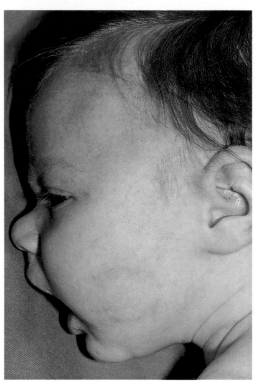

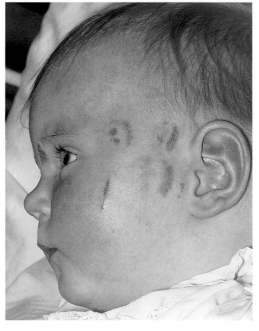

◀ 3.70 Female aged 12 months

Taken to see a doctor because she was 'irritable'. She was also reported to have been 'assaulted' by her disturbed, abused 4-year-old cousin. The photograph shows a bruised pinna, a graze to the nose, a superficial scratch to the cheek and three paired, elliptical lesions with surface abrasion. They are possibly caused by bites.

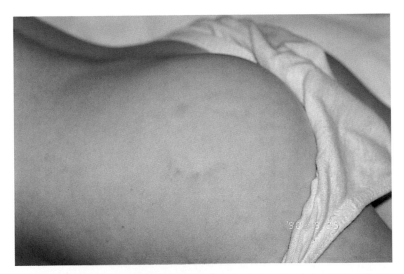

◀ 3.71 Male aged 6 years

He presented having fallen off a gate. The photograph shows an incomplete bite with individual tooth marks visible. This is probably an adult bite. The boy had also been sexually abused.

▼ 3.72 Female aged 11 months

Mother showed marks on the baby's shoulder to a health visitor. A double bite mark can be seen on the outer aspect of the upper arm/shoulder. The father admitted biting the child after being approached by a forensic odontologist.

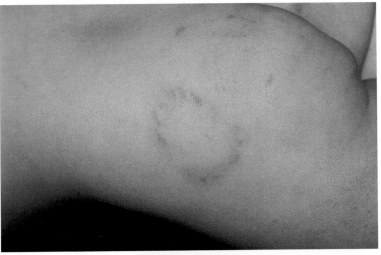

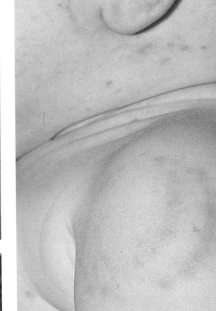

▲ 3.73 Male aged 3 years

He presented as a neglected child with a healing burn on the chest and a mark on the bottom. A bite mark is seen with individual tooth marks visible, caused by an unidentified perpetrator.

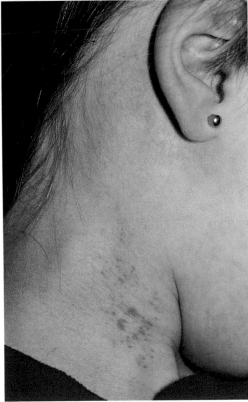

◀ 3.74 Female aged 4 years

She was said to have fallen out of bed. The child had been repeatedly sexually abused at home where her mother lived with a female partner. There is multiple petechial bruising over a circumscribed area of the neck, due to a 'love bite'.

▶ 3.75 Female aged 4 years

She had been previously sexually abused. Two bite marks are seen on her arm, probably child bites obtained in the day nursery.

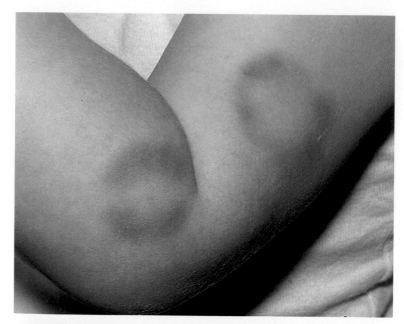

▶ 3.76 Female aged 3 years

A small radius bite with a central suction mark, on the back of the thigh, was a chance finding at a routine follow-up appointment following sexual abuse. This is a worrying unexplained bite because of the type of bite and position.

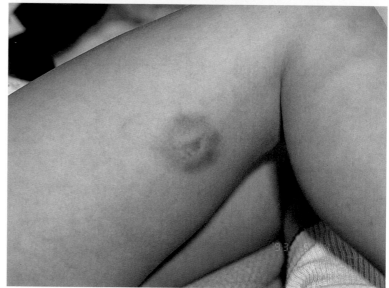

▶ 3.77 Male aged 8 years

He was bitten by a neighbour's Rottweiler. A faint healing semicircular mark with scarring is seen on the knee, and an inferiorly deeper laceration not yet healed.

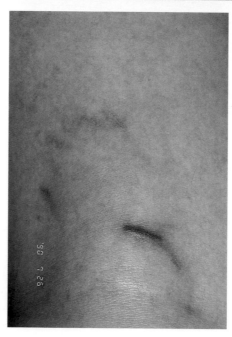

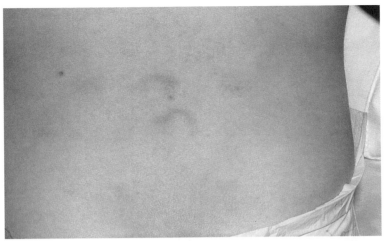

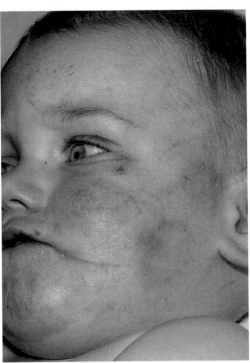

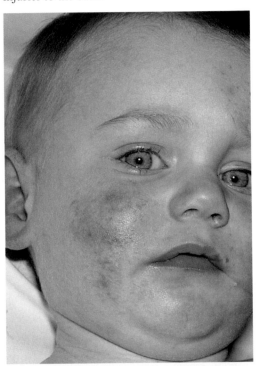

◀ ▼ ▼ 3.78–3.80 Male aged 14 months
His grandmother noticed bruises and scratches when caring for the child. The mother was known to be abusing drugs. There are multiple healing, semilunar facial scratches; an old yellowing bite on the left cheek; a linear, purple/blue bruise on the right cheek, and semicircular bruises on the back. These are due to fingernail scratches and an old bite (probably adult), in addition, there are unexplained old injuries to the back.

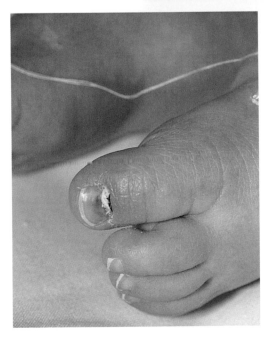

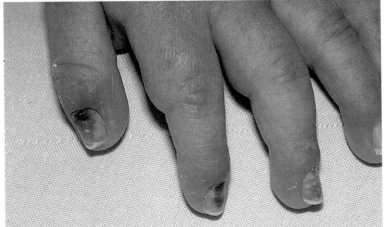

◀ 3.81, ▲ 3.82 Male aged 6 months
His father took him to hospital because of vomiting. Bruises can be seen under the nails of the hand and foot. The child was very ill with intestinal obstruction, but also had, on skeletal survey, unexplained fractures, an old subdural haematoma, and these inflicted injuries on the hands and feet.

▶ 3.83 Male aged 17 years

He was resident in hospital because of severe learning difficulties. Day staff found unexplained marks on his back. The photograph shows extensive bruising over the back, of characteristic linear shape and 'key shape'. This was an inflicted injury, although the actual weapon used was not discovered. (Note: people with disability of any sort are more vulnerable to all forms of abuse.)

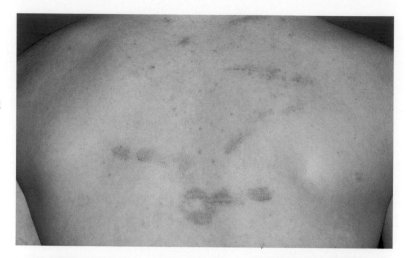

▶ 3.84, ▼ 3.85 Female aged 6 months

Her older brother was seen to have multiple bruising on his face, arms and back in the day nursery, and therefore she was seen in the clinic as well. Petechial bruising seen round neck, caused by strangulation. (Note: strangulation may cause petechiae round the neck, upper eyelids and behind the ears, but it should be remembered that in many cases of strangulation there are no abnormalities seen on the neck.)

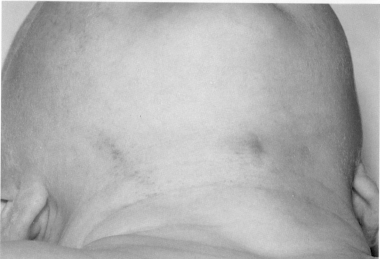

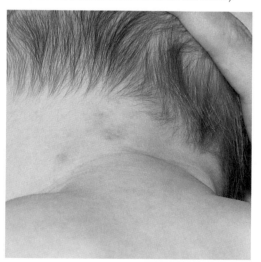

▶ 3.86 Female aged 7 years

She was referred to social services by her school, because of concern that the child was withdrawn and had repeated scratch marks on her face. There is bruising over the bridge of the nose and infra-orbitally on the right, and scattered scratch marks in various stages of healing across the face and chin. These were due to unexplained injury: the parents explained that the children kept fighting. (Note: further investigation was unsatisfactory and the child was not protected.)

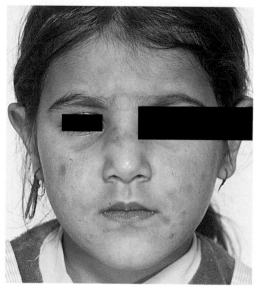

▶ 3.87, ▼ 3.88 Female aged 14 years

She told her teacher that her mother had attacked her the previous evening. The photograph shows fingernail scratches to the side of the face and extensive lacerations with petechial bruising around the neck, caused by serious physical assault. (Note: lacerations were caused by long fingernails, an extremely scaring assault for this child.)

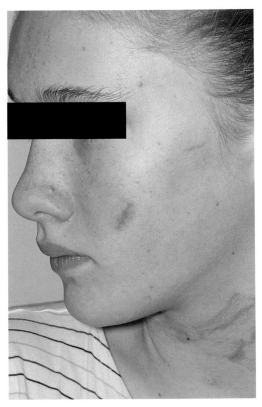

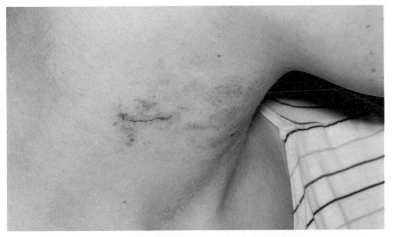

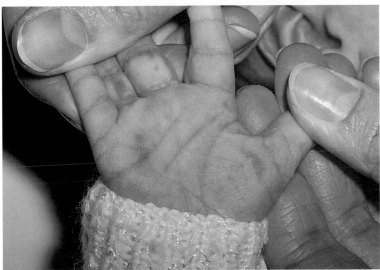

◀ 3.89 Female aged 4 weeks

Her mother asked the health visitor about a bruise on the palm of the hand. The photograph shows multiple abrasions and a bruise with superficial abrasion on the palm of the left hand. This is an unexplained injury in a very young baby.

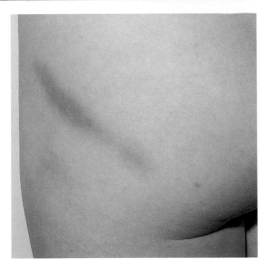

◀ 3.90 Male aged 9 years

He complained to his teacher at school that his father had beaten him up. An old linear bruise can be seen extending across the lateral aspect of the left buttock, consistent with history of being hit with a stick.

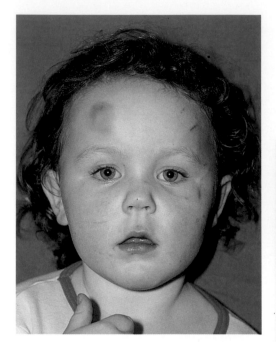

◀ 3.91, ▼ 3.92 Female aged 3 years

Her parents had a fight one evening, the police were called and observed injuries to the children. The child said her mother had banged her head on the cupboard door. An old circular bruise is seen on the right frontal area, and multiple fingernail marks in various states of healing on the forehead and cheeks. The bruise is consistent with a bang against a hard surface as described; the scratches were inflicted by fingernails.

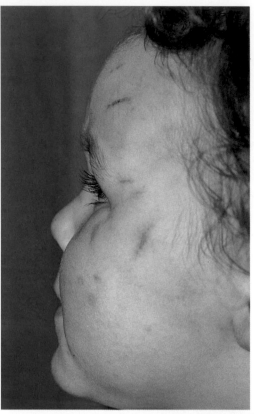

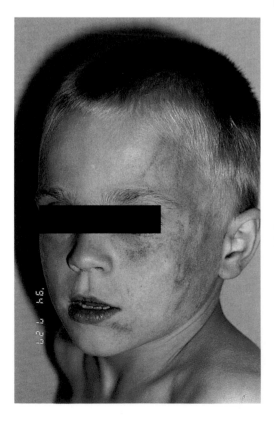

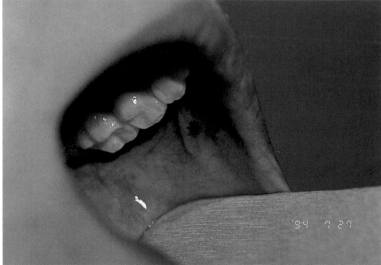

◀ 3.93, ▲ 3.94 Male aged 5 years

He claimed that his mother had hit him. The photographs show a slap mark on the left side of the face and bruising on the buccal surface on the left cheek due to the cheek impacting on the teeth. This was diagnosed as a non-accidental injury.

(Note: When bruising of lips or cheeks is seen then remember to look inside the mouth.)

▶ 3.95 Male aged 12 months

Child had a history of feeding problems. A traumatic ulcer of the hard palate is shown in the photograph, it was probably caused by a spoon.

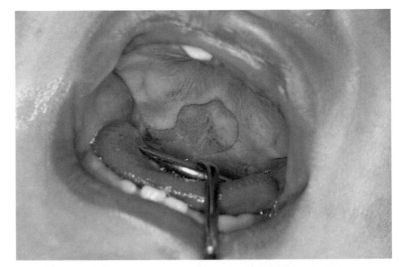

▶ 3.96a, ▼ 3.96b Male aged 5 years

He was referred by a psychologist during a therapy session because of marks around neck. Child had a history of emotional, physical and sexual abuse. The photograph shows an incomplete circumferential abrasion around neck (Fig. 3.96a) with a similar lesion under the chin (Fig. 3.96b). The lesions had the appearance of a cord burn but the exact nature of the 'accident' was unknown.

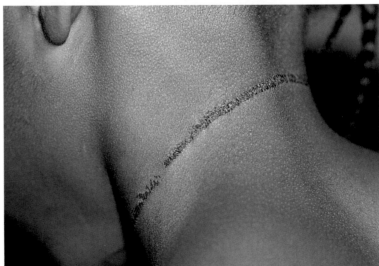

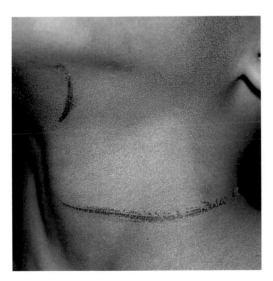

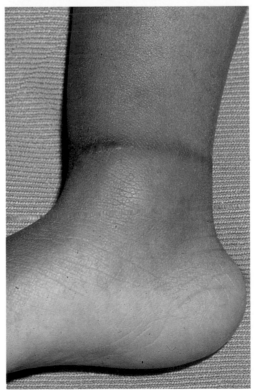

▶ 3.97 Male aged 4 years

He was referred because the neighbours had heard a child screaming at night. He had a pigmented circumferential band round lower leg with keloid scarring anteriorly. The ligature mark was caused when the child was tied to his bed.

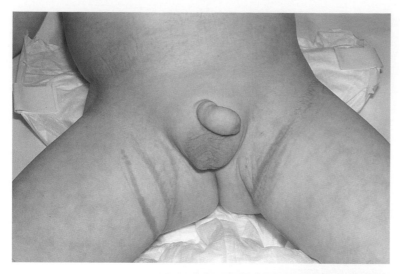

◀ **3.98 Male aged 2 years**

He was referred by his nursery because of unexplained marks in groin. The linear red marks encircling inner thighs were caused by the child being sealed into his nappy at night with parcel tape. This was done to prevent the child removing his nappy in the morning.

▼ **3.99 Female aged 5 years**

The torn, ulcerated frenulum of lower lip was an incidental finding at a paediatric follow-up clinic following previous sexual abuse by the mother's partner. The mother said doctor had diagnosed an aphthous ulcer. This indicated physical abuse.

▶ **3.100 Male aged 2 years**

He presented with facial bruising, fracture and signs of sexual abuse. Examination revealed hair loss that had been caused by the child's hair being pulled.

▼ **3.101 Female aged 3 years**

She was referred because of multiple bruises. Examination revealed an area of hair loss (as shown in photograph) resulting from the child's hair being pulled; there were also signs of physical and sexual abuse.

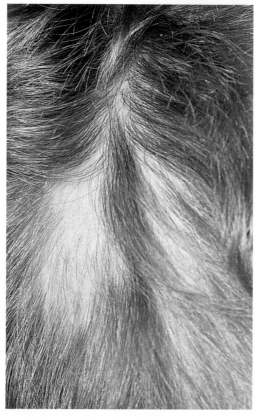

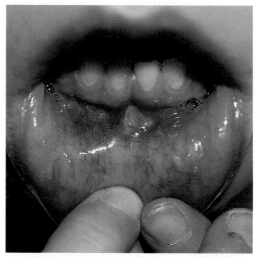

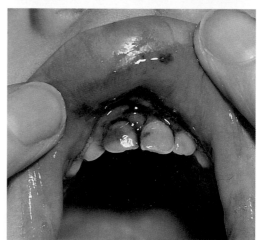

▲ **3.102 Male aged 4 years**

He was taken to hospital's emergency department by his parents with a history of having fallen against the toilet. Examination showed a swollen upper lip with abrasions, bleeding from the gum, and also chipped incisor teeth. The injury was compatible with a fall against a hard surface or a blow to the mouth. But there were numerous other bruises not typical of accidents.

Chapter 4

Fractures

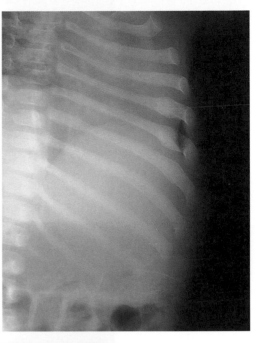

▶ 4.1 Female aged 3 months

She was brought by her parents to the hospital emergency department with a serious head injury. The radiograph shows healing fractures of the 5th, 6th and 7th ribs, with well developed callus so that the fracture line is not visible. This is a typical shaking/crush injury – injuries of this order are only seen in serious non-accidental injury and crush injuries such as in road traffic accidents.

▼ 4.2 Female aged 3 months

She was brought by her parents to the hospital emergency department with a serious head injury. The radiograph shows a healing fracture of the left clavicle with well-developed callus. There is a possible fracture of the posterior end of the 5th and 6th ribs on the left side. The opinion of a paediatric radiologist is essential in assessing cases such as this. The question of possible birth injury will be raised concerning the clavicle, but the additional skull fractures and head injury made the diagnosis of non-accidental injury a clear one (see Fig. 4.3). The child survived the injuries and at the age of 10 years has a moderate learning difficulty, a mild right hemiparesis but good vision in spite of occipital contusion.

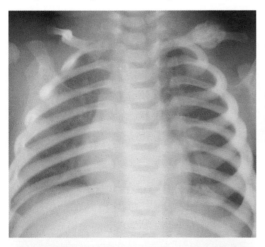

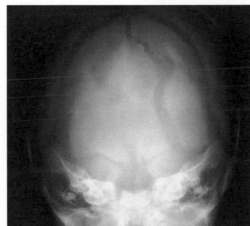

◀ 4.3 Female aged 3 months

The same child as in Fig. 4.2. This radiograph shows an extensive occipital fracture, measuring up to 0.5 cm in width.

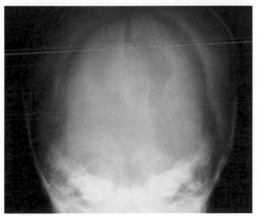

◀ 4.4 Female aged 3 months

The same child as in Figs 4.2 and 4.3. This is a follow-up skull X-ray 2 weeks later showing that the occipital fracture has now grown in width, i.e. this is an example of a growing skull fracture in infancy.

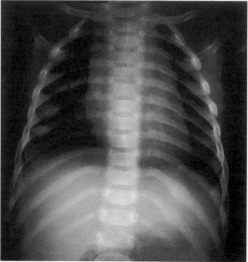

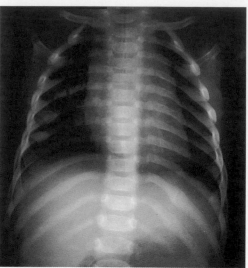

◀ 4.5 Male aged 4 months

He presented as a battered baby, with multiple rib fractures. Note the recent fracture of the right 5th rib with the fracture line visible and healing fractures of the left 10th and 11th ribs with marked callus formation and the fracture line just visible.

▼ 4.6 Male aged 4 months

He presented with bilateral rib fractures of the left 6th and 7th and the right 7th, 8th and 9th ribs.

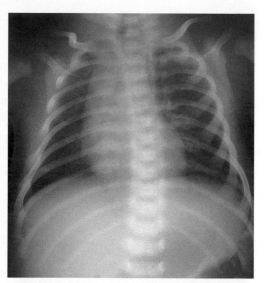

▶ 4.7 Male infant aged 2 months

His mother, while suffering from severe post-natal depression, threw him on the floor, hitting his head on a stone fireplace. A long wide linear parietal fracture can be seen extending into the occiput. This was a severe intra-cranial injury from which the child died.

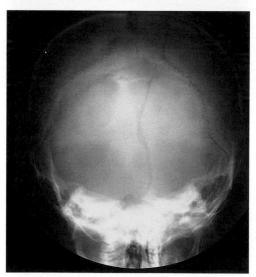

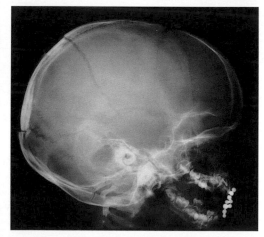

▲ 4.9 Female aged 18 months

The same child as in Fig. 4.8, showing the occipital fracture clearly. Depressed occipital fracture in infancy is virtually pathognomonic of abuse.

▲ 4.8 Female aged 18 months

She was taken to the hospital emergency department by her parents who said the child had fallen off a chair. Multiple bruises on the buttocks and back were seen, as well as a right parietal/occipital fracture with a large depressed segment of the skull. The child had a persistent right hemiparesis.

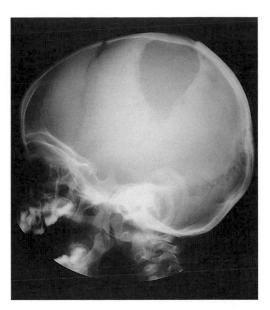

◄ 4.10 Male aged 18 months

He was referred to neurosurgeons with a large fluctuant swelling over the left parietal region and minimal weakness in the right arm. At the age of 7 months he had been dropped down the stairs by his sister, and was seen in the hospital emergency department with a 4 mm wide linear parietal fracture. Surgical repair was required at 18 months. (Note: this is an unsatisfactory history, i.e. at presentation the infant had a wide fracture implying that considerable force had been applied to the skull. Fuller investigation at the time of initial presentation was needed.)

▶ 4.11 Female aged 8 months

She had tipped herself up attempting to go downstairs in a baby walker. Long linear parietal fracture is seen, with maximum width of 2 mm. There is no intra-cranial injury. This was accepted as an accidental fall.

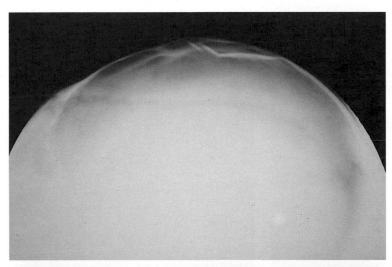

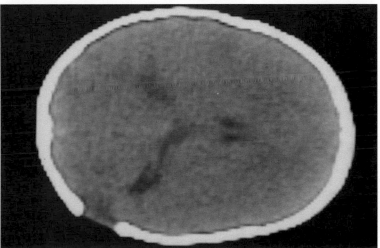

◄ 4.12 Male aged 10 months

He had a history of being dropped onto the corner of a central heating radiator. There is a localized depressed fracture of the parietal bone, with no intra-cerebral injury. This was accepted as an accidental injury.

◄ 4.13 Female aged 19 months

She received a significant head injury aged 4 months when the wind blew her pram over a ledge and she fell 5 feet (1.5 m) onto concrete. She initially showed localized neurological signs with focal fits. The child was followed up and the computerized tomography (CT) brain scan at 19 months shows a 1.5 × 8 cm deficit in the skull. At operation the dura was adherent to the pericranium at the skull edge. The brain was gliotic, the arachnoid herniating and pulsating and probably connected to the lateral ventricle. A repair was undertaken but the child has continued to have convulsions.

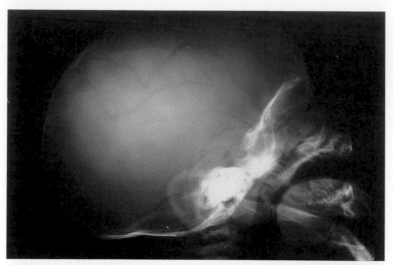

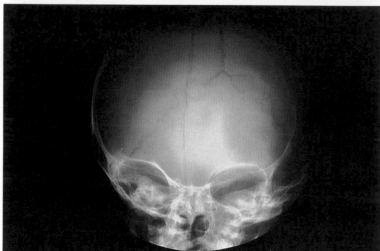

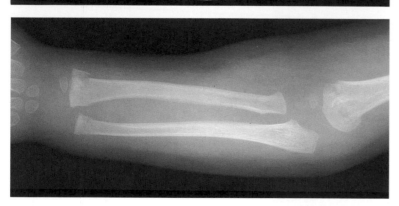

◀ 4.14 Female aged 6 weeks

Her grandfather was said to have dropped her onto a linoleum-covered floor while he was feeding her. Bilateral linear parietal fractures are evident up to 2.5 mm in width. (Note: non-accidental injury was not suspected at the time of presentation, but at 16 months the child sustained 6% scalds to the neck, chest and upper arm from spilt tea, and at 2½ years was hit across the buttocks and back resulting in severe non-accidental bruising.)

◀ ◀ ▼ 4.15–4.17 Female aged 14 months

She was left unsupervised and fell through a gap in a broken banister from the first floor landing to the floor below. The distance of the fall was estimated to be 10–12 feet (3–3.5 m). There was bruising to the forehead and a linear frontal fracture. The skull X-ray shows a long, narrow, mid-line frontal fracture (Fig. 4.15). The X-ray of the right forearm (Fig. 4.16) shows a fracture of the distal end of the radius and also an epiphyseal fracture of the humerus. Bruising of the upper eyelid (Battle's sign) is seen in Fig. 4.17. This was a preventable accident, due to neglect.

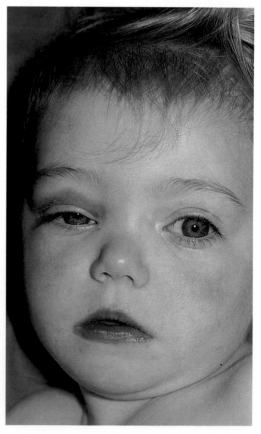

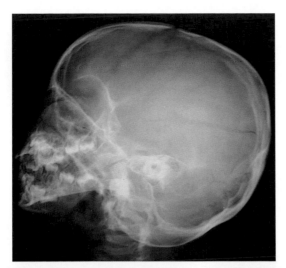

◄ 4.18 Male aged 19 months

He fell 13-14 feet (approx. 4 m) from a first floor window onto the garden below. He was taken straight to hospital where he was found to be drowsy and bleeding from the ear. The radiograph shows a linear parietal/temporal fracture involving the base of the skull, 2 mm maximum width × 9 cm in length. The child spent 3 days in hospital and made a full recovery. (Note: children falling from one or two stories frequently escape major injury; at four to five stories there is a real threat to life.)

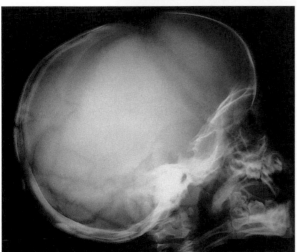 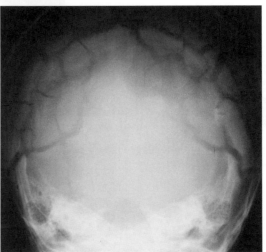

▲ 4.19, ▲ 4.20 Male aged 11 months

He was taken to the hospital emergency department where it was claimed he had fallen from a settee. The skull X-rays show multiple, convoluted crazy-paving fractures of the parietal and occipital bones with a parietal fracture measuring 11.5 cm long and 0.8 cm wide. The injury was complicated by intra-cerebral haemorrhage resulting in hydrocephalus and 6th nerve palsy. The child's father admitted to causing the injury.

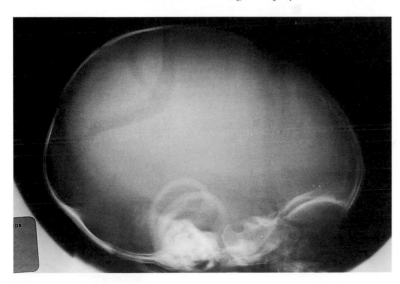

◄ 4.21 Male aged 6 weeks

It was claimed that he had fallen from a bed onto the floor. The radiograph shows two parietal fractures towards the vertex, 4 and 3.5 cm long with a maximum separation of 0.4 cm. The CT brain scan showed cerebral contusion to the left parieto-occipital areas. A skeletal survey showed fractured ribs and ulnar fracture — the father admitted to injuring the baby.

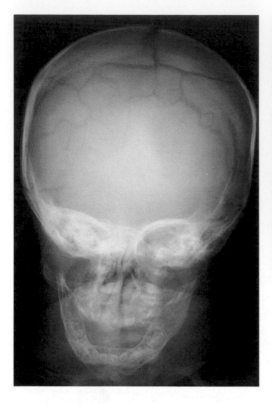

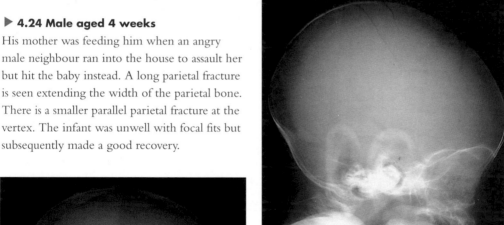

◄ 4.22, ▲ 4.23 Female aged 5 months

She was brought by her parents to the hospital emergency department having died. The skull X-rays show multiple, bilateral skull fractures with crazy-paving appearance (parietal bones). In addition to the fatal head injury she had a torn frenulum and multiple bruises over her body. In addition there was gross abnormality of the anus consistent with anal abuse.

▶ 4.24 Male aged 4 weeks

His mother was feeding him when an angry male neighbour ran into the house to assault her but hit the baby instead. A long parietal fracture is seen extending the width of the parietal bone. There is a smaller parallel parietal fracture at the vertex. The infant was unwell with focal fits but subsequently made a good recovery.

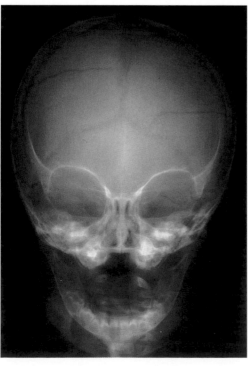

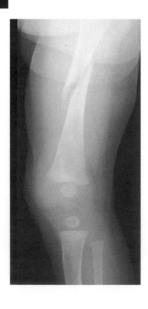

◄ 4.25, ▶ 4.26 Female aged 6 months

She was brought to the hospital emergency department with multiple unexplained injuries. The skull X-ray (Fig. 4.25) shows bilateral linear parietal fractures, and the sutures may be slightly widened. Other injuries included a rib fracture and a long bone fracture (Fig. 4.26). The pattern of injuries is typical of severe physical abuse in infancy.

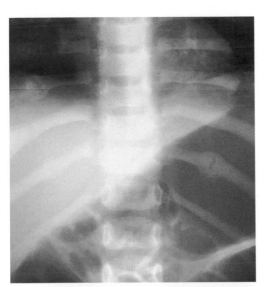

◀ 4.27 Male aged 18 months

The health visitor referred the child to hospital after she had seen him with an untreated scald on the forehead when visiting at home. When examined the child also had multiple bruises of different ages and therefore a skeletal survey was performed. The chest X-ray shows bilateral rib fractures. The clinical picture is one of clear non-accidental injury.

▶ 4.28, ▶ 4.29 Female aged 6 years

She was taken to see her doctor because of abdominal pain and was referred to hospital for investigation. The clinical picture was one of chronic pancreatitis. Further examination showed evidence of bony injury with an old fracture of the humerus and characteristic notching of the anterior/superior surface of the vertebral bodies and narrowed disc spaces, the result of a spinal injury. (Reproduced with permission from Meadow S.R. (ed.) (1989) *ABC of Child Abuse*, British Medical Journal, London.)

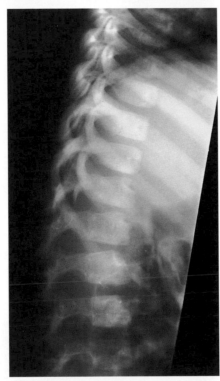

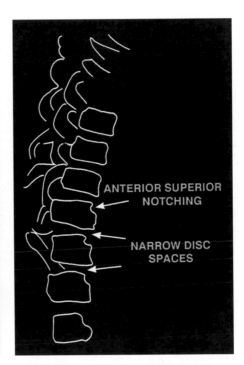

ANTERIOR SUPERIOR NOTCHING

NARROW DISC SPACES

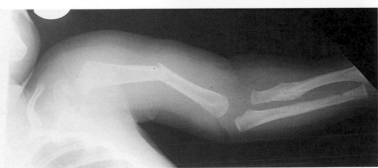

◀ 4.30 Female aged 5 months

Her parents took her to the hospital emergency department as she was not moving her left arm. A recent fracture of the left humerus and healing fractures of the radius and ulna can be seen. (Note: although spiral fractures of the humerus are the more usual fractures in non-accidental injury transverse fractures may also be seen.)

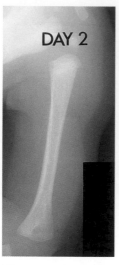 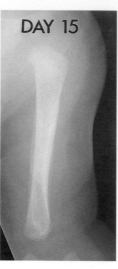

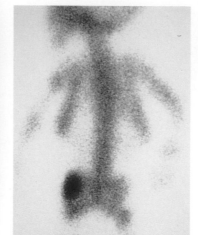

◀ **4.31**, ◀ **4.32 Male aged 3 months**

He presented in the hospital emergency department with his parents who said he would not move his left arm and seemed to have pain on movement. The initial X-ray showed no abnormality but by Day 15 a clear periosteal reaction can be seen. A radioisotope bone scan (Fig. 4.32) was done on Day 3 which showed increased uptake of ^{99m}Tc. The injury was due to the arm being twisted causing damage to the periosteum.

▼ **4.33 Male aged 3 years**

His history was of tripping and falling onto his outstretched arm. The X-ray shows a greenstick fracture of the ulna. This was an accidental injury.

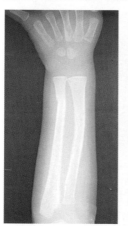 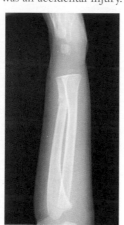

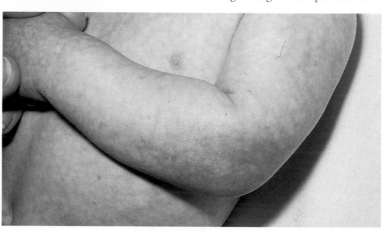

▲ **4.34 Male aged 3 months**

He was taken to the hospital emergency department because of a red, painful arm. The photograph shows a reddened painful swollen elbow; the child resisted movement. The diagnosis was of a pulled elbow. The child was subsequently seriously physically abused (skull fractures and bruised face).

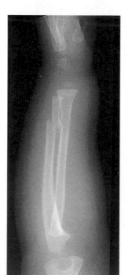 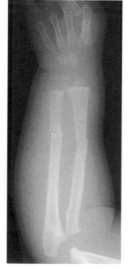

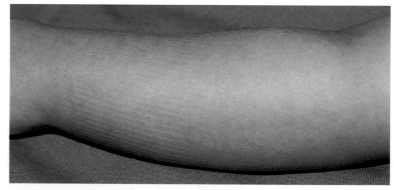

◀ **4.35**, ▲ **4.36 Male aged 14 months**

His mother took him to the hospital emergency department 3 days after he had received contact burns to the abdomen. On examination he also had multiple bruising to the face, body and legs and bilaterally swollen forearms which were non-tender. He also had penile abrasions. He was failing to thrive. The X-ray shows fractures of both forearms with some healing reaction; possibly fractures have occurred at different times and healing has started. Swelling of the forearm is evident in Fig. 4.36. The diagnosis is a multiply injured emotionally abused child who is failing to thrive.

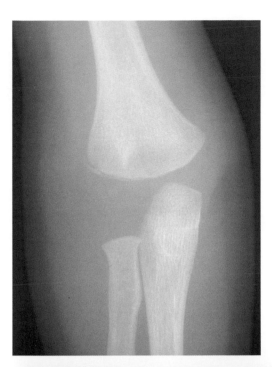

◀ 4.37 Male aged 2 years

He was taken to the hospital emergency department by his parents when he 'wouldn't stand up'. A metaphyseal fracture of the lower end of the humerus is seen on the radiograph. There was also a spiral fracture of the tibia. The usual mechanism for these fractures is rotation or wrenching. These two unexplained fractures were due to non-accidental injury.

▼ 4.38 Male aged 2 years

He was taken to the hospital emergency department by his mother because he was not using his arm. Bruises were seen on his ear, face and trunk. The X-ray shows a metaphyseal fracture (bucket-handle type). This was diagnosed as a non-accidental injury. This type of fracture is thought to be almost pathognomonic of abuse. The child had also been sexually abused.

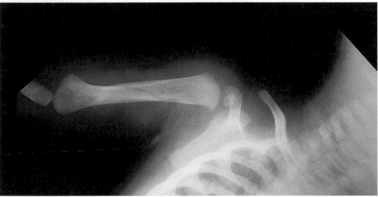

▲ 4.39 Female aged 4 months

She was taken to the hospital emergency department by her father because she seemed to be in distress when her arm was moved. He gave a history that the previous day he had been bathing her when she slipped and he grabbed her by the arm. The radiograph shows a spiral fracture of the right humerus. There were also healing fractures of the right 5th rib. Spiral fractures of the humerus are highly correlated with physical abuse. The combination of a spiral fracture of the humerus and rib fractures is physical abuse. (Note: originally the child was sent away from hospital until the radiologist noted the rib fractures, which were beginning to heal.)

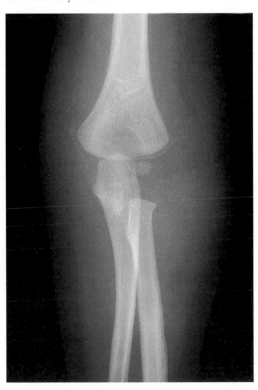

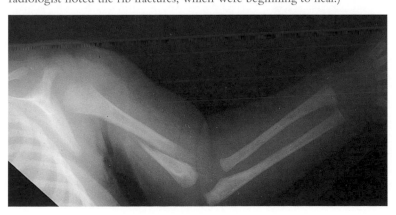

◀ 4.40 Female aged 6 weeks

Her mother claimed she felt her arm 'give way' when she put it through the sleeve of a babygrow. A spiral displaced fracture of left humerus is evident. Skeletal survey showed that the baby also had a linear parietal fracture which was unexplained. The diagnosis is non-accidental injury.

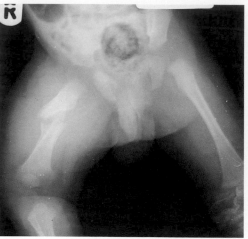

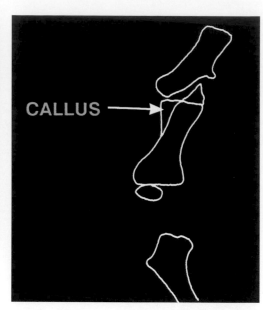

▶ 4.41, ▶ 4.42
Male aged 2 months
He was taken to the hospital emergency department by his parents who noticed that his right leg was swollen. A fracture of the right femur can be seen through a previous fracture which had started to heal. This was a non-accidental injury. The child had initially been seen by an orthopaedic surgeon who had discharged him home without taking any child protection initiatives.

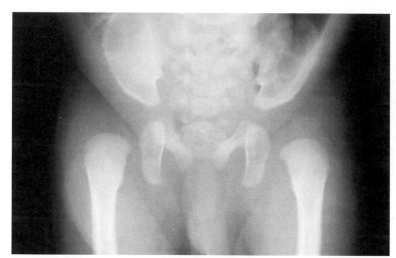

◀ 4.43 Male aged 4 months
Social services referred the child to a paediatrician after he had been seen with multiple facial bruising. A skeletal survey revealed a fracture of the right pubic ramus.

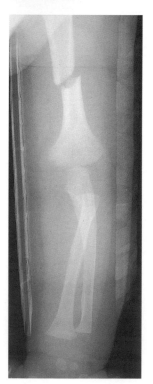

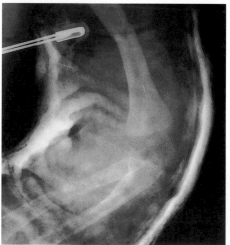

◀ ▲ ▲ 4.44–4.46 Male aged 5 months
He was taken to the hospital emergency department, two days after having been picked up from his cot by his father in the middle of the night. The father complained that the child disliked his arm being moved. The X-ray (Fig. 4.44) shows a transverse fracture of the left humerus with displacement (Day 2). The X-ray taken on Day 11 shows early healing (Fig. 4.45). Figure 4.46 taken on Day 23 shows marked callus formation. The child also had a fractured left clavicle. The father later admitted to having performed a karate chop on the child's arm.

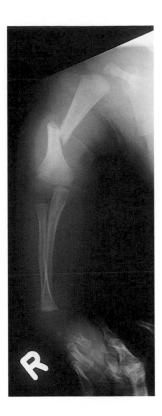

◄ 4.47 Male aged 3 months

He was taken to the hospital emergency department because he seemed in pain when he was picked up. The baby had been well in the mother's care earlier that morning but he was irritable and crying when she came home. The X-ray shows a spiral fracture of the right humerus. The parents vehemently denied causing any trauma to their baby, but spiral fracture of the humerus is almost always due to non-accidental injury and in a 3-month old there is little space for an alternative diagnosis.

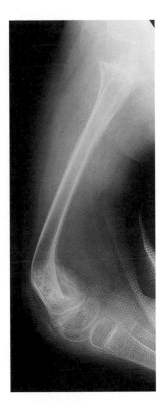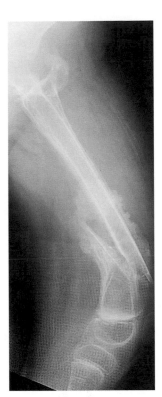

▲ 4.48, ▲ 4.49 Female aged 8 years

The mother found her daughter, who was handicapped with cerebral palsy, sitting in an unusual position on a beanbag. The child's hips were adducted normally but she was described as sitting 'ordinary fashion'. The child appeared to be both miserable and in pain. The X-rays were taken several days later and show bilateral fractures of the femur with different rates of healing. She was diagnosed as having markedly osteopenic bones.

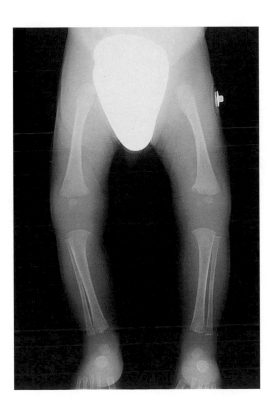

◄ 4.50 Male aged 8 months

He was brought to hospital unconscious by his parents after he had had 'a fit' at home. Investigation showed that he had retinal haemorrhages and a subdural haematoma. A skeletal survey showed metaphyseal corner fracture at the distal end of left femur. The combination of severe head injury and fractures is diagnostic of abuse.

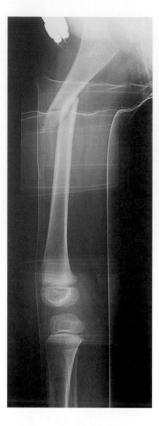

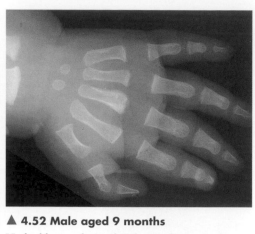

▶ 4.51 Male aged 4 years

The history initially given in the hospital emergency department was that the child had fallen downstairs. Later the father admitted grabbing at the child as he ran away from him down the stairs. The child had been seen previously because of failure to thrive, unexplained burns and apnoeic attacks in early infancy. The X-ray shows a spiral/oblique fracture of the right femur. This was probably a non-accidental injury.

▲ 4.52 Male aged 9 months

He had been admitted to hospital two weeks earlier with a skull fracture after a fall. Subsequently he was seen with facial bruising by a health visitor. Investigation following the second admission showed rib fractures and an old healing fracture of the second left metacarpal. The skull fracture, the rib fractures, the finger fracture and the facial bruising all indicate non-accidental injury. Fractures involving the hands and feet are uncommon and probably represent a very sadistic injury.

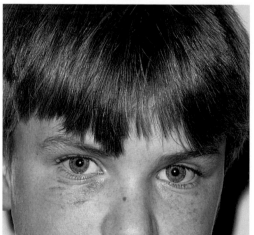

◀ ▼ ▼ 4.53–4.55 Male aged 13 years

He had gone to his uncle's house to say that he was fed-up of being beaten up by his father. His injuries included a bruised right eye, injury to the side of his face and neck and recent bruising to his legs caused by kicks. Investigation confirmed an old fracture to his clavicle. The boy had suffered repeated physical assaults by his father. Assaults on teenagers should be taken very seriously.

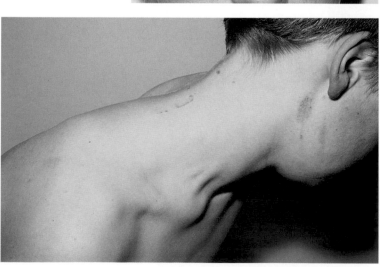

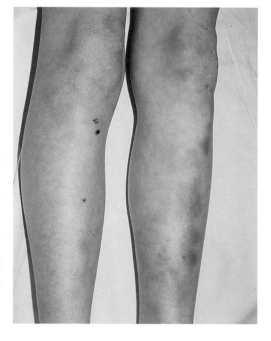

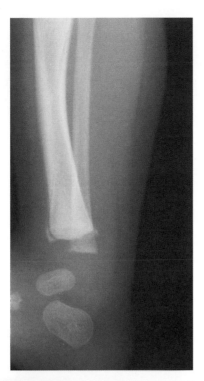

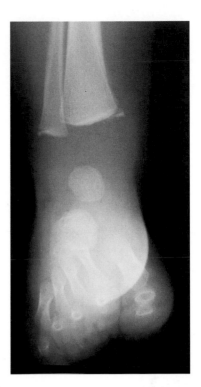

◀ **4.56,** ▶ **4.57 Female aged 3 weeks**

She was taken to the hospital emergency department because she was crying inconsolably. A skeletal survey was performed because bruises were seen on the child's face. The X-rays revealed a long undisplaced spiral fracture of the left tibia extending to include metaphysis, and a second fracture. Also shown are distal metaphyseal fractures at the lower end of the tibia and fibula. These indicate physical abuse of a young baby.

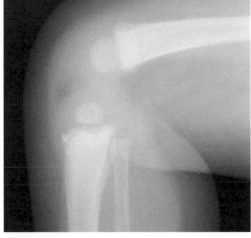

◀ **4.58 Male aged 5 months**

The parents brought the child to the hospital's emergency department because of a lack of movement of the arm. A skeletal survey revealed a metaphyseal fracture of the upper end of tibia. There was a total of 25 separate injuries in this child, which indicates serious physical abuse of a young baby.

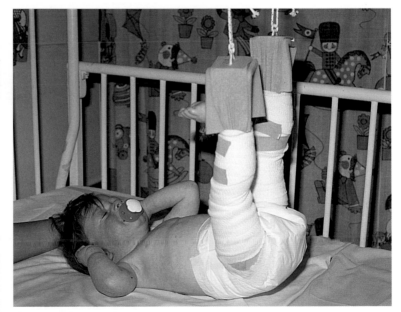

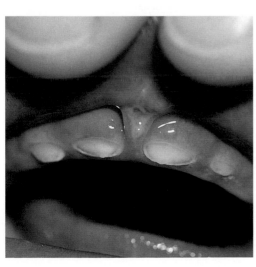

▲ **4.59,** ◀ **4.60 Male aged 12 months**

The history given by his mother was that he had been jumping up and down in his cot, but later she had found him sitting in the cot on his legs and with a bleeding mouth. Investigation revealed a fracture of the lower end of the shaft of the femur. Further investigation showed a recently torn frenulum, an old bite mark and bruising to the right arm; he was also failing to thrive.

Chapter 5

Burns and scalds

Contact burns

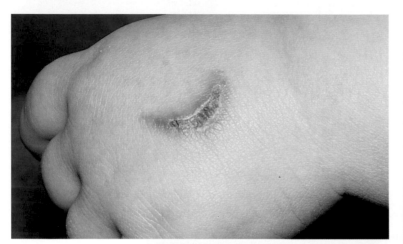

◄ 5.1 Male aged 14 months
He had been left in the care of a 35-year-old female babysitter, who claimed that he had touched the fire with his hand. (The babysitter's own daughter had been deliberately burned by being made to stand too near to the fire at 5 years of age.) A curved healing contact burn is seen on the dorsum of the left hand, probably an inflicted injury.

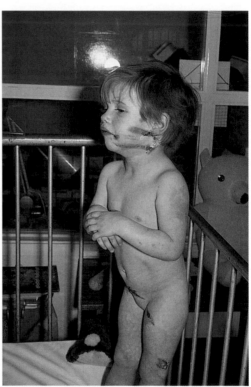

▲ 5.2 Female aged 2½ years
She was burned with a poker. Linear burns are seen to the side of the face, lower abdomen and thigh. The distribution would suggest sexual abuse but this was not investigated. The diagnosis is an inflicted, extremely sadistic injury.

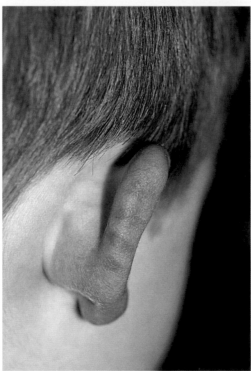

▲ 5.3 Male aged 5 years
He told his teacher that his father had heated a fork and applied it to his ear, while laughing. The photograph shows four parallel superficial contact burns on the outer aspect of the pinna. This indicates sadistic abuse.

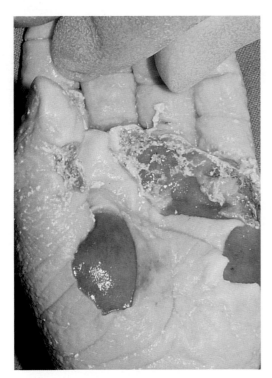

◀ 5.4 Male aged 2½ years

He was taken by his parents to the hospital emergency department, because he 'put his hand on the convector heater'. There was a past history of neglect and physical abuse. He was in the sole care of his father at the time of the incident. The photograph shows a superficial contact burn to the palm of the hand. It was taken on the ward after 24 hours of treatment and consequently resembles a scald rather than a contact burn. The cause of the burn remained unexplained but abuse was suspected.

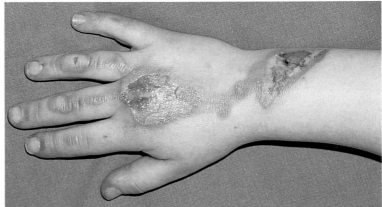

▲ 5.5 Female aged 7 years

She went to school with her hand wrapped in a dirty bandage; her parents subsequently speculated that while she was doing the ironing she must have burned herself on the back of the hand. The girl had moderate learning difficulties. There was no history of the child complaining of pain, but on examination there were also signs consistent with sexual abuse. There was also previous serious physical abuse to a sibling. The photograph shows an extensive burn over the dorsum of the fingers, hand and wrist with a full thickness burn over the wrist. The injury is too severe and extensive for the history given and the response of the child and the parents is inappropriate. This is likely to be an inflicted injury by a hot iron, rather than an accidental injury.

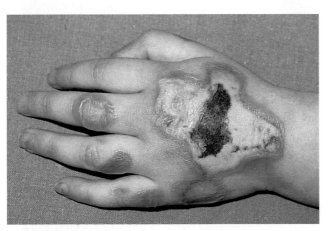

▲ 5.6 Female aged 2 years

Her mother speculated that the 7-year-old brother had put the iron on his younger sister's hand while she was out of the room. The brother denied doing this. He also had a history of soiling and emotional difficulties. The girl also had physical signs consistent with vaginal and anal abuse. The photograph shows an extensive full thickness burn on the dorsum of the hand and more superficial burning on the dorsum of the fingers. Grafting was needed. The diagnosis is an iron burn: probable abuse.

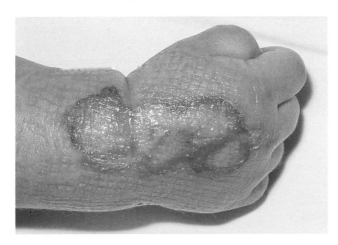

◀ 5.7 Female aged 8 months

The history given was that whilst in the care of teenage siblings she was sitting by the side of the hot stove and reached out and touched it. A contact burn of variable thickness can be seen over the dorsum of the hand and wrist. (Note: when children explore and grasp it is usually the palmar surface of the hand which comes into contact with the hot surface. Burns on the dorsum of the hand are thus always suspicious.)

▼ 5.8, ▶ 5.9 Male aged 5 years

He was profoundly deaf, hyperactive and with difficult behaviour. He presented with burns of different ages on his hand and buttock. Fig. 5.8 shows three parallel healing burns on the dorsum of the left little finger and a healing burn extending onto the dorsum of the hand. Fig. 5.9 shows an extensive burn on the right buttock demonstrating a grill pattern. This child has had at least two burns due to contact with the grill of a portable room heater. (Note: as with burns on the back of the hand, burns on the buttocks are always suspicious; in this case there was no history of a witnessed injury but repeated burns imply neglect or inflicted injuries.)

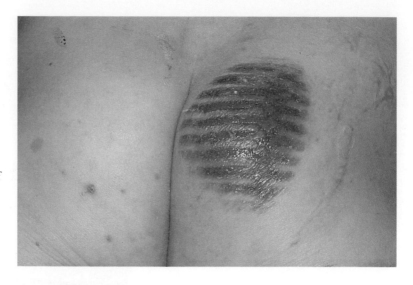

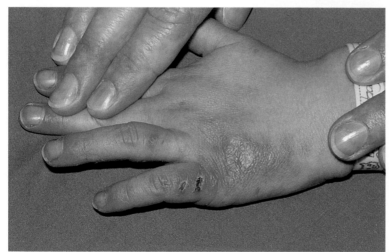

▼ 5.10 Male aged 5 years

His parents said that he had inflicted this burn deliberately by holding himself against a radiator. Superficial contact burns of the outer aspect of the left buttock can be seen. This boy had also been seen on several previous occasions with unexplained bruising and his younger sister was found to have been sexually abused. If this burn was self-inflicted, i.e. self-mutilation, it is of extreme concern, and further investigation is clearly warranted.

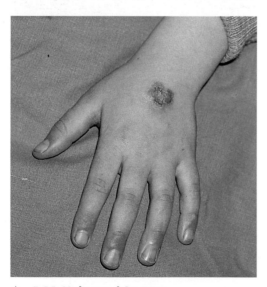

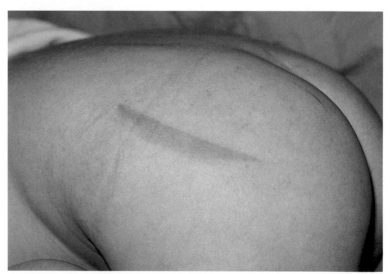

▲ 5.11 Male aged 8 years

He had an unexplained mark on the back of his hand seen while the family were visiting an a child walfare charity family unit. The photograph shows an irregular shaped healing burn on the dorsum of the left hand, possibly caused by multiple cigarette burns. (Note: it is not always possible to establish the cause of a burn, but unexplained burns on the back of the hand are always of concern.)

▶ 5.12 Female aged 3 years

Her nursery nurse noted a burn and an excessive number of bruises during routine care in a day nursery. A clearly demarcated arc with an inner parallel burn, of uniform thickness, of several days duration is seen on the left lower back. Scattered petechial bruising over both buttocks and bruises were also noted on the left thigh and right loin. All the marks are unexplained, but the burn suggests contact with, for example, a kettle, and the petechial bruising over the buttocks suggests a hand slap.

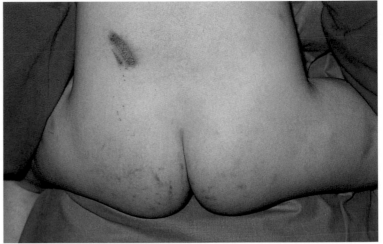

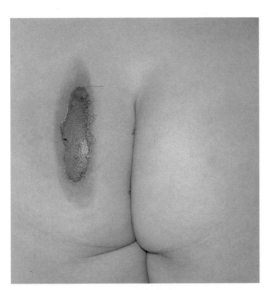

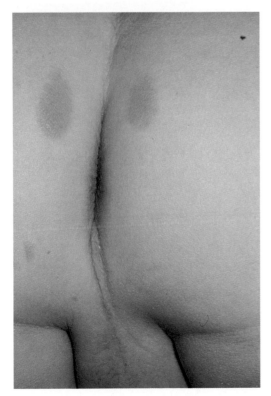

◀ 5.13 Female aged 5 years

Her mother said the child had fallen backwards against a heated towel rail while getting ready for her bath. The mother is schizophrenic, and became very agitated when the 'accident' was discussed. The photograph shows a superficial burn of the left buttock, with surrounding erythema and signs of recent blistering. This is consistent with the history, but the reason for the fall is unclear.

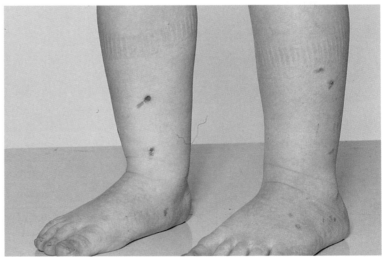

▲ 5.14 Female aged 3 years

The grandmother was caring for this child and her brother when she found the children had bruises on their faces and burns on their hands and contacted the a child walfare charity. The photograph shows multiple contact burns over the lower legs and feet in various stages of healing. (Note: the similar shape of all the burns – the inflicting implement was not discovered. The older brother had signs consistent with anal abuse.) These were sadistic inflicted burns; there is a high correlation between injuries like this and sexual abuse.

◀ 5.15 Male aged 4 years

He returned home after an access visit with his father with two black eyes and multiple burns. Paired superficial contact burns on the buttocks are seen. There were similar burns on the scrotum and legs. The child subsequently gave a very clear history of sexual abuse and deliberate burning by his father.

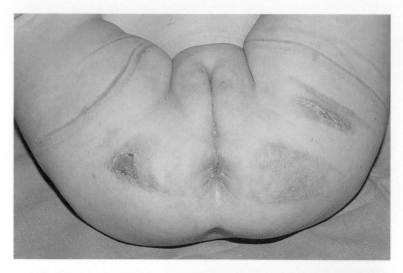

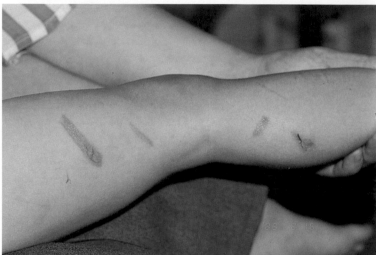

◄ 5.16 Female aged 10 months

Her 6-year-old brother was seen at his school for children with emotional difficulties with a burn on his back. A doctor diagnosed this as a burn; the mother then sought a second opinion and the further examination of the younger sibling showed unexplained burns on the baby too. The mother explained that the boy had burned himself on the washing line, and the baby had crawled backwards in to the radiator. She had not sought treatment for either child. The photograph shows an old, almost healed contact burn over the buttocks and left upper thigh. These were unexplained contact burns in both children. Further investigation was difficult but showed a severely dysfunctional family. The burns were thought to be inflicted but no further information was forthcoming.

▲ 5.17, ▶ 5.18 Male aged 4 years

He was seen by a paediatrician as part of a planned follow-up following earlier neglect, and his mother mentioned that he had been sitting too close to the fire. Paired linear contact burns of the outer aspect of the thigh and lower leg are seen. Note that when the leg is flexed the pattern is seen clearly (Fig. 5.18). It is difficult to see how the injury was caused with the child's leg bent.

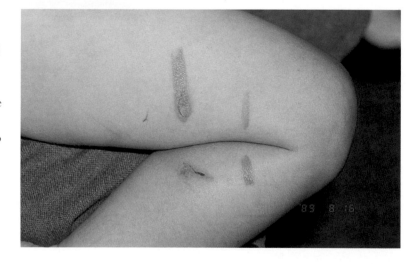

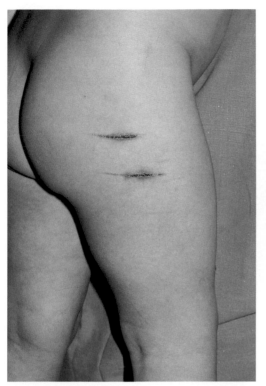

◄ ◄ ▼ ▼ 5.19 – 5.22 Male aged 4 years

When the health visitor was visiting routinely she was shown a burn, and the child's father commented that he was always falling against the fire. Multiple linear burns are seen, both recent and well healed, on the outer aspect of thigh. These were deliberately inflicted with a hot implement over a period of time. (Note: accidental burns rarely occur more than once to the same child.)

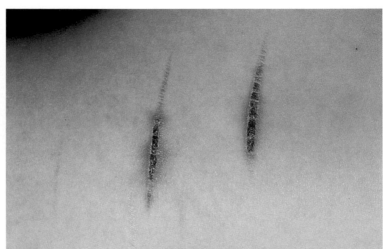

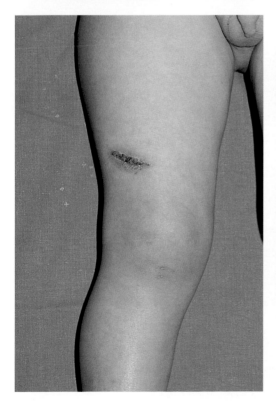

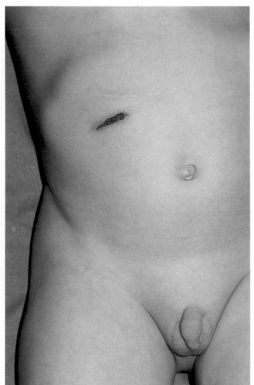

▼ ▶ ▶ **5.23–5.25 Female aged 11 years**
She attended a school for children with moderate
learning problems and was already known
because of emotional difficulties in relation to
her stepmother. She presented in school with
bruising to the face, burns on the back of the
hand and neck, and signs of sexual abuse.
Healing burns can be seen on the dorsum of the
hand and back of the neck. The stepmother
admitted burning the child with a spatula while
frying eggs. Figure to the right shows healed skin
at the back of the neck with depigmentation,
which ensures differentiation from superficial
skin infection, e.g. impetigo.

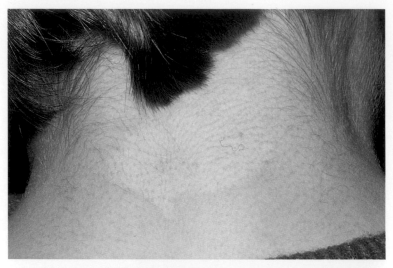

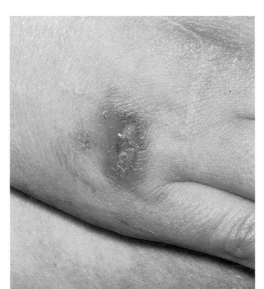

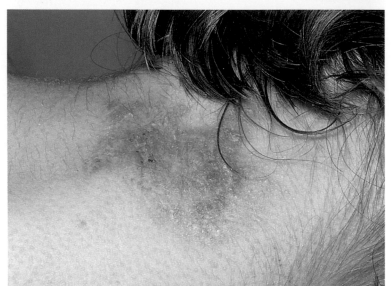

▶ **5.26 Female aged 7 years**
Burns were an incidental finding when she was
being examined in the follow-up clinic because
of a vaginal discharge. There was a past history of
physical, sexual and emotional abuse and neglect.
The photograph shows a burn from a grid mark
which has healed with linear hyperpigmentation.
This is a very worrying injury, especially in the
context of the other abuses.

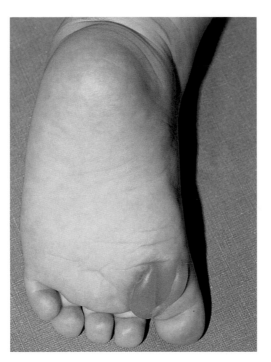

▶ 5.28 Female aged 6 years

She was referred because of possible sexual abuse, and burns were an incidental finding. Parallel linear contact burns are seen on the outer aspect of the elbow, which were unexplained.

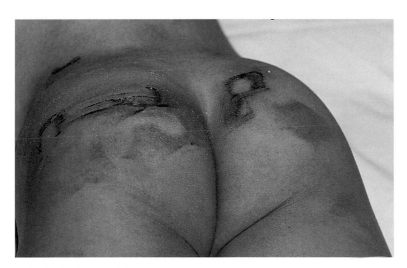

▲ 5.29 Male aged 5 years

He had a history of being beaten by his father. Extensive bruising of both buttocks is seen, but also skin loss; on the left buttock, seen as linear healing marks, and on the right buttock a roughly rectangular area of skin loss without evident healing. This is a difficult case to interpret but there is a probability of a burn superimposed on a beating.

▶ 5.30 Male aged 2 years

He was referred because of neglect and failure to thrive, along with his siblings. The parents said he had picked up a hot iron and burned himself, but they had not sought medical help. The photograph shows a long linear healing burn on the anterior aspect of the right thigh, of partial thickness. The burn is consistent with contact with the edge of a hot iron; the history however needs further investigation.

◀ 5.27 Male aged 12 months

He was seen with his 2-year-old brother at the request of the social services after a convicted child abuser had become part of the household. The older brother was demonstrating disturbed behaviour including soiling. Examination of the older boy showed signs consistent with anal abuse and the baby had an unexplained burn. The photograph shows a superficial blistering burn on the sole of the foot, which was unexplained.

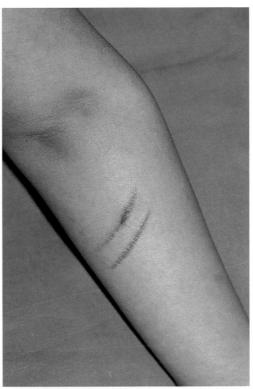

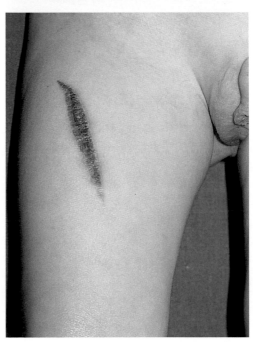

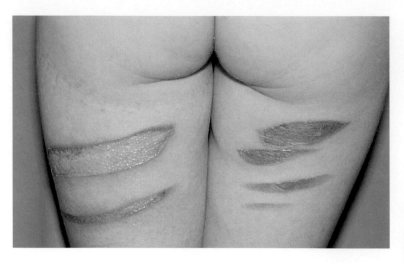

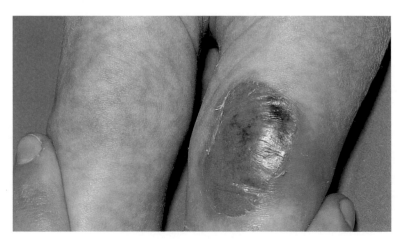

◀ 5.31 Female aged 6 years

She was severely mentally handicapped. The history given was that she 'sat on the fire' but medical help was not sought. Linear contact burns are seen on the back of the thighs, of several days standing and of variable thickness. There was a previous history of unexplained bruises and scratches. This is a significant injury in a vulnerable child who is not being protected.

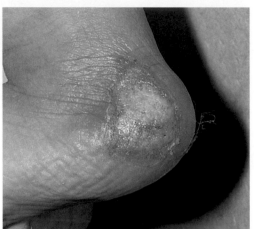

▶ 5.32 Male aged 8 months

It was claimed that he had 'crawled against the fire'. The photograph shows a healing contact burn on the outer aspect of the left heel. Accidental contact burns are usually trivial as the child removes the limb quickly; this is a deep burn and of great concern.

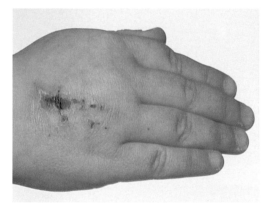

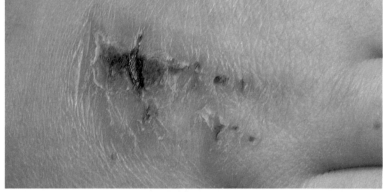

▲ 5.33, ▲ 5.34 Female aged 4 years

She presented as having 'touched the fire with her hand'. A healing contact burn of the dorsum of the left hand is seen, of several days duration. Contact burns of the hand are usually on the palmar aspect, therefore this is an unusual site. There is also a past history of sexual abuse, physical abuse causing a fracture of the tibia, and emotional abuse of this child.

◀ 5.35 Female aged 3 months

The burn was found by a health visitor on a routine visit. The parents speculated that they had perhaps put the baby's feeding bottle in the carrycot with the baby and this had caused the injury. An extensive healing contact burn is seen over the left lower thigh and knee, which is unexplained. It is also not clear if this a scald or a contact burn.

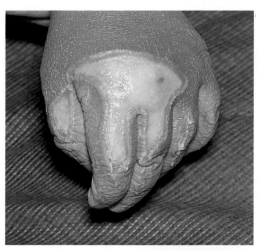

◀ **5.36 Male aged 18 months**

He was said to have touched the fire. There is an extensive irregular contact burn on the back of the left hand. The injury looked superficially like a scald, but note the burn is over bony prominences, and the alteration in skin texture due to treatment. The cause is unknown.

▼ **5.37, ▼ 5.38 Female aged 2 years**

Her history as given by teenage babysitters was that the child had fallen asleep on a settee and slipped so that her foot touched the fireguard. An extensive burn with blistering outer aspect of the right forefoot with clearly demarcated edge is seen. This is a serious, unexplained injury possibly due to immersion in hot water.

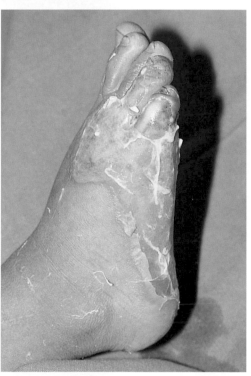

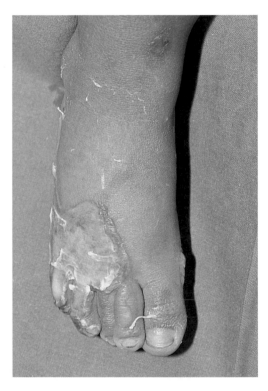

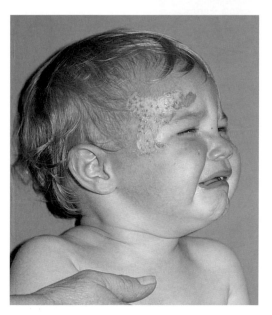

◀ **5.39 Female aged 15 months**

She was taken to the hospital emergency department several hours after the parents said that she had been injured falling against a fire whilst left alone in a room. The photograph shows an irregular, roughly triangular scald to the front and side of forehead. The history was inconsistent with a contact burn – later her parents said she had been eating very hot pizza. Additionally there was a fresh, unexplained burn on the child's arm and unusual bruises on the thighs and feet.

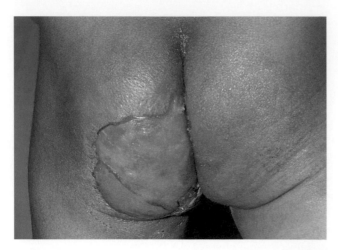

◀ 5.40 Male aged 6 years

He presented with a history of having 'leant against a convection heater'. The photograph shows an immersion scald primarily affecting the left buttock but extending into the natal cleft. The history is inconsistent with the injury, particularly as the child was already known to be failing to thrive and also suffering severe emotional abuse.

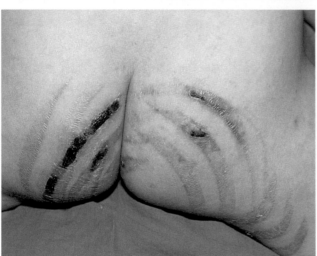

◀ 5.41 Female aged 13 months

She presented as having climbed onto the worktop and then sat on the cooker. Her father had heard her crying and had lifted her down. Concentric circular burns to both buttocks and to the top of the right thigh can be been seen in the photograph. The injury is not consistent with the history given. More than one contact has occurred, and in a position not consistent with sitting. A serious and sadistic injury.

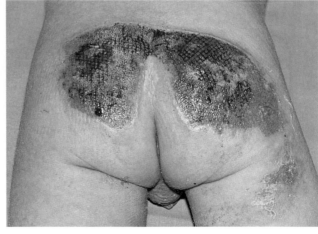

▲ 5.42 Male aged 4 years

The history given by his foster father was that the child was found in a bath of hot water, the father having left the room to get a towel. There is an extensive contact burn of the buttocks and right upper thigh with healing already apparent. This injury is not consistent with the history given, and this has the appearance of a contact burn, complicated by delayed presentation.

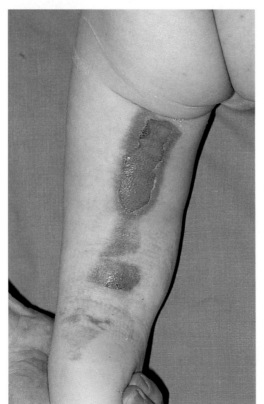

◀ 5.43 Male aged 14 months

He presented with a history of being 'wedged' between a storage heater and the back of a settee; however on a visit to the home a distance of 3 feet (0.9 m) was observed between the furniture and the heater. There is an extensive superficial contact burn on the back of the left thigh but sparing the back of knee. This is an unsatisfactory history in a child who had previously had unexplained apnoeic attacks, failure to thrive, and at the age of four an unexplained fractured femur.

Scalds

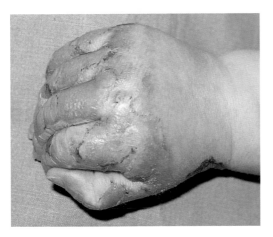

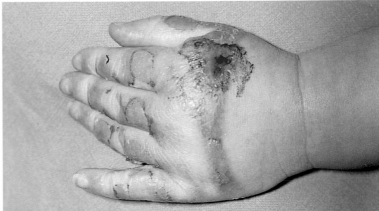

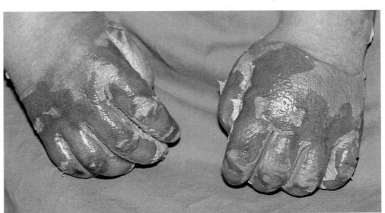

▲ 5.44, ▲ 5.45 Female aged 3 years

She was claimed by her mother to have climbed into a hot bath fully clothed, where she was found sitting upright with her hands immersed in the water. The photographs show immersion injury to the distal part of both hands only – a symmetrical injury with a clear tide mark. This is a typical forced immersion scald.

▲ 5.46 Male aged 21 months

The history given was that he fell forwards into the bath. He was treated at home by his mother, who was a nurse, for 4 days. He was also found to be failing to thrive. This is a typical forced immersion scald. (Note: bath scalds do not occur in non-impaired adults.)

◄ 5.47 Male aged 3 years

He was said to have put his hand into a kettle of boiling water. An immersion scald of the hand and wrist is seen, with extensive skin loss. The history given is unacceptable.

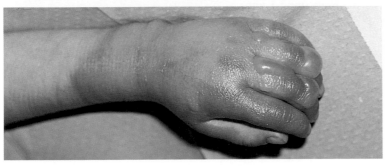

◄ 5.48 Male aged 3 years

The history given was that he fell into a hot bath. There is an immersion scald of the hand and wrist with blistering and swelling. A clear tide mark can be seen. This is an unacceptable history. Other members of the family have failed to thrive and there is also history of sexual abuse.

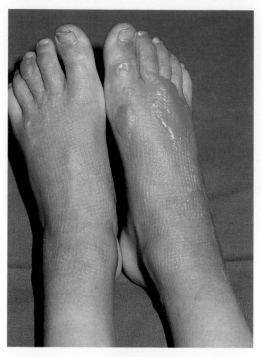

◀ 5.49 Male aged 5 years

He was made to stand in a bath of hot water by his mother's partner. He had a long previous history of emotional abuse. An immersion scald of both feet is seen with a faint tide mark and blistering. The injury is consistent with the history given.

▼ 5.50 Male aged 4 years

A changing history was given; initially the mother said she left him to play in the bath when she went to fetch the soap, and he must have turned on the hot tap and then got himself out of the bath. When she dried the child's foot the skin came off. The mother assaulted the policewoman during an interview and then admitted that she had put him into the hot bath to teach him a lesson. There is a typical immersion scald of both feet and the bottom (only the right foot is shown here). The injury was deep and the foot required grafting. The injury is consistent with the history, i.e. abuse

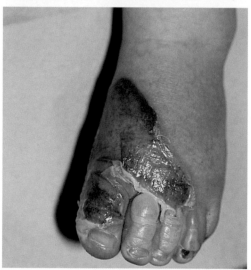

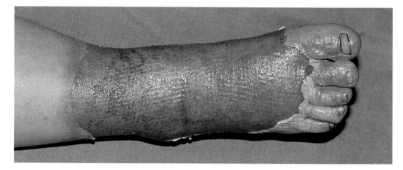

◀ 5.51 Male aged 18 months

He was said to have put his foot in a bowl of porridge which was on the floor. There is a clear immersion injury of the left forefoot. No other features of the history suggest abuse, but this is a worrying injury and a preventable one. Adherent porridge caused an enhanced injury.

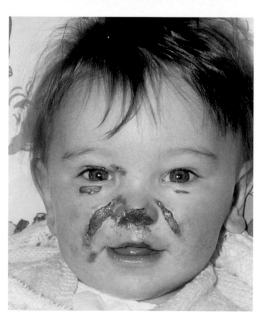

◀ 5.52 Male aged 1 year

The history given was that he picked up a mug of hot soup and tipped it over himself. The child was failing to thrive and had feeding difficulties. His father initially refused admission to hospital. An extensive scald to the face is seen in an unusual pattern. The mechanism for this injury is not clear; the mug may have been pushed in his face, the soup thrown, or the child could have caused this injury to himself.

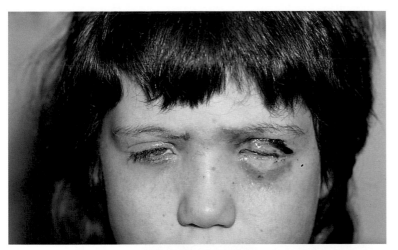

◀ **5.53 Female aged 6 years**

The history given was that she 'looked into a kettle of boiling water'. There is a scald injury to both eyes, worse on the left, with early infection evident. This is an unusual and worrying history, not previously encountered.

 **5.54, ▶ 5.55**
Male aged 2 years
The history given was that he pulled a mug of hot tea over himself. There is a scald to the side of the face, ear, left shoulder and upper arm. This is a typical pour scald, though more severe than usual.

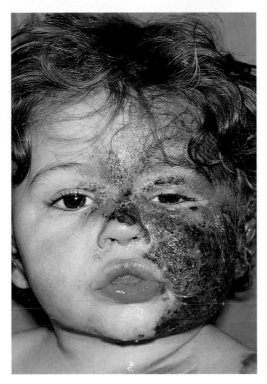

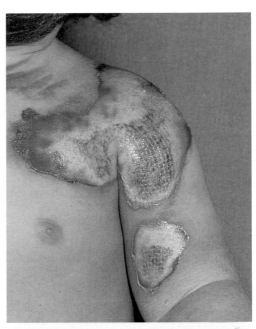

▶ **5.56 Male aged 1 year**
He presented as having pulled a kettle of hot water over himself. There is an extensive scald of variable thickness with skin loss and swelling over the face, upper chest and upper arms. This is a common accidental injury, which should be preventable with coiled kettle flexes.

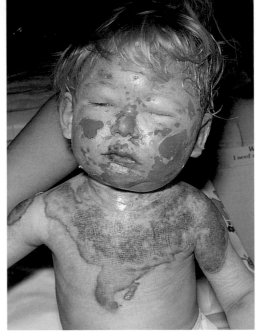

▶ 5.57, ▼ 5.58 Female aged 3 years

The child is severely mentally and physically handicapped. She was scalded while being bathed in a bath appliance (Fig. 5.57). Her family are known to have a history of child sexual abuse, physical abuse and murder. A patterned recent superficial scald is seen with blistering over the trunk. This is consistent with the history of being washed with excessively hot water.

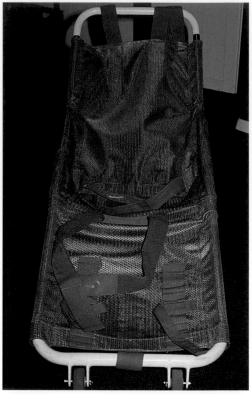

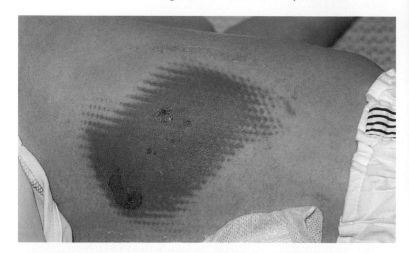

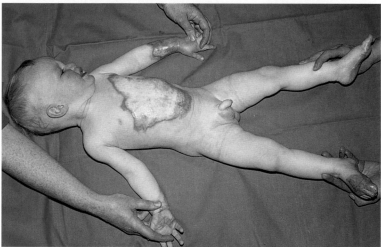

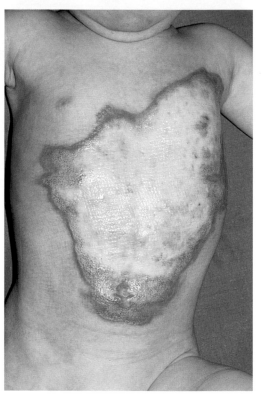

▲ 5.59, ▶ 5.60 Male aged 18 months

The child had a past history of severe failure to thrive. The history given was that he pulled a kettle of boiling water onto himself, with the water splashing his abdomen, foot and arm. There are widespread scalds to the abdomen, arms and foot, which are showing signs of healing. The accident was due to serious neglect.

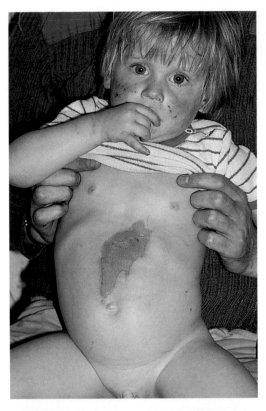

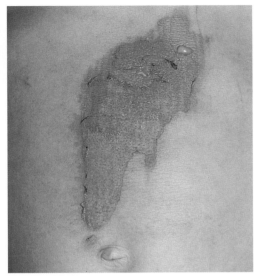

▲ 5.61, ◀ 5.62 Male aged 2½ years

He was seen to be scalded by the health visitor on a routine visit. An older sibling was said to have poured a mug of hot tea on her brother. A healing scald with blistering and healing is seen on the upper abdomen. This is probably an accidental scald, but note the bite on the right forearm, and a younger child in the same household died of bronchopneumonia following measles. The care of this scald had been neglected.

◀ 5.63 Male aged 20 months

It was claimed that he had 'reached over the edge of the bath and fell forward with his hands in the hot water'. The mother, a nurse, pulled him out and treated him at home initially; then took him to the hospital emergency department. There is marked, previously unrecognized failure to thrive, as well as partial thickness bilateral immersion scalds in glove distribution. This is a forced immersion scald. (This is the same child as in Fig. 5.46)

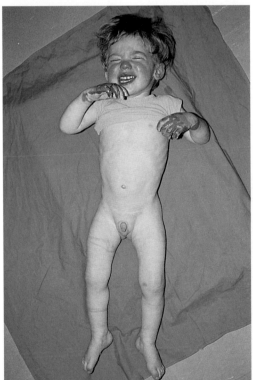

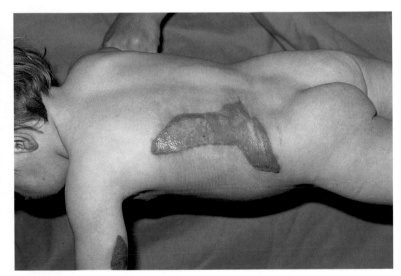

▲ 5.64 Male aged 16 months

He was 'found screaming in the kitchen'. An extensive scald is seen over the back and left upper arm posteriorly. The distribution of the scald suggests a splash injury, but this is an unusual distribution and there is a worrying lack of history.

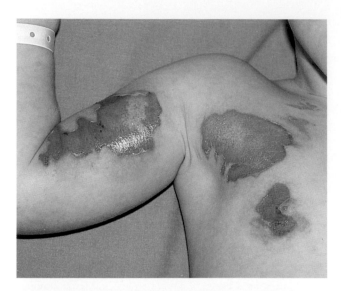

◀ 5.65 Female aged 3 years

She was taken late at night to hospital emergency department with a recent scald. It emerged that the drunken father had thrown a cup of coffee at the child because he felt 'she was up too late'. The photograph shows the splash effect with scattered, separate areas of superficial scalding..

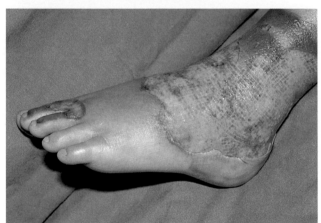

◀ ◀ ▼ ▼ 5.66–5.69 Male aged 3 years

His father claimed that the child had fallen into the bath of hot water with his shoes and socks on. Bilateral, severe partial to full thickness scalds of both feet can be seen. There are no splash marks and the dorsum of the feet have been spared. All of this indicates a typical forced immersion injury.

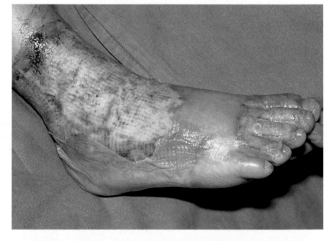

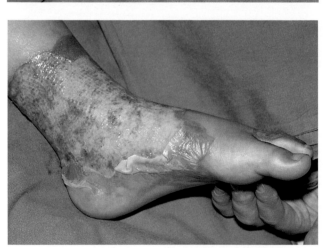

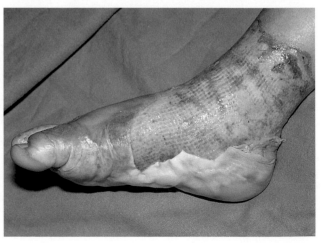

Friction burns

▼ 5.70 Female aged 6 months
She presented to the hospital emergency department with an unexplained lesion on her forehead. She was a healthy, well-nourished, thriving baby with a superficial, circular burn on the prominence of her forehead and a graze above the nose. There was also recent diffuse blue bruising of the buttocks. A carpet burn was diagnosed, and the mother subsequently gave a history of dragging the child across the floor by her feet.

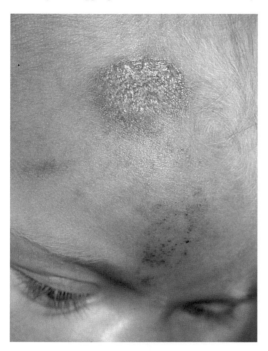

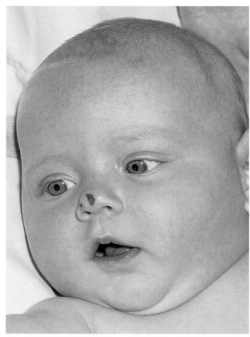

◀ 5.71 Female aged 6 weeks
She had been pulled across the floor by an arm. Superficial skin loss of the nose can be seen. This is a carpet burn. The child also had a spiral fracture of the humerus.

Scars

▶ 5.72 Female aged 13 years
She presented with a history of previous physical abuse by the mother. The girl recalled that her feet had been burned by her mother's partner with whom she had been left as a toddler. Extensive scarring of both feet can be seen, which was an incidental finding. This demonstrates how abuse by burning leaves life-long scars.

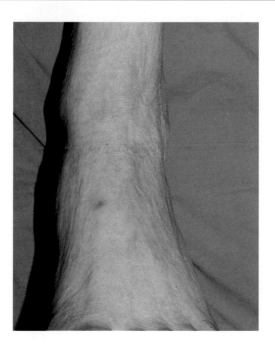

▶ 5.73, ▼ 5.74 Male aged 4 years

He was seen because of bruising to his face. Scarring was noted on the anterior chest, and he was claimed to have pulled a cup of hot fluid over himself. There was also a history of physical and sexual abuse involving his mother. The photographs show scarring on the anterior chest and right upper arm with keloid formation. Note the unusual distribution of the injury. Note: Burns are now well recognized to be part of the wider picture of child abuse, particularly child sexual abuse. Accidents also occur more commonly in abusing families.

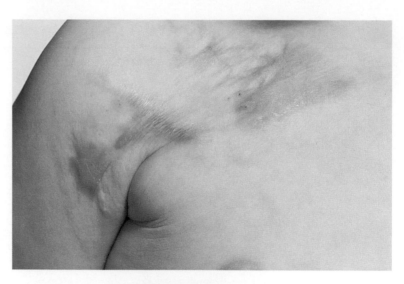

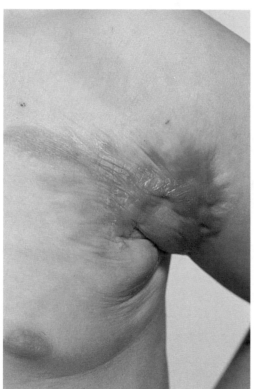

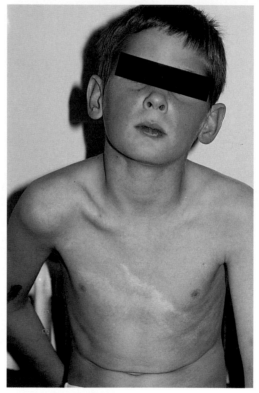

◀ 5.75 Male aged 11 years

Scarring was found incidentally after he had been referred because of emotional abuse and failure to thrive. Extensive old scarring can be seen over the centre of the chest. The mother recalled the history of scalding when the child was very young and pulled a cup of tea over himself

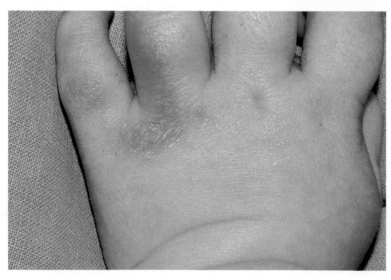

◀ 5.76 Female aged 18 months

She was examined with her siblings because of black eyes, failure to thrive and sexual abuse. A healed burn is seen on the dorsum of the fourth and fifth fingers of the left hand. The appearance is consistent with a healed burn. Note the unusual site for accidental injury. No explanation was offered.

Cigarette burns

▶ **5.77 Male aged 6 months**
He was referred because of unexplained lesions on the face. This is a typical cigarette burn, round with a punched out centre and showing early healing. The child had several similar burns on his face, all consistent with cigarette burns.

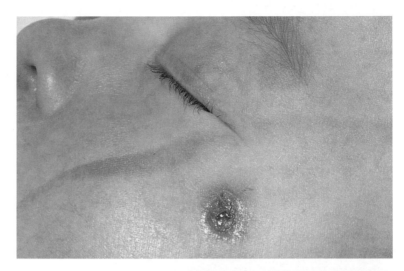

▼ **5.78 Female aged 6 weeks**
She was with her mother in a child and mother's home. The mother said she dropped ash accidentally on the baby when she was smoking. A typical punched out cigarette burn can be seen on the lower jaw and neck. These two lesions are superimposable; the cigarette may have been held forcibly against the child while the neck was flexed.

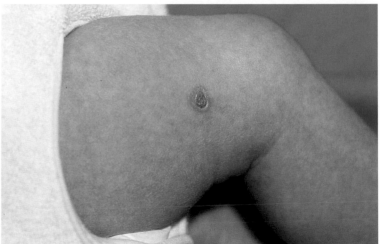

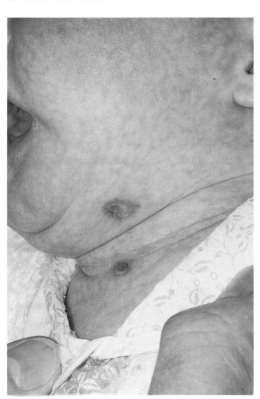

▲ **5.79 Female aged 6 weeks**
The mother had initially wanted the child to be adopted. The mark was found incidentally by the midwife. A typical punched out cigarette mark is seen on the outer aspect of the right upper thigh.

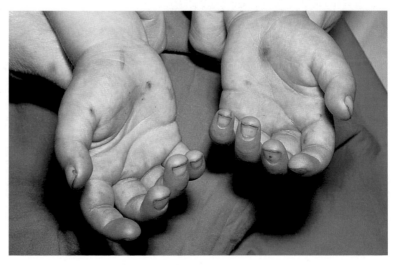

▶ **5.80 Male aged 5 years**
He presented a history that he had been playing out with older boys and he said they had burned him with matches. There are several small burns on the palmar aspect of hands. These injuries are consistent with burns from match ends. The child is from a large, extended, neglected family.

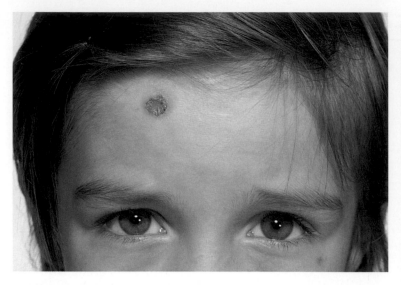

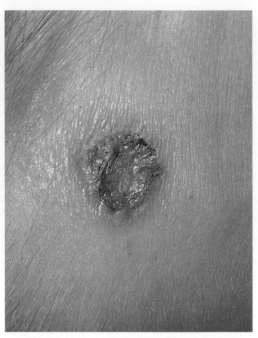

▲ 5.81, ▶ 5.82 Female aged 7 years

The child told her school teacher that her father had burned her with a cigarette. There is a typical cigarette burn on the forehead.

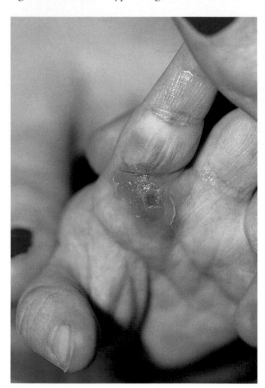

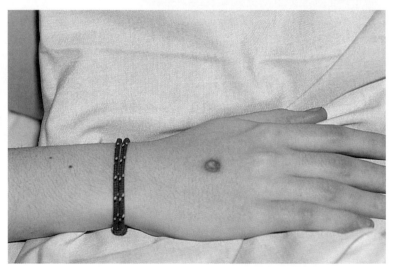

▲ 5.84 Female aged 16 years

She had a long history of physical and sexual abuse at home. She refused to say who had caused the cigarette injury to the back of the hand as shown, and 16 other similar lesions found on limbs, breasts, back, thighs, etc. The lesions were seen when she returned to a safe house from home. This is a typical punched out cigarette burn.

▲ 5.83 Male aged 3 months

The history was that the child grasped hold of a cigarette. There is a superficial burn with blistering over the metacarpal-phalangeal joint of the index finger. This is a very worrying injury in a young infant, consistent with a cigarette burn.

▶ 5.85 Male aged 2 years

He presented in the hospital emergency department with a metaphyseal fracture of the humerus. There was unexplained bruising of the face and ear, and the lesion as shown. There were also signs of sexual abuse. This is a typical healing cigarette burn with heaped up skin, over the front of the left knee. This was a multiply abused child.

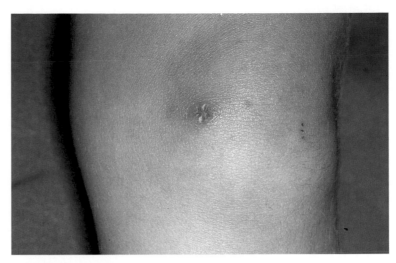

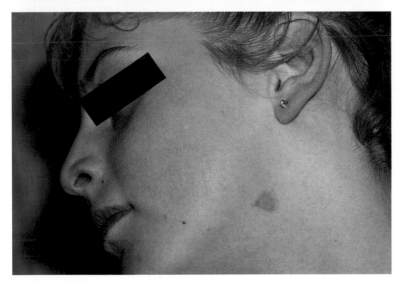

◀ 5.86 Male aged 2 years

He had a history of playing in the garden when he brushed against an adult neighbour's cigarette. An eccentric but moderately deep burn is seen on the left cheek, consistent with glancing contact with a cigarette.

◀ 5.87 Female aged 15 years

She was deliberately burned by her older brother with a cigarette during 'horseplay'. The girl made a complaint at school about the injury. There is an asymmetrical burn below the lower jaw, showing healing, which is consistent with the history. This is abuse.

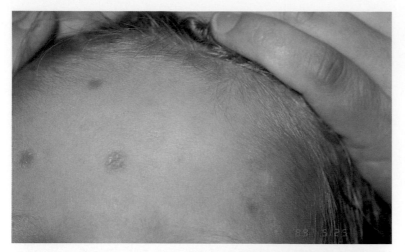

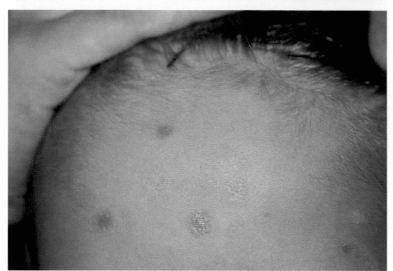

◀ ◀ ◀ ▼ **5.88–5.91 Brothers aged 3 years and 5 years**

The boys presented to the paediatrician after the younger child was found wandering in the street and was referred by police. A doctor had been 'treating' the lesions on the boys for the previous 2 years. Multiple circular, punched out lesions are seen at various stages of healing, some with paper-thin scarring. The lesions are all on the upper half of the face. They are consistent with cigarette burns at various stages of healing. The mother had several cigarette burns on her forearms; she initially admitted to causing these lesions but then retracted. Several expert opinions were obtained; these included a diagnosis of chickenpox, acne excoriée and impetigo. The lesions all healed quickly in care, and the final diagnosis was cigarette burns.

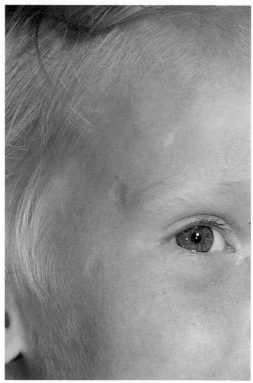

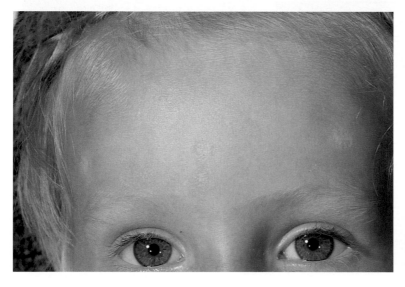

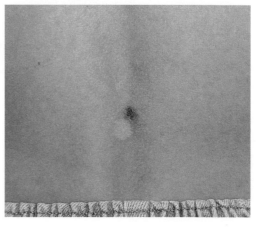

▶ **5.92 Male aged 8 years**

The child was profoundly deaf. He presented saying he had been burned in the street by a stranger. There was a history of previous sexual abuse by an older brother. A circular scar is seen on the lower back with depigmented scar tissue. There is also a recent irregular burn just superior to the scar. These appear to be a healed and a recent cigarette burn. (Note: children with disability are at high risk of abuse.)

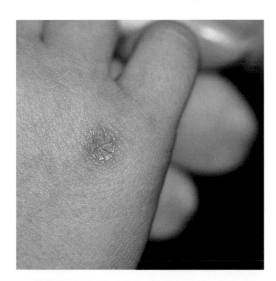

◄ 5.93 Male aged 4 years

He presented in the context of a custody dispute, where both parents made allegations of sexual abuse. The physical signs were consistent with anal abuse. There is a healed circular cigarette burn at the base of the fifth finger. Note the association with sexual abuse.

▼ 5.94 Female aged 10 months

The child was examined as part of an investigation in a family where older siblings were failing to thrive and had been severely abused. A healing circular scar is seen in the palm of the right hand, consistent with a cigarette burn. No history was available: this is an unacceptable injury.

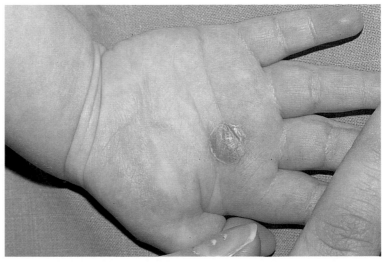

◄ 5.95, ▼ 5.96 Male aged 5 years

It was claimed that he had been burned with a match by an unknown assailant. There is a circular, deep burn in the left cheek with charring. This is consistent with a match burn, but it is not acceptable to have no named assailant.

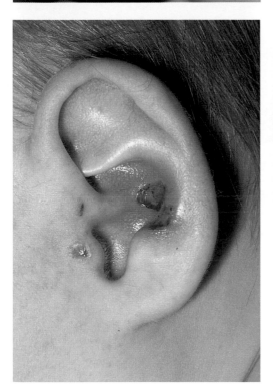

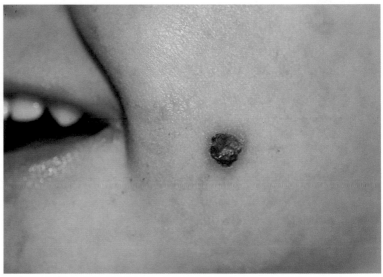

◄ 5.97 Male aged 4 months

He was seen by a health visitor with unexplained marks on the face and ear. A cigarette burn is seen in the inner aspect of the left pinna. Two smaller burns, one partially healed, and a small laceration can also be seen. This is a non-accidental injury, and a serious sadistic repeated physical assault.

Miscellaneous

▶ 5.98 Male aged 6 years

He was taken to the hospital emergency department with a history that he had been playing outside with older boys when a canister was thrown on the fire and exploded. There are multiple burns on the face with blistering and skin loss consistent with explosion injury. The child had had previous other minor injuries, and was poorly protected.

▼ 5.99 Male aged 2 years

The history given was that the child had poked a piece of paper in the fire and set himself on fire. The photograph shows a burn to the left upper ear with skin loss. Singed hair is also seen. These injuries are consistent with flame burn of the ear in a non-protected child.

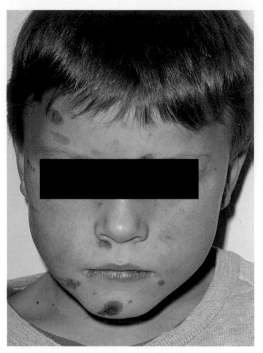

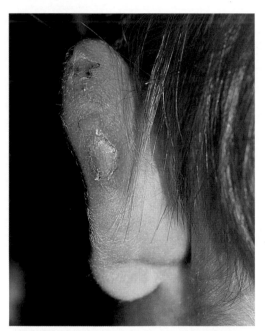

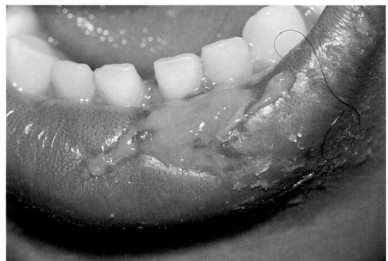

▲ 5.100 Male aged 3 years

He was brought to the hospital emergency department with a history that he had fallen into the bath. However there were burns on four separate areas, i.e. lower lip, arm, foot and leg. There was previous history of a bilateral wrist drop from a suspension injury. The photograph shows a burn with skin loss and marked swelling of the lower lip. This injury is not explained by the given history. The mother later confirmed abuse by her partner.

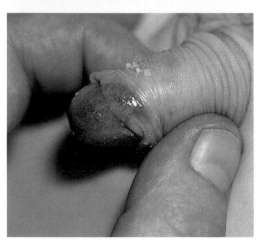

◀ 5.101 Male aged 2 years

The child was taken to the hospital emergency department with an unexplained lesion on the penis. Recent superficial burn of the foreskin and glans penis can be seen, only visible with the foreskin retracted. This is a contact burn. The parents later said that he must have caught his penis on the radiator while standing micturating in the WC. The diagnosis is sadistic injury.

▶ **5.102 Female aged 2 months**

She was taken to the hospital emergency department with a history that the mother's partner had fallen on the stairs, banging the child's head. Examination showed severe facial bruising, a fractured skull and eye injury. The photograph shows clouding of the cornea and injected conjunctivae. This is an unexplained burn to the eye, in the context of severe physical abuse. The child lost sight in the eye.

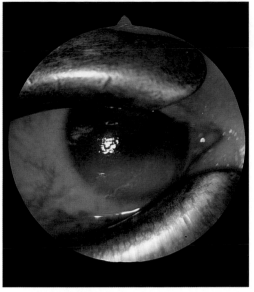

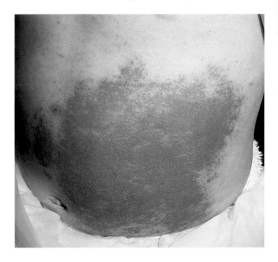

◀ **5.103 Female aged 1 year**

The mother admitted to putting bleach in the bath water. There are extensive superficial chemical burns over the abdomen. This is abuse.

▼ ▼ ▼ **5.104–5.106 Female aged 14 months**

Her teenage parents, both heroin addicted, noticed 'smoke and the sound of frying bacon' when the child stood on a cool fire surround. The parents suggested a bare electrical wire had touched the surround and electrocuted the child. There was no evidence of this. There is an extensive, very deep burn of the sole and instep of the right foot. The injury was estimated to be 3–4 days old, and required a skin graft. This is a severe contact burn, not acquired as described.

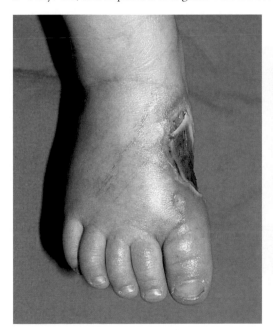

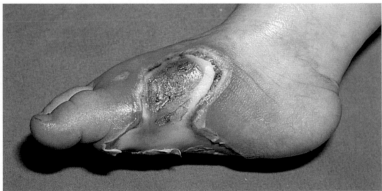

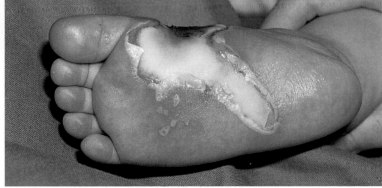

◄ 5.107, ▲ 5.108 Female aged 3 years

The child was burned after a family outing to the seaside, where she spent the whole of a sunny day on the beach. The child was taken to the hospital emergency department 1 week later. There is an extensive burn covering the entire back, with blistering and healing evident. The burn is limited to the area usually covered by clothing. The diagnosis of severe sunburn was made after considerable thought, with recognition that the skin underlying clothing had not received any previous tanning and therefore was susceptible to burn.

◄ 5.109 Female aged 13 years

The child, with spina bifida and impaired sensation in lower limbs, presented with a sudden and unexplained breakdown of 'bedsore in right groin'. There is an area of ulceration resembling a burn in the middle of healed, reddened skin following an earlier bedsore. This is a chemical burn due to antiseptic cream on previously injured skin.

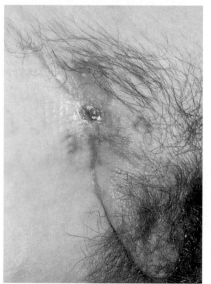

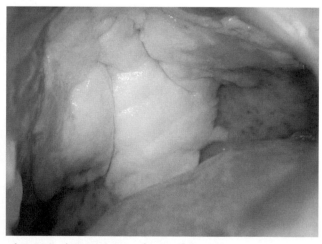

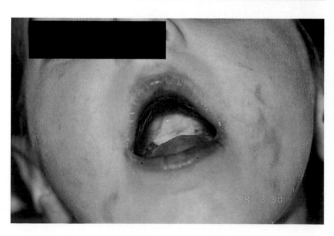

◄ 5.110, ▲ 5.111 Female aged 4 years

The child was in foster care because of a failure to thrive, emotional abuse and sexual abuse. The foster mother stated that the child had picked up a hot drink and had thus burned her mouth. Investigation revealed an extensive slough across the palate, and red marks on the cheek and above the upper lip. The indications are that the child has probably been forcibly fed hot food.

Differential diagnosis (other than accidental burns)

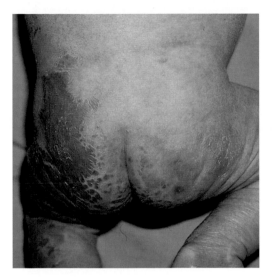

▶ 5.113 Male aged 3 years
He presented in day nursery with unexplained lesions on the abdomen and thigh. Circular red lesions with crusting can be seen, and small satellite lesions are visible. The diagnosis is impetigo.

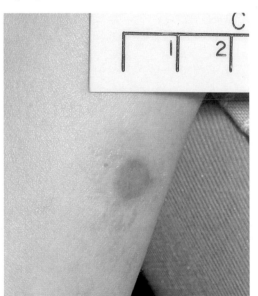

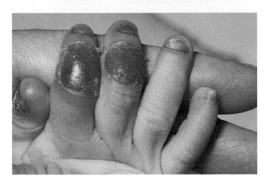

◀ 5.112 Male aged 1 month
He was referred because of poor weight gain and a skin rash. There is severe failure to thrive and an extensive ammoniacal burn. The diagnosis is a severe chemical burn due to neglect.

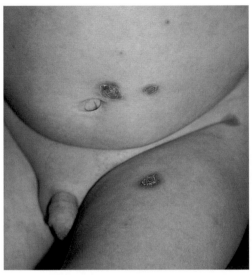

◀ 5.114 Male aged 4 years
He was seen in nursery with an injury to the left forearm thought to be a cigarette burn. The photograph shows a circular lesion with skin loss and blistering (scale in centimetres). The diagnosis is impetigo. (Note: this was an early impetigenous lesion, which healed without scarring. If this lesion had been a cigarette burn it would have almost inevitably healed with scarring.)

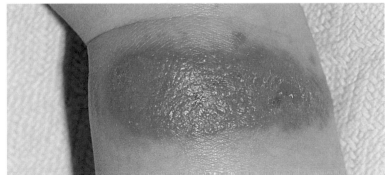

▲ 5.115 Male aged 6 months
He had been wearing a hospital name band. A reddened swollen area with superficial skin loss is seen in an area in contact with the band. Note the similarity to a contact burn.

◀ 5.116 Neonate
Presented with unexplained blistering of the skin. The diagnosis is epidermolysis bullosa.

Chapter 6

Head and eye injuries

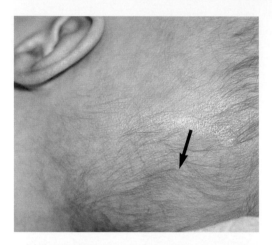

◀ 6.1 Female aged 2 months

The child was brought by her parents to the hospital emergency department because she was unresponsive and fitting. She was deeply unconscious with a small bruise on the occiput (arrow). No other external injuries were evident. The child subsequently died from serious head injuries including skull fracture, subdural haematoma and retinal haemorrhages. (Note: young infants in particular may present without signs of external injury, and physical abuse must always be considered in a differential diagnosis of unexplained fitting, 'ill baby' or sudden collapse.)

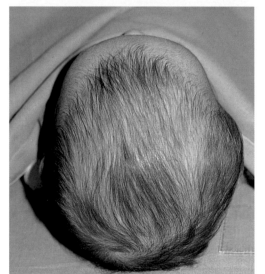

◀ 6.2 Male aged 5 months

The mother noticed a large bump on the side of his head. She later gave a history of the television falling on his head 3 days previously, a fall against a coffee table, and a relative then said that the child's head had been kicked. There is a large fluctuant swelling over the parietal eminence. Further investigation showed a long parietal fracture with overlying haematoma. This injury would be consistent with a kick from a boot. Young infants seen with a swelling on the side of the head and no history of trauma are likely to have been abused.

▶ 6.3 Female aged 5 months

The child was brought to the hospital emergency department by parents because she was 'unrousable'. She was deeply unconscious with multiple injuries to the face, scratches and early bruising with oedema of the face. Further investigation revealed retinal haemorrhages and subdural haematoma on CT scan. This baby had been physically assaulted causing the injuries to her face, and she had also been shaken.

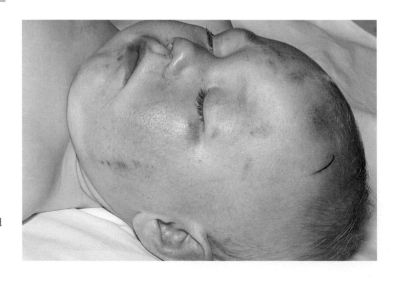

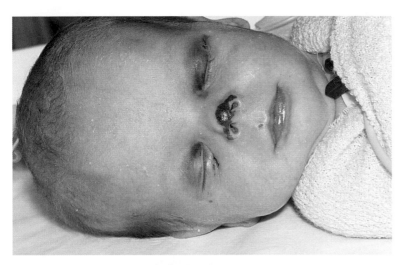

◀ 6.4 Female aged 3 months

The child was found fitting when her parents awoke in the morning. The photograph shows a deeply unconscious infant with peri-orbital haematoma and an extensive carpet burn to the nose. This infant had suffered a severe head injury with skull fracture and intracerebral haemorrhage. She survived but now has severe cerebral palsy and significant learning difficulties.

▶ 6.5, ▶ 6.6 Female aged 2 months

The mother's male partner accidentally dropped her on the stairs. A laceration above the right eye is seen, showing signs of healing, with marked oedema to the right side of the face, infra-orbital and cheek bruising. There is dried blood about the nose, and an injury to the lip (not shown on this photograph). Further examination showed a burn of the right cornea, demonstrated

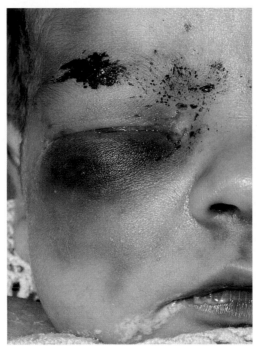

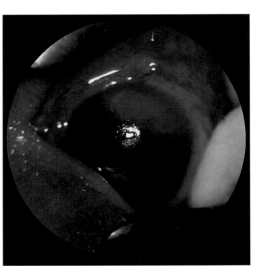

using fluorescein (Fig. 6.6). Further investigation showed a complex parietal skull fracture, caused by impact with a firm object. The other injuries are consistent with blows to the face and head. The cause of the corneal burn is unknown, but the presumption was that it was a cigarette burn. She subsequently suffered a detached retina to the right eye and is now blind in this eye.

▶ 6.7 Female aged 2½ years

The child presented with unexplained bruising, which had been noted by a social worker on a routine visit. There is marked swelling across the forehead with bruising and tracking of blood giving bilateral peri-orbital haematoma. The eyes are not injured. (Note: fading bruise around the angle of the right jaw; bruises were also seen on the upper arms, abdomen, back and thighs.) This child had been punished for not using her potty by having her head banged against the floor. She was thus the victim of physical assault, emotional abuse and subsequent investigation showed she had also been sexually abused.

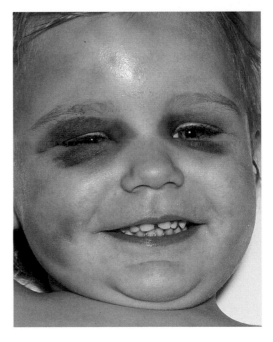

▶ 6.8 Male aged 4 years

The boy returned from an access visit to his father with unexplained black eyes and multiple burns. There is swelling of the forehead and bilateral peri-orbital haematoma, with no injury to the eyes. He also had burns to the genitalia, buttocks and lower legs, and he gave a history of attempted buggery. (Note: there is an association between sadistic burns and sexual abuse.)

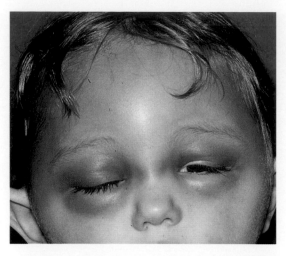

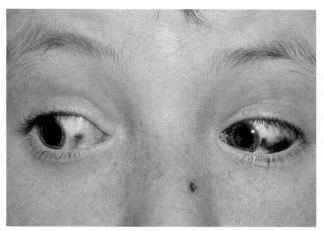

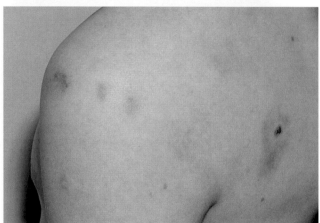

▲ 6.9, ▲ 6.10 Male aged 13 years

The child told his teacher at school that he had been 'beaten up' by his father. Bilateral subconjunctival haemorrhage can be seen with a small area of skin loss over the bridge of the nose, and extensive diffuse bruising over the back. Subconjunctival haemorrhage may be caused by blunt trauma, e.g. a fist causing direct damage to the orbit, or a similar injury may be seen due to strangulation, where there may or may not be associated petechiae of the upper eyelids. Subconjunctival haemorrhage may also be caused by bouts of paroxysmal coughing, e.g. whooping cough. The combination of injuries here is consistent with the boy's history, i.e. he has been beaten up.

▶ 6.11 Male aged 3 years

The child was taken to the hospital emergency department by his parents because of bleeding from his mouth. He was said to have fallen off the settee. There is subconjunctival haemorrhage, but also bruising around the orbit. This eye injury is consistent with a blunt injury, e.g. a fist. The child also had a markedly swollen upper lip, also consistent with blunt trauma. (Note: this pattern of injury is not caused by a simple fall as described.)

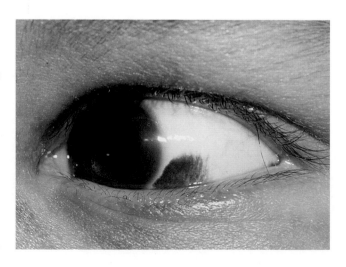

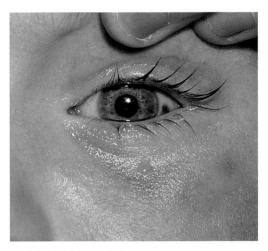

▲ 6.12 Male aged 4 years

The child returned home crying saying he had been hit by older boys. The photograph shows subconjunctival haemorrhage, with peri-orbital swelling and bruising. The injury is consistent with a blunt impact, e.g. a fist in the orbit. (Note: the changing colour of the bruising, suggesting this bruise may have been more than 1 day old, i.e. at variance with the history.)

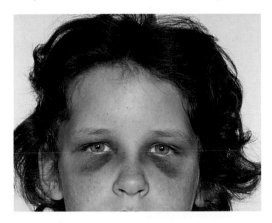

▲ 6.14 Female aged 12 years

The parents took the child to the doctor complaining of an allergic reaction to bath cleaner which had accidentally fallen into the bath. The doctor confirmed this diagnosis. The photograph shows bilateral peri-orbital haematoma, which is consistent with a blunt injury to the forehead. (Note: the father, who was a convicted child abuser, had 2 years earlier admitted to banging the girl's head against a wall causing a similar injury. The girl was also self-mutilating, and was thought to have been sexually abused although this was not confirmed.)

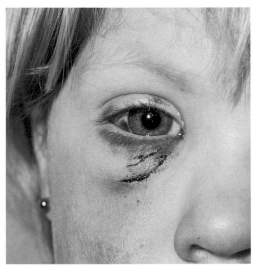

▲ 6.13 Female aged 4 years

The history given was that her mother's male partner was putting her to bed when he accidentally poked her in the eye. There is peri-orbital haematoma with two parallel lacerations below the eye and a subconjunctival haemorrhage. The injury is not compatible with the history given but likely to have been caused by a clenched fist, and the lacerations due to rings on the fingers of the assailant. (Note: this child was later found to have been sexually abused; in any child where there has been a physical injury sexual abuse should also be considered.)

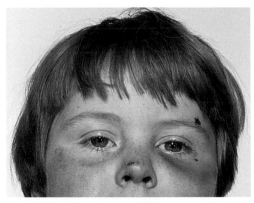

▲ 6.15 Male aged 7 years

The child told his class teacher that his father had hit him when he had wet the bed. There is bilateral old infra-orbital bruising with minor abrasions with skin loss about the orbit at the left and on the nose. The injuries are consistent with multiple blows to the face.

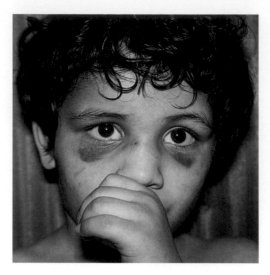

▶ 6.17 Male aged 3 months

The child was seen in an infant welfare clinic with rapid head growth. This is a classic picture of abuse 20 years ago, showing sites where diagnostic and therapeutic subdural taps have been performed. (From 1974: Dr M.F.G. Buchanan.)

▶ 6.18 Male aged 4 years

The mother returned from a shopping trip to find the child in her male partner's arms and unable to rouse the child. He was deeply unconscious with bruising of the face, bleeding from the nose and bruising to the back. The bruising is of different ages. Further investigation revealed recent retinal haemorrhages. There were also signs of anal abuse. The boy died of his head injury.

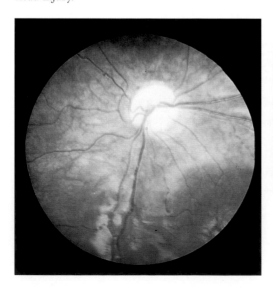

◀ 6.16 Male aged 3 years

The health visitor observed injuries when visiting the house to see a new baby. The photograph shows bilateral infra-orbital haematoma with a small laceration to the bridge of the nose. Old linear scarring of face is also noted, and he was also failing to thrive. The injuries suggest a blow to the frontal area with blood tracking downwards. There was a history of previous physical abuse in this family and also failure to thrive.

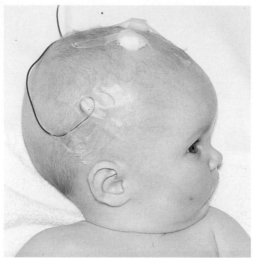

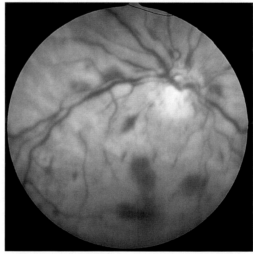

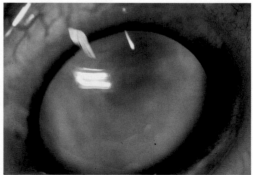

◀ 6.19, ▲ 6.20 Male aged 2 years

This photograph shows optic atrophy resulting from a severe shaking injury in a child who survived. (Photograph provided by Mr R.M.L. Doran.) Another complication of non-accidental injury is cataract as shown in Fig. 6.20.

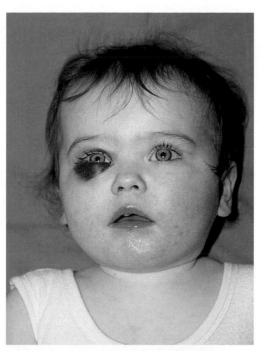

◄ 6.21 Female aged 2 years

The injury to the eye was noticed by a health visitor. A recent right peri-orbital haematoma with swelling is seen. This is a serious unexplained injury in a very young child. There were other bruises on examination of the child but none were diagnostic of physical abuse.

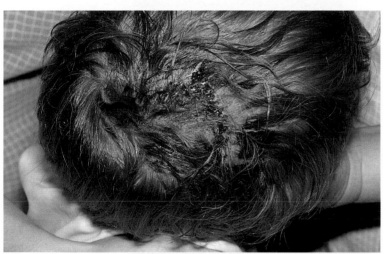

◄ 6.22 Male aged 9 years

The child was bouncing up and down on his bed; his father told him to stop and when he didn't he lifted the boy bodily and threw him onto the bed. His scalp was then lacerated on the bed springs. The photograph shows a long, irregular, deep laceration of the scalp. This is an unusual, worrying history and injury.

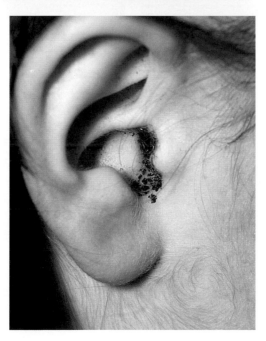

◄ 6.23 Female aged 3 years

The history given was that she fell off a settee. Her parents admitted giving her alcohol. She was drowsy with bleeding from the ear and bruising around the right eye. Fracture of the base of the skull was considered, but bleeding was in fact due to a ruptured eardrum. The diagnosis was physical abuse.

Chapter 7

Fatal abuse

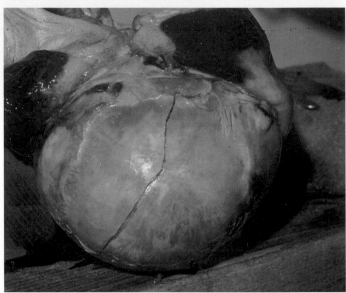

▶ 7.1 Female aged 3 months

The child was brought to hospital having stopped breathing. The given history was that she had rolled off the settee. She was dead on arrival at hospital. The skeletal survey showed fractured ribs and a skull fracture. At post-mortem it was seen that the child had a long, wide, parietal fracture. Initially it was accepted that this was an accident but the mother later injured a child whilst baby sitting and admitted to the murder of her baby.

◀ 7.2 Male aged 6 months

The child was brought to hospital after an emergency call. There was extensive bruising on the face (cheek and behind the ear), the front of the chest and around the knees, and subhyaloid haemorrhages. He had cerebral swelling and coning and died after 48 hours. There was a single old rib fracture, and multiple and complex skull fractures including a depressed fracture leading from the parietal into the occipital bone. The adoptive mother admitted to the murder of the baby.

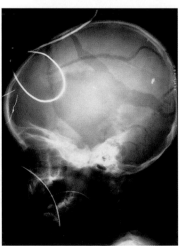 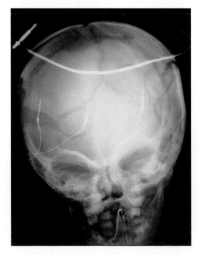 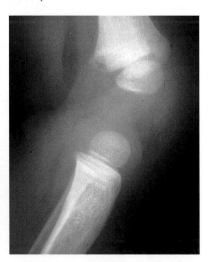

▲ ▲ ▲ 7.3–7.5 Male aged 15 months

The child was admitted as an emergency to hospital. He was a thin, underweight child, failing to thrive. There were bilateral retinal haemorrhages, and 34 bruises over the face and body and a torn frenulum. A subdural haematoma was treated surgically. He had five skull fractures in the parietal bones and occiput. There was also a metaphyseal fracture at the lower end of the femur. The child died and the mother later admitted to his murder.

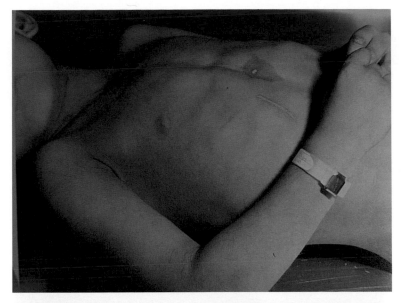

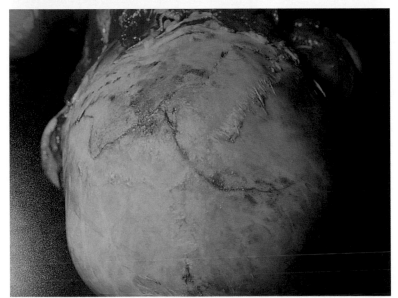

◀ ◀ ◀ ◀ 7.6–7.8 Male aged 4 years

The child was brought to hospital dead. The history given was that he had slipped in the bath and banged his head. On examination he was thin and wasted and had unexplained marks on his body. At post-mortem he had a complex parieto-occipital fracture. He also had bleeding into the base of the mesentery. Ordinary falls such as falling in the bath do not cause complex skull fractures including the occiput. This child died of a massive head injury, and there were also signs of previous injury, including bilateral healing fractures of the distal part of the radius and ulna. He was also thin and wasted. A police prosecution for manslaughter was successful.

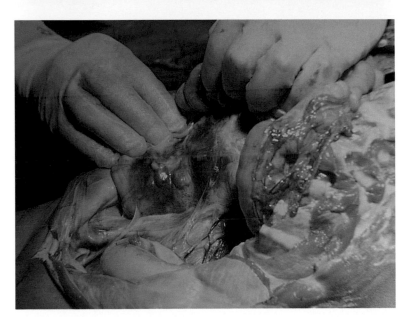

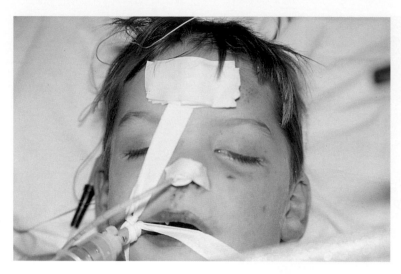

▲ ▶ ▼ ▼ 7.9–7.12 Male aged 4 years

The child arrived at hospital after an emergency call but was dead on arrival. He was resuscitated but died several hours later. His injuries included facial bruising, bruising to the back, bilateral retinal haemorrhages, and an abnormal anus. The CT scan showed gross cerebral oedema. The bruising on the back has the appearance of fingertip bruising. The anus showed some perianal reddening, a very irregular margin and dilated veins. This boy died of a shaking injury. The bruises on his back, retinal haemorrhages and cerebral oedema are consistent with this diagnosis. The anal changes and an acute anal fissure seen at post-mortem are consistent with recent anal penetration.

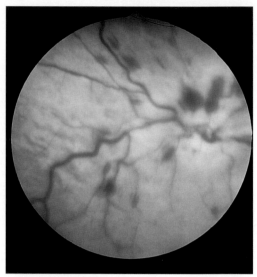

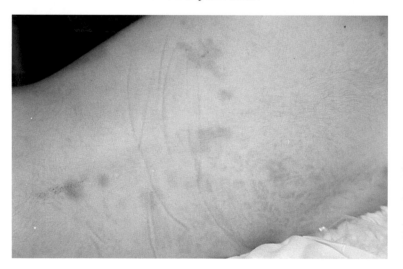

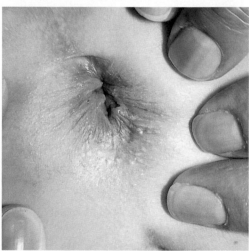

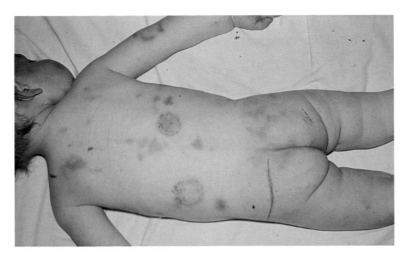

◄ **7.13 Female aged 18 months**

The child was brought into the hospital emergency department dead. Resuscitation was unsuccessful. Her body and limbs were covered in bites, bruises and lacerations. (This is an old photograph and signs of sexual abuse were not sought.) Post-mortem showed signs consistent with suffocation.

▼ **7.14, ▼ 7.15 Male aged 6 months**

The child was brought into the hospital emergency department dead. He was resuscitated but died several hours later of anoxic brain damage. A ball of nylon fibres was retrieved from the posterior nasal space (Fig. 7.15). The fibres were thought to have come from a toy. This was treated as an accidental death.

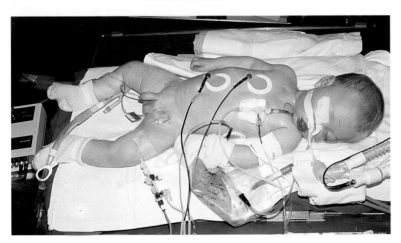

▼ **7.16, ▼ 7.17 Female aged 4 months**

The child was brought into hospital collapsed and was resuscitated. She was ventilated but died several days later of massive head injury. The only bruises were one small bruise to the side of the spine (Fig. 7.17) and a similar one behind the ear. Further examination showed retinal haemorrhages and the CT brain scan showed gross cerebral swelling and subdural haematoma. Skull X-ray showed a complex skull fracture. The clinical findings are consistent with a shaking and impact injury.

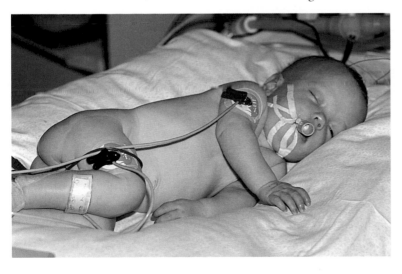
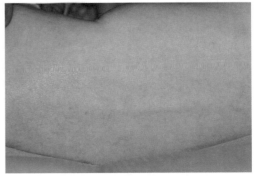

▼ ▼ ▼ ▼ 7.18–7.21 Female aged 14 months

The child began to fail to thrive from around 1 year. She was brought into hospital dead. The history given was that she slipped in the bath and drowned. Her hair was dry on admission to hospital and she was very cold. She had bruising round the mouth, several fingertip bruises round the knees and a grossly gaping dilated anus (Figs 7.18, 7.19 and 7.20). A skeletal survey showed an old healing mid-shaft fracture of femur (which had never been presented clinically). The growth chart (Fig. 7.21) showed failure to thrive. Her 2-year-old sister had had a recent burn on the back of her hand and following the death of their sister this child and the 5-year-old brother both disclosed sexual abuse. The post-mortem findings were consistent with suffocation but not drowning. The interpretation of the anal signs is difficult but in view of the history of penetrative sexual abuse involving the older siblings abuse has to be considered.

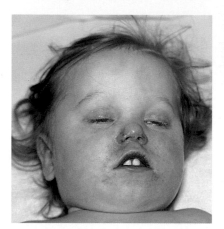
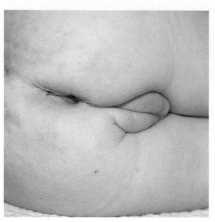
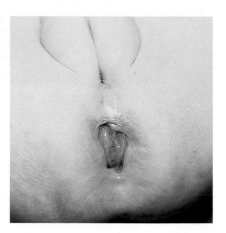

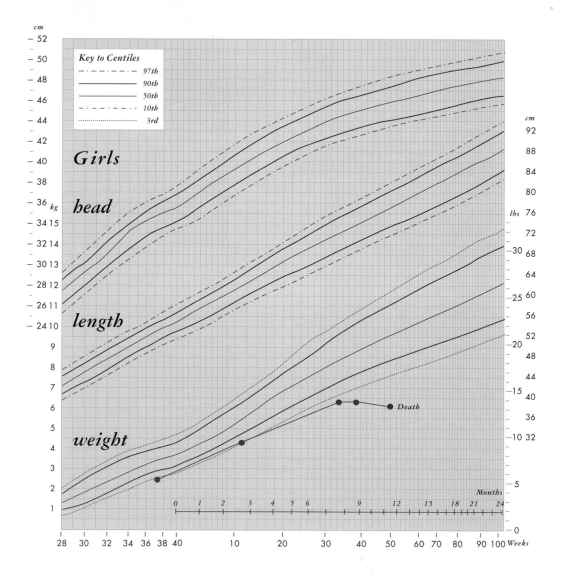

▶ ▼ ▼ ▼ ▼ **7.22–7.26 Female aged 5 months**

The child was brought in to the hospital emergency department dead. The photographs show new and old bruises around the face and trunk, including pinch marks on the front of the chest and a torn frenulum. A skeletal survey showed a fractured skull and fractured ribs. Post-mortem revealed she had died of a massive head injury. (Note: this infant had labial fusion (Fig. 7.25) which is not uncommon in infancy but is long and thick in this child.) The apparently abnormal anal findings (Fig. 7.26) are due to post-mortem changes. An older sibling had been sexually abused.

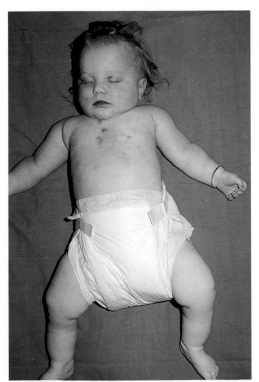

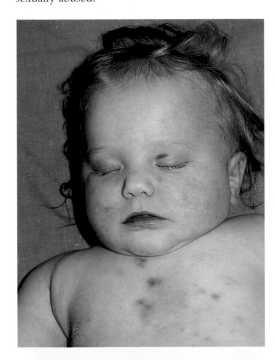

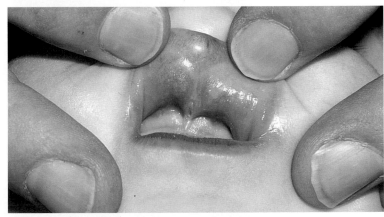

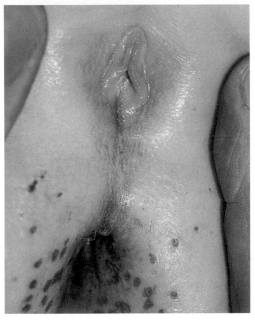

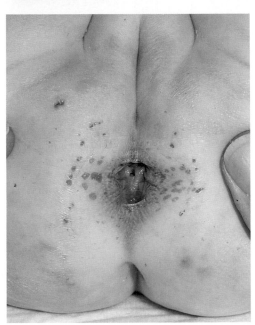

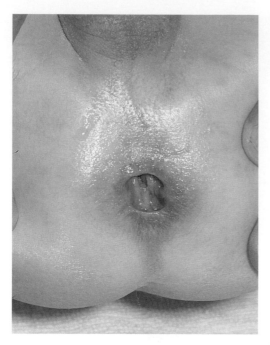

◀ 7.27 Male aged 8 months

The child was brought into the hospital emergency department collapsed and was resuscitated, but died several days later of a massive head injury. The photograph shows a markedly dilated anus with some venous congestion. This slide was taken before death. The question of possible sexual abuse was raised but not investigated, and remains unanswered.

▼ 7.28 Female aged 3 months

The child was brought into the hospital emergency department dead. The post-mortem suggested a diagnosis of sudden infant death syndrome but the pathologist was concerned about the anus. A further history was obtained from the parents who said that the baby had been constipated and they had used a spoon to remove faeces from the rectum. (With permission of Dr S. Siva.)

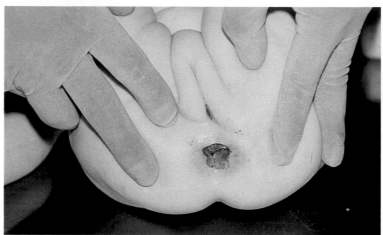

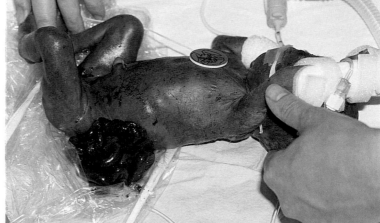

▲ 7.29 Extremely pre-term infant

The baby was born by Caesarean section after the mother was admitted to hospital having been stabbed in the abdomen. The baby's abdomen was perforated and the guts eviscerated. The baby died some days later. This is a form of pre-natal child abuse. (With permission of Dr K. Brownlee.)

◀ 7.30 Female aged 2 years

The child was admitted to hospital collapsed with a history that she had fallen across a loudspeaker. On examination there was bruising on the lower abdomen and at laparotomy a ruptured duodenum. This injury is caused by blunt force to the abdomen. The duodenum is vulnerable because it is located near the bony spinal column.

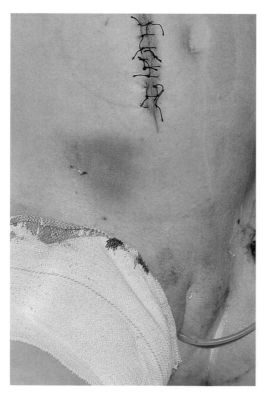

◄ 7.31 Male aged 2 years

The child was brought to hospital collapsed. On examination there were deep full skin thickness burns from the side of the mouth round the neck. This child had been given a corrosive substance to drink and died of the injuries.

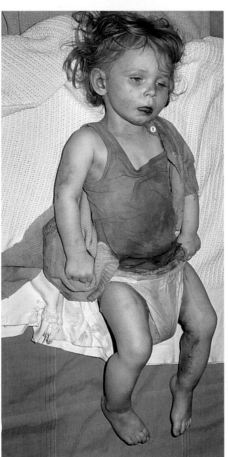

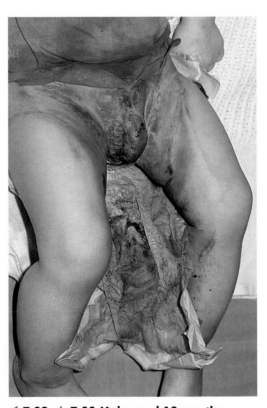

◄ 7.32, ▲ 7.33 Male aged 18 months

The child was brought into hospital dead following an emergency call. The child was of normal nutrition but was very cold, wet and the nappy contained the equivalent of 4 days of normal stool. The nappy area showed evidence of post-mortem gangrene. The mother was a drug addict and the baby had been last seen alive 4–5 days earlier.

Chapter 8

Differential diagnosis of physical abuse

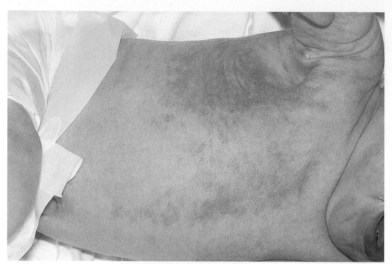

◀ **8.1 Neonate**

Purple discoloration on the chest was noted at birth. This is a port wine stain.

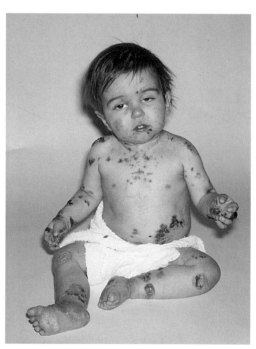

▲ **8.2 Male 18 months**

The child was anonymously reported to a child welfare charity as being battered. There are multiple bullous lesions in various stages of healing. This is a known case of epidermolysis bullosa.

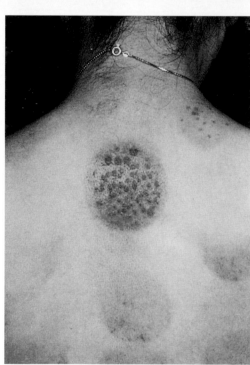

▲ **8.3 Female 16 years**

She was referred because of unusual lesions on her back. Circular lesions can be seen across the back with numerous purpura, due to cupping.

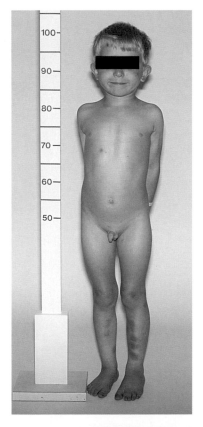

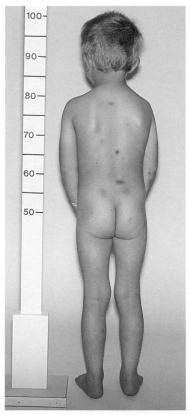

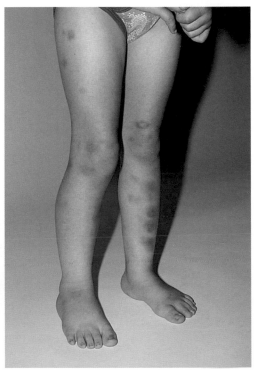

◀ ◀ ◀ ▼ 8.4–8.7 Male aged 5 years

The child was referred by his doctor because of concern about physical abuse. There is extensive large purple bruising in a well cared for child. The diagnosis is idiopathic thrombycytopenic purpura.

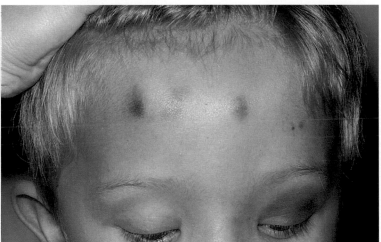

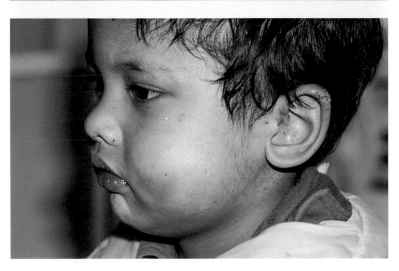

◀ 8.8 Male aged 2 years

The child was referred to the paediatrician because of a swollen, bruised cheek. The photograph shows a very swollen left cheek with bruising at the corner of mouth and a crusted lesion on the pinna. The medical opinion was haemophilia and impetigo. There was also physical abuse in this family and the children were all later put on the Child Protection Register.

▶ 8.9, ▼ 8.10 Female aged 2 years

The child was referred from day nursery because of bruising on her back. Scattered Mongolian blue spots are seen over the back and buttocks. A depigmented area is also seen on the lower back (Fig. 8.9).

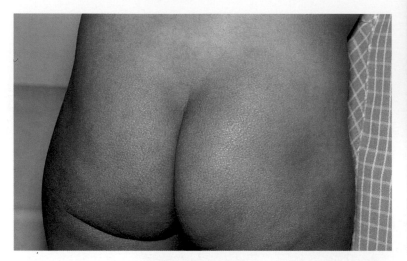

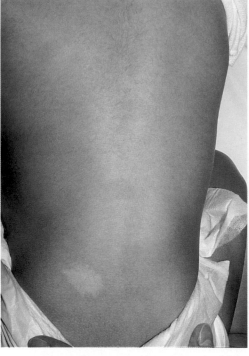

◀ 8.11 Male aged 5 years

The child was referred after his foster mother said she had bitten him. A circular lesion is seen on the left lower back with flaking skin. A Mongolian blue spot is also seen on the sacrum. The medical opinion was a fungal infection and Mongolian blue spot.

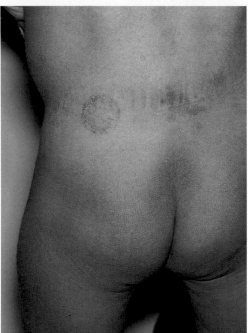

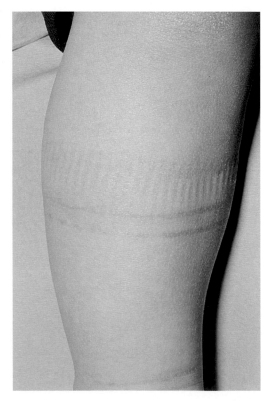

▶ 8.12 Male aged 7 years

The child was referred because of unexplained red marks around his lower leg. Linear erythematous parallel marks are seen below marks caused by elastic in socks. The marks were due to tapes applied too tightly to keep the socks up.

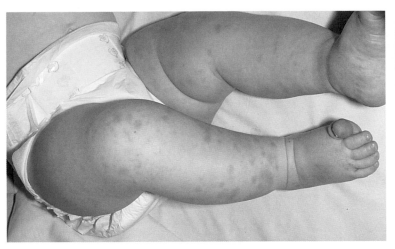

▲ 8.13 Female aged 6 months

Child was referred to hospital by her doctor because of febrile illness. The photograph shows extensive purpuric marks on the legs, due to meningococcal meningitis.

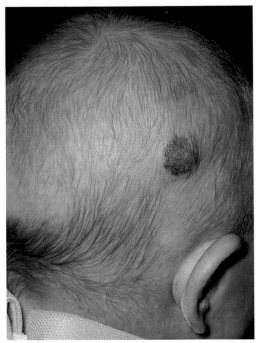

▲ 8.14 Female aged 3 months

Child was seen in the clinic after she had become involved in a fight between her parents. The strawberry naevus shown was an incidental finding.

◀ 8.15 Female aged 4 years

Child was referred by her doctor because of a rapidly spreading lesion on the buttock. This was diagnosed as a staphylococcal infection resembling a burn.

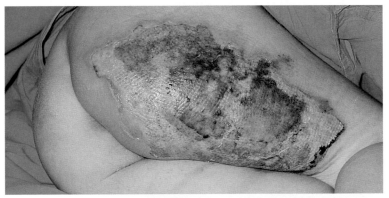

◀ 8.16 Female aged 2 months

The photograph shows a healing lesion on the left buttock. This lesion had been present at birth and subsequently healed. It superficially looks like a healing burn. The diagnosis is congenital abnormality.

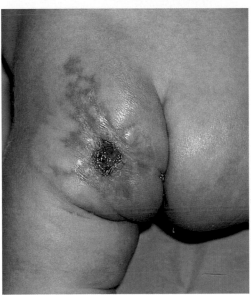

▶ 8.17 Female neonate

The photograph shows a lesion on the buttocks which was present at birth and resembles a burn. This is a congenital abnormality.

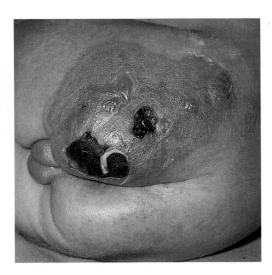

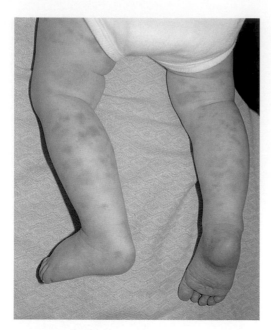

◀ 8.18 Female aged 10 months
Doctor referred child to hospital with extensive bruising on legs. The scattered bruises are due to Henoch–Schönlein purpura.

▼ 8.19 Male aged 6 weeks
Child was referred as a possible physical abuse victim. The diagnosis is extensive scabies.

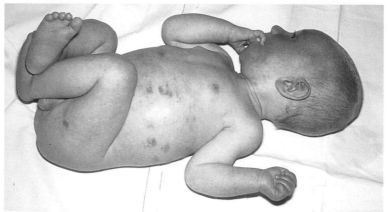

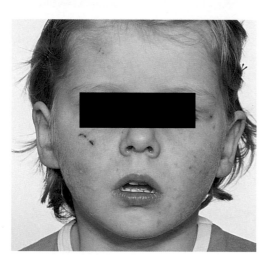

◀ 8.20 Male aged 8 years
Child was referred by social services because of a number of bruises on his face and body. The diagnosis was idiopathic thrombocytopenic purpura. However, this boy also had scratch marks on his face allegedly because of fighting with his brothers. The whole family was neglected.

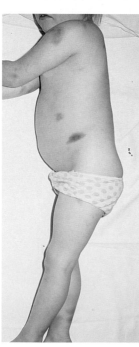

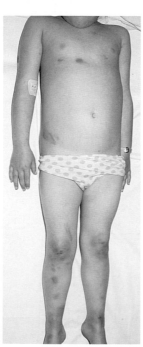

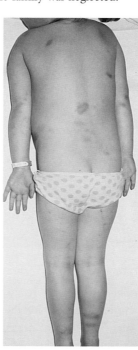

◀ ◀ ◀ 8.21–8.23 Female aged 5 years
Child was referred because of possible physical abuse in a family where the children were already on the Child Protection Register. The photographs show multiple bruises in unusual sites, and several bruises of unusual severity. The diagnosis is idiopathic thrombocytopenic purpura in a child known to have been previously physically abused.

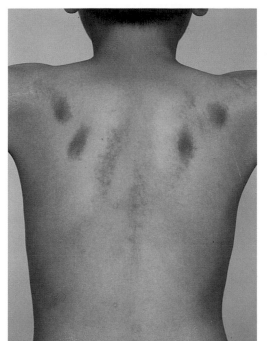

◄ 8.24 Male aged 8 years
Child was referred because of unusual markings on his back. Four roughly oval linear haemorrhagic areas are seen on the upper back. These lesions are due to coil rubbing.

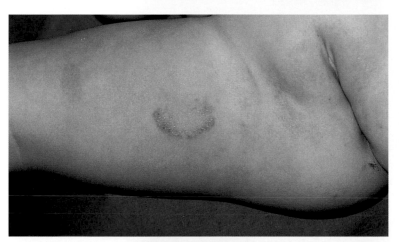

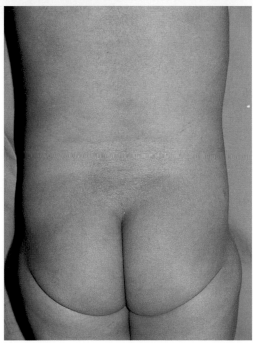

◄ 8.25, ▲ 8.26 Female aged 6 months
Child was referred by her nursery because of a possible bite. A semicircular raised lesion with some scaling is seen, caused by seborrhoeic eczema.

◄ 8.27 Female aged 3 years
Child was referred because of a burn on her hand. She has a white mother and Asian father. The photograph shows a Mongolian blue spot.

▼ 8.28, ▼ 8.29 Female aged 6 years

Child was referred by her doctor because of rectal bleeding. Crops of lesions are seen on the back of the lower leg and small irregular scaly lesions on the back of the leg. This is a fictitious rash caused by the mother scratching the skin in a child with mild eczema. The child was also sexually abused, probably by her mother.

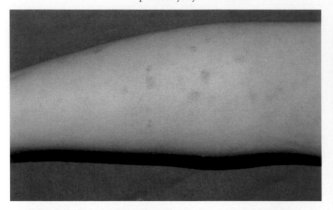

◀ 8.30 Female aged 12 years

She was referred because of bruising on her upper arm. A vertical row of three bruises on the inner aspect of the right upper arm and one bruise on the anterior aspect of the left upper arm are seen. The diagnosis is self-inflicted bruises. This girl was being sexually abused.

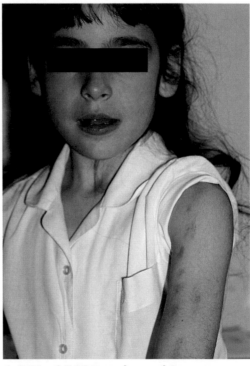

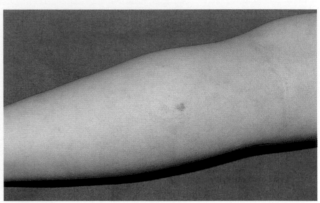

▲ 8.31, ◀ 8.32 Female aged 9 years

Child was referred because of unusual lesions on her left upper arm. There are several lesions on the inner and anterior aspect of the left upper arm and abrasions with some bruising. These are self-inflicted injuries. Fig. 8.32 shows her drawings to be those of an emotionally disturbed child.

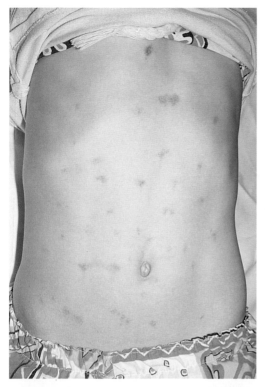

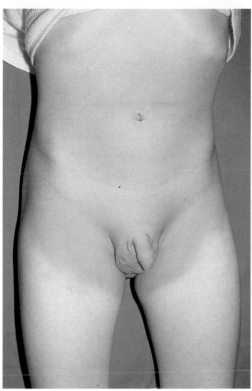

▶ **8.36 Male aged 13 years**

He was referred because of an unusual rash on his forearms, and because he was sexually abusing other children. Linear scratches are seen on the outer aspect of both forearms, which were self-inflicted. The boy was also being sexually abused by an uncle.

◀ **8.33 Female aged 9 years**

Child was referred because of a rash on her abdomen. There are paired and single lesions over the anterior chest and abdomen with the appearance of small abrasions. The diagnosis is self-inflicted injury. This child's father was a chronic alcoholic.

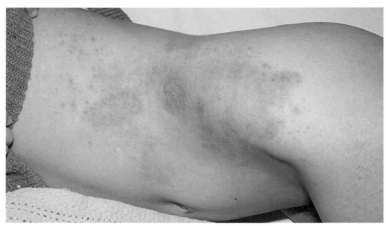

▲ **8.34 Female aged 13 years**

She was referred because of an unexplained rash on her abdomen and upper thigh. The girl was known to have been sexually abused for several years previously. This is an extensive erythematous rash with some scaling, which is self-inflicted. This girl has become very distressed after recent further sexual assault at her special school.

◀ **8.35 Male aged 8 years**

He was referred because of rash possibly due to physical abuse. The photograph shows a generalized erythematous rash over the abdomen and upper thighs, which remains unexplained.

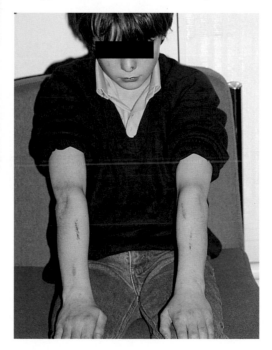

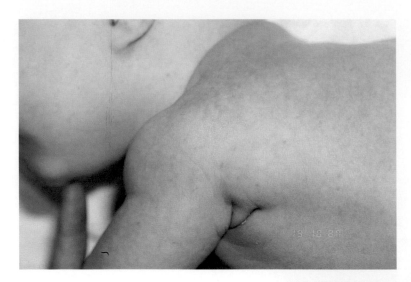

◀ 8.37 Female aged 5 months
Child was referred from her nursery with a possible bruise in the left axilla. The diagnosis is haemangioma.

▼ 8.38 Male aged 15 months
He was referred because of a 'bruise' seen at day nursery. The diagnosis is haemangioma.

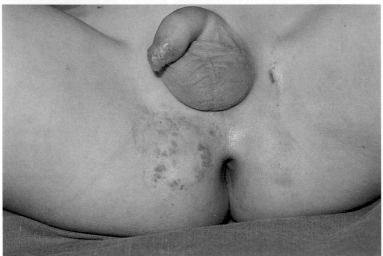

SECTION 3

NEGLECT

Chapter 9

Neglect

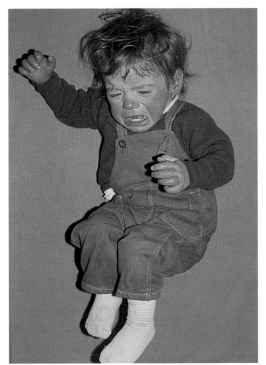

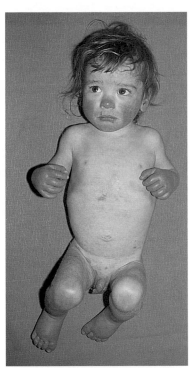

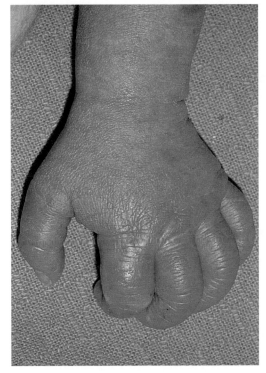

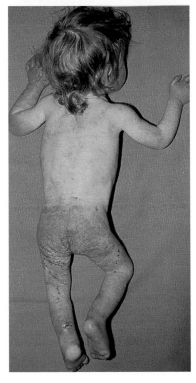

◄ ◄ ▼ ▼ ▼ 9.1–9.4 Male aged 22 months

The social worker and paediatrician made a home visit after the family had failed to attend the clinic. The older child (see Figs 9.11–9.18) had been at nursery that day. Professional concern was around the failure to thrive and neglect. A previous child who was very underweight had died from sudden infant death syndrome at 6 months. The father had an addiction to gambling. Fig. 9.1 shows a small, unkempt child, in a flexed position, with red swollen hands and straggly hair. Note that the same posture is maintained when undressed (Fig. 9.2). Fig 9.3 shows a swollen red oedematous hand, cold to the touch (deprivation hands and feet remain red and swollen even after heating up). Fig. 9.4 shows how the child is emaciated; note the wasted buttocks and severe chronic nappy rash extending down the posterior part of leg. Swollen lower legs are also seen.

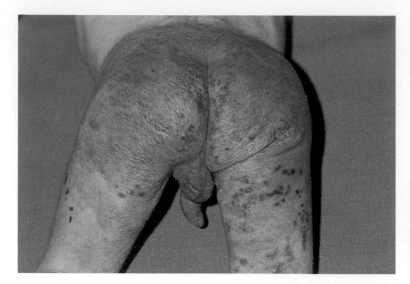

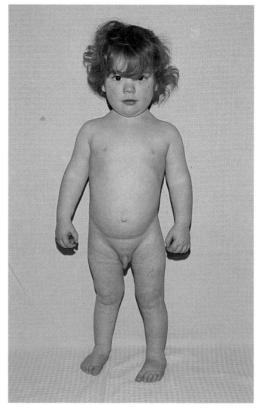

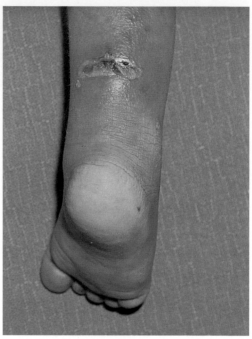

◀ ◀ ◀ ▼ ▼ 9.5–9.8 Male aged 22 months
The same child as in Figs 9.1-9.4. Note the chronicity of the nappy rash (Fig. 9.5). An old ulcerated cold injury is seen in Fig. 9.6. Note the pallor of the heel which was extremely cold to the touch. There was rapid weight gain in hospital over a period of 2–3 weeks (Fig. 9.7). Fig. 9.8 shows the same child a year later after being in foster care.

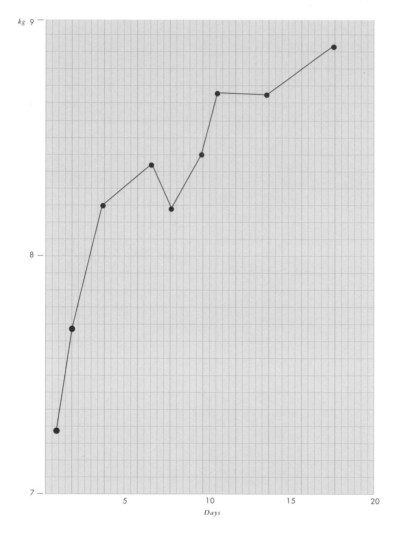

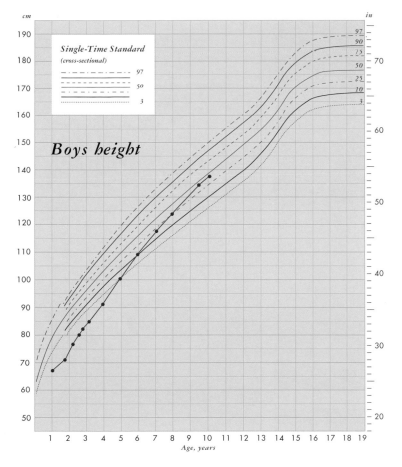

◀ **Fig 9.9 Male aged 22 months**
Growth chart to 10 years of child in Figs 9.1–9.8.

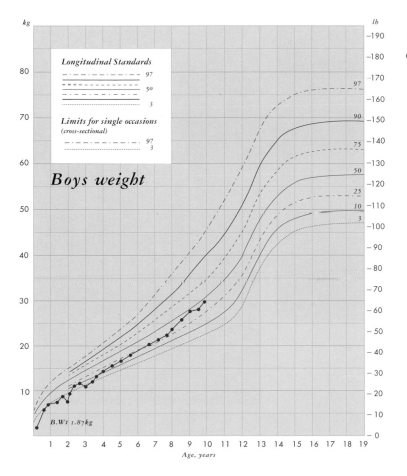

◀ **Fig 9.10 Male aged 22 months**
Growth chart to 10 years of child in Figs 9.1–9.8.

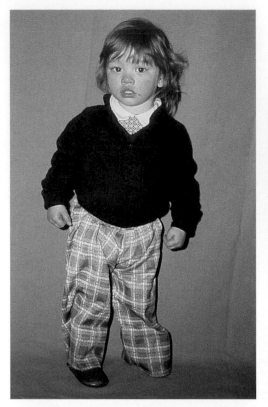

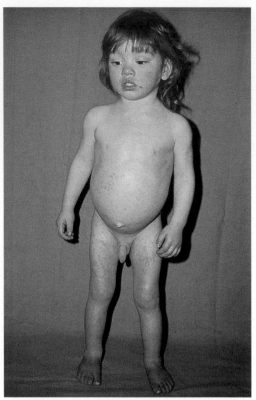

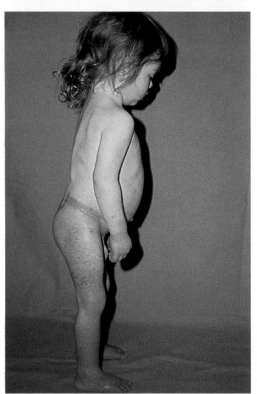

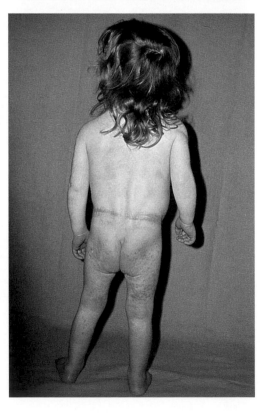

▲ ▲ ▲ ▶ **Male aged 2 years and 10 months**

(Caption opposite)

9.11–9.16 Male aged 2 years and 10 months (continued)

The older sibling of the child in Figs 9.1–9.10. He had been at day nursery the day these pictures were taken. The photographs show a scruffy child with long hair, and over-size clothes concealing malnutrition. He has frozen body posture with watchfulness and clenched hands. There is gaze avoidance, and a swollen abdomen with very thin arms and legs. Note the passivity, and gross malnutrition. Nappy rash is evident, and red swollen feet are seen with early ulceration (Fig 9.15). There was no weight gain during 3 weeks in hospital.

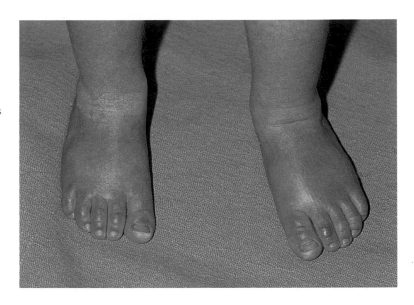

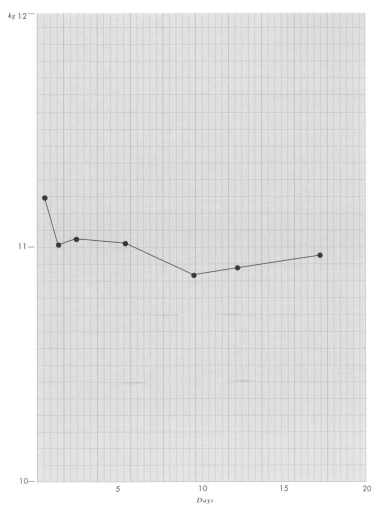

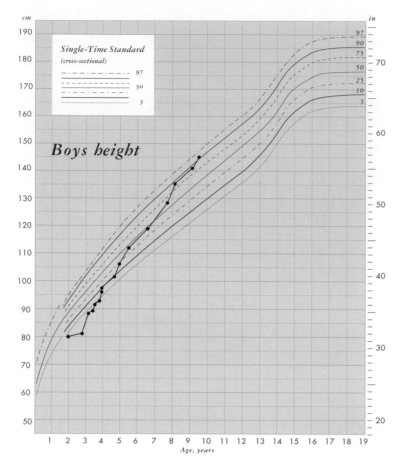

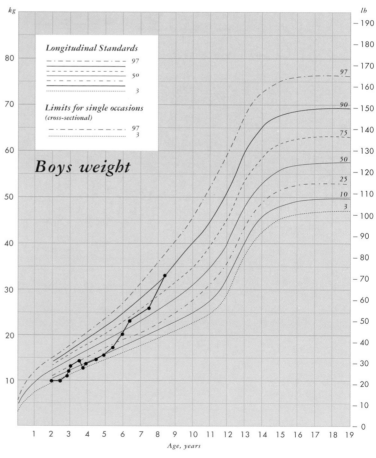

◀ **Fig 9.17 Male aged 2 years and 10 months**

Growth chart to 8 years of child in Figs 9.11–9.16

▼ **Fig 9.18 Male aged 2 years and 10 months**

Growth chart to 8 years of child in Figs 9.11–9.16

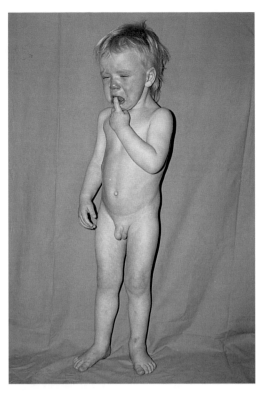

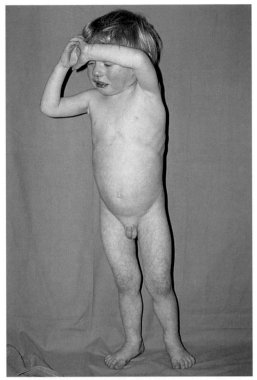

▲ ▲ ▶ 9.19 – 9.21 Three brothers aged 2 years 4 months, 3 years 5 months and 4 years 8 months (a further two siblings were not photographed). There was longstanding concern about neglect and failure to thrive. All five children were found in the house alone, the house was extremely dirty and the children were playing in dog excrement. These photographs were taken a week after admission to foster care. Younger children were unhappy and fearful in the clinic, and sat crying, refusing to play. The youngest child (top) is stunted with infantile proportions, masking a degree of malnutrition. The middle child adopted a fearful posture (middle). He has thin arms, protuberant abdomen and a reticular skin pattern on the legs. The oldest child is smiling, passive and wishing to please (bottom). He is seen to be thin. All the children in this family had developmental delay and in particular poor language development.

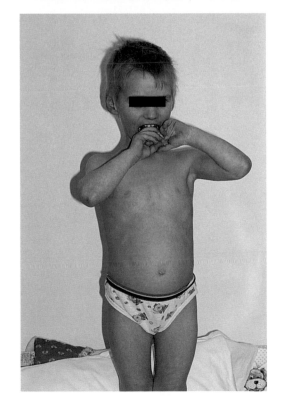

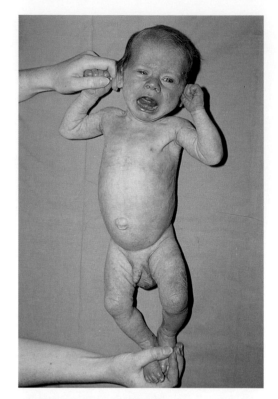

◀ ▼ ▼ ▼ **9.22–9.25 Male aged 4 weeks**

He was the fifth child in a family living in a house without gas or electricity in extreme poverty. The mother who was aged 22 years had been refused a termination. The photographs show a pale, emaciated, worried baby giving an appearance of rooting. Loose skin folds around the neck and upper arm are seen. There is a distended abdomen, extensive nappy rash and deprivation hands and feet. This baby put on weight very rapidly in hospital. (Note: infants who are failing to thrive and have not yet given up the attempt to find food will usually put on weight very rapidly in hospital. The older the child the less certain that the weight gain will be rapid in the early stages. If the child does receive good care almost all children will then grow in spite of severe emotional deprivation in the longer term.)

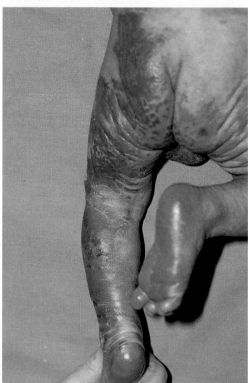

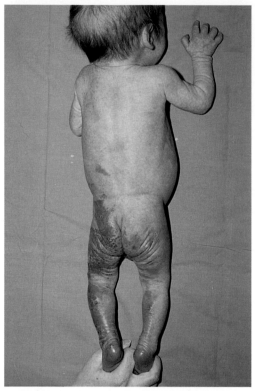

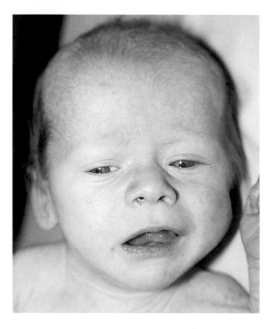

▶ 9.26 Male aged 3 years

The brother of the child in Figs 9.22–9.25. A large head and short limbs of stunted growth are seen. He is emaciated, and has flexed posture. He was also developmentally delayed.

▼ 9.27 Male aged 10 months

He was followed up following skull fracture aged 3 months, having missed several appointments. The photograph shows a watchful, emaciated baby. Note the flexed posture and immobility. He gained weight rapidly in hospital.

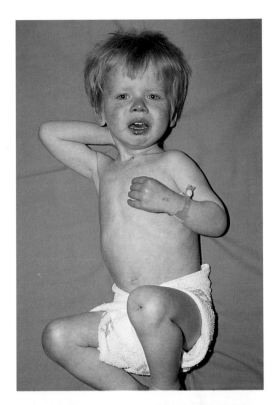

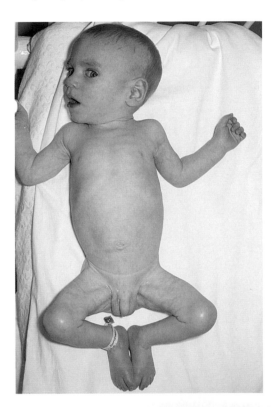

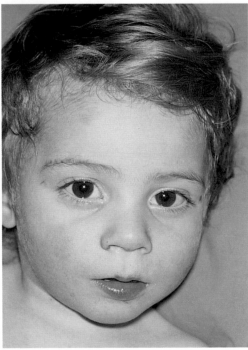

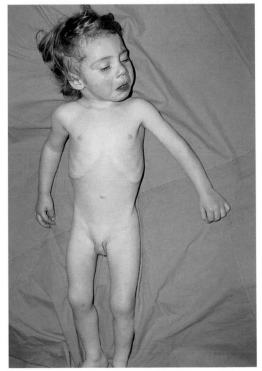

▲ 9.28, ◀ 9.29 Male aged 2 years

Child was referred by his doctor because of poor growth. The family was known to be impoverished and the mother had poorly controlled epilepsy. The photographs show a passive, emaciated child with anxious facies. Note that unless this child were to be undressed he does not look particularly thin.

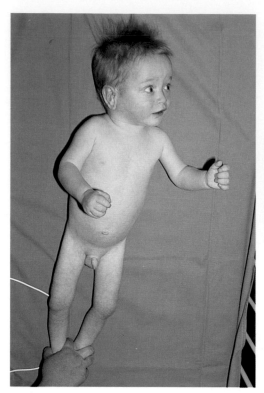

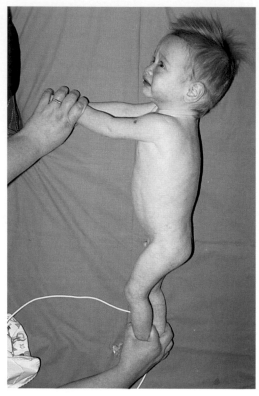

◀ 9.30, ▼ 9.31 Male aged 9 months

He was referred to hospital because of bronchiolitis. His mother said that she did not like this child who was one of twins. The photographs show a watchful, interested child, but with a distended abdomen. This child had also been previously physically abused, and his older siblings had been sexually abused.

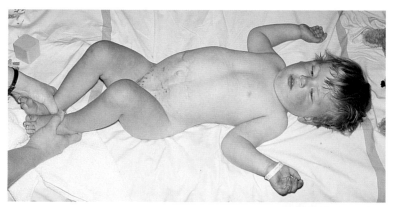

◀ 9.32, ▼ 9.33 Male aged 2 years

His older siblings were found to have been sexually abused and taken into care. This child remained with his emotionally disturbed mother while his father was in prison. His nutrition was adequate but note the flexed posture. He also had severe bleeding nappy rash, and was developmentally delayed.

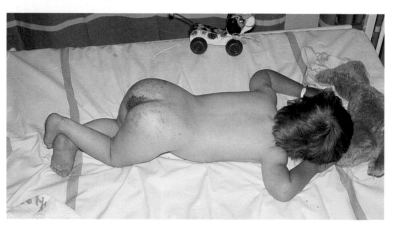

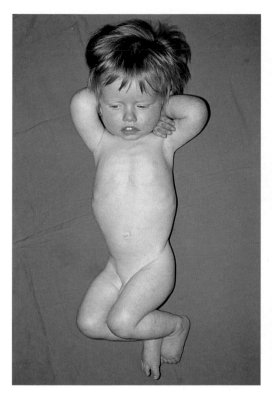
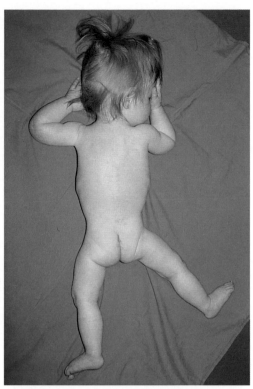
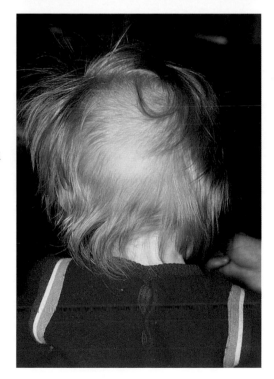

▲ ▲ ▶ **9.34–9.36 Male aged 15 months**
The child was referred by the health visitor
because of concern about poor weight gain. He
had very uncooperative parents, and in particular
an angry father who was threatening towards all
professionals. The child was very passive and still.
The photographs show a stunted child,
malnourished with wasted buttocks. A bald
patch is seen on the occiput, caused by being left
for long periods alone in his cot. The child was
fostered for several months before being returned
home. He subsequently had language delay and
behavioural difficulties.

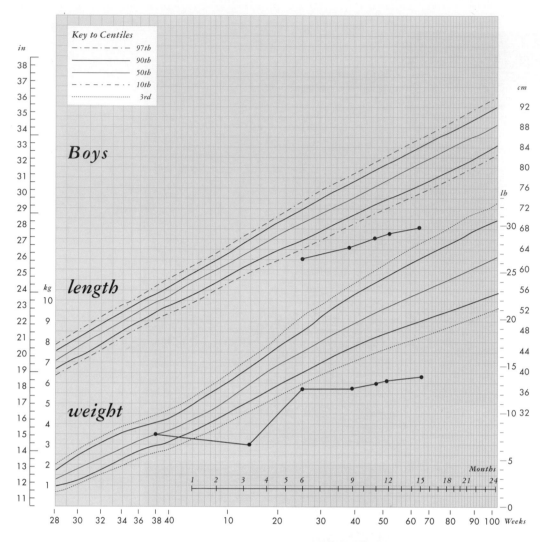

▶ **9.37,** ▲ **9.38 Male aged 15 months**

The younger of two brothers under social services supervision because of concern about neglect. He failed to thrive in spite of a 5-day placement at day nursery. He had a violent, threatening father who appeared on the ward with a knife when the child had been admitted for investigation. The photograph shows a watchful, anxious expression. Nutrition looks adequate but the growth chart (Fig. 9.38) shows growth failure.

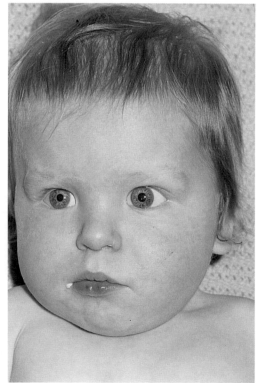

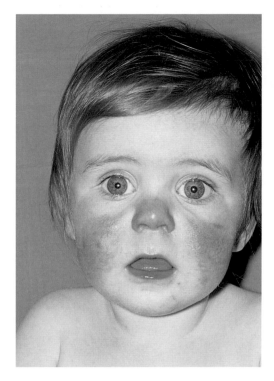

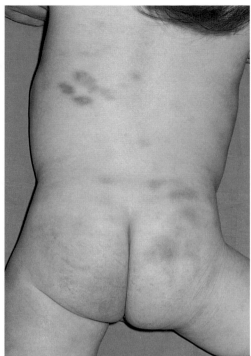

▲ 9.39, ▲ 9.40 Male aged 2 years

He was referred from a battered wives hostel with his older sister after bruising had been noticed on both children. The photographs show a tiny child with a worried expression and stunted growth. There is extensive bruising on the back of the buttocks consistent with hand marks. (Note: neglected children may be short and appear adequately nourished. This child demonstrated rapid catch-up growth in care. Children adapt to their circumstances, and may appear to have deceptively good nutrition.)

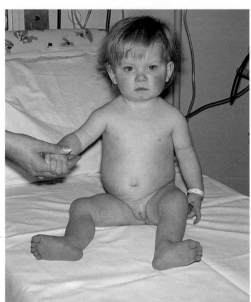

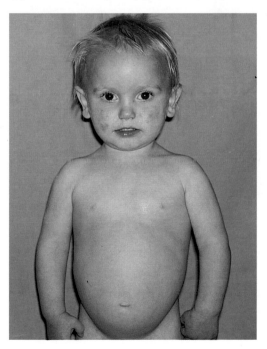

▲ 9.41 Female aged 18 months

She was referred from a child welfare charity special unit where a family assessment was being undertaken. She was the middle one of three; the other siblings were thriving. She was a quiet, passive, undemanding child with marked developmental delay. Note the appearance of a large head and thin arms. The mother had a very poor emotional relationship with this child who was neglected and emotionally deprived.

◀ 9.42 Male aged 3 years

Child was seen in a follow-up clinic because of previous non-accidental injury. His weight gain at home was poor. He is seen to have a challenging expression, distended abdomen, thin arms and poor height. This child was failing to thrive, but his mother's main complaints were of his hyperactive, destructive behaviour.

▶ 9.43 Male aged 2 years

He was referred by the health visitor to local clinic because of poor weight gain. He was one of three; the mother described the older brother as being 'the devil'. These three boys were later taken into care and described a lot of cruelty including being tied to the bed at night. The photograph shows a smiling, friendly boy with thin limbs and protuberant abdomen. All three boys subsequently had serious behaviour problems. One was sent to a residential school, and another to a day school for children with emotional problems.

▼ ▼ ▼ 9.44–9.46 Female aged 14 months

Child had been admitted to hospital several times with intercurrent illness, but no intervention was planned with reference to the failing to thrive. She was referred by the community health doctor to the community paediatrician. She had a history of difficult feeding and vomiting during and after meals. She was a passive child, and distressed with eye avoidance. She made attempts at indiscriminate attachment to all staff working on the ward. The photographs show a thin child with grossly distended abdomen, wasted buttocks and thin hair. There was also developmental delay. Her follow-up growth in foster care was good, and Fig. 9.46 shows a lively, friendly child. She still had difficult feeding patterns, but was interested and alert and much more confident.

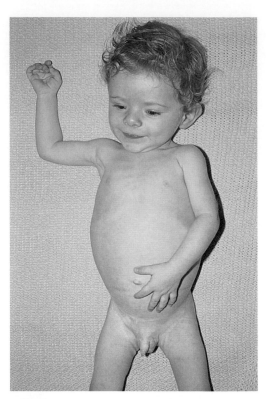

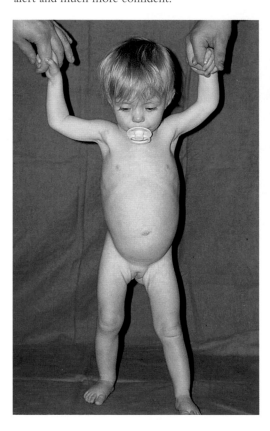

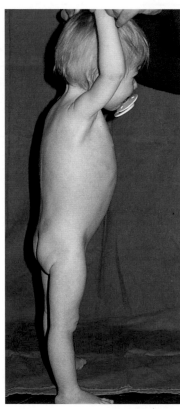

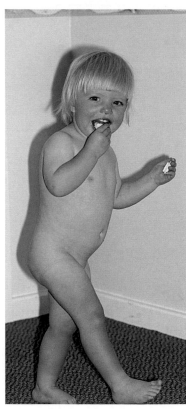

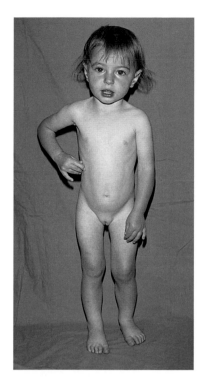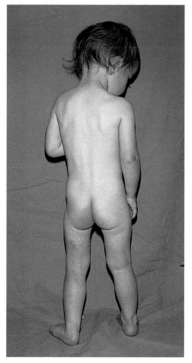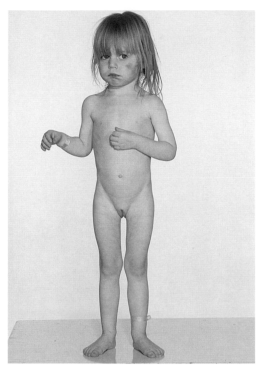

▲ 9.47, ▲ 9.48 Female aged 2 years

At 10 months this child was sexually abused by her father. She remained in the care of her mother with whom she had a very poor relationship, and was repeatedly bruised and shouted at. She is an alert, thin child with fine hair, and indiscriminately friendly. Bruises are seen on the back of the left thigh. She was eventually taken into care by the local authority at the age of 4 years. She did not thrive in care, and further assessment showed her to be very emotionally disturbed following prolonged emotional abuse at home. At the age of 5 years plans for adoption have not yet succeeded. (Note: it is becoming evident that the damage caused by early maltreatment is not all reversible, and children may have persisting emotional difficulties.)

▲ 9.49 Female aged 2 years

Child was referred by the health visitor after the mother had asked for help because the child refused to feed. The parents had recently split up, and the father had taken over the care of the baby. The mother was force feeding the child, who responded by biting. The photograph shows a flexed, frozen, wasted child. Note wasting of the upper arms and thighs.

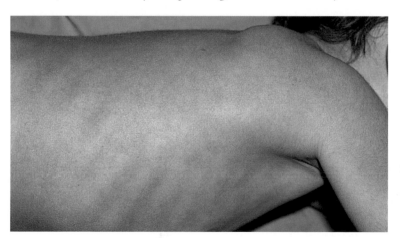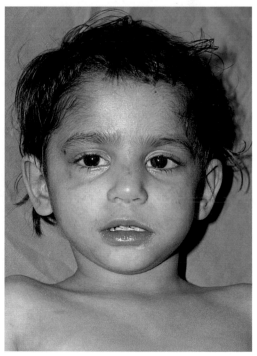

▶ 9.50, ▲ 9.51 Female aged 3 years

The family was known to social services because of previous physical abuse and failure to thrive. The child was referred back to the paediatrician when the black eye was seen in school. It was also known that this girl gained weight when cared for by the extended family but failed to gain weight when at home with her mother. Fig. 9.50 shows a thin, watchful child, with a peri-orbital bruise. Note the lack of subcutaneous fat and prominent rib cage (Fig. 9.51)

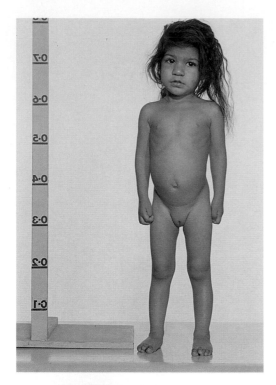

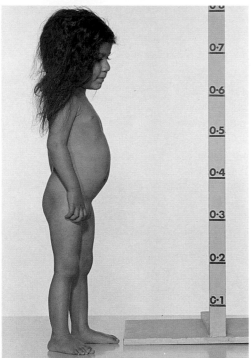

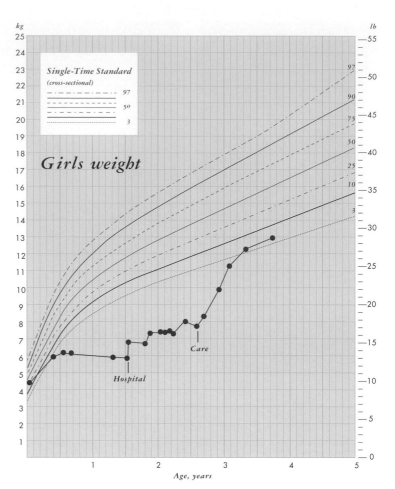

Girls weight

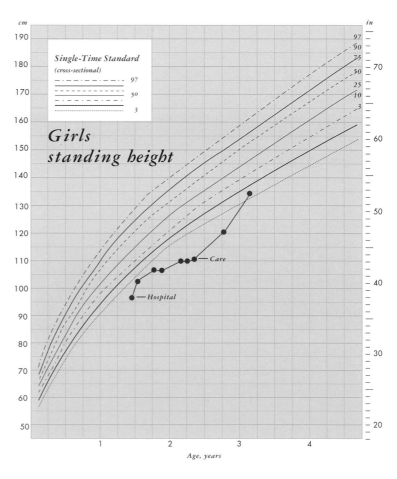

Girls standing height

▲ ▲ ▶ ▶ **9.52–9.55 Female aged 2½ years**
She was referred by the health visitor to the
paediatrician because of concern about poor
weight gain. An older sibling was found to be
stealing food in school. She is seen to be a silent,
watchful, apathetic, passive child with long
straggly hair. She also had delayed development.
Note the stunting with infantile proportions, and
distended abdomen. She is thin, with prominent
ribs. This child and her older sister put on weight
and grew rapidly in care (Figs 9.54–9.57).

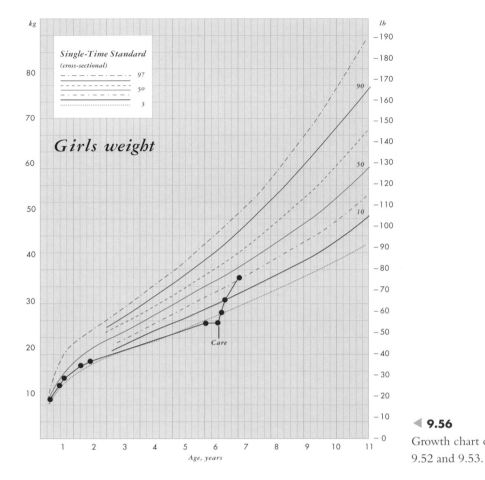

◀ **9.56**

Growth chart of older sibling of child in figs 9.52 and 9.53.

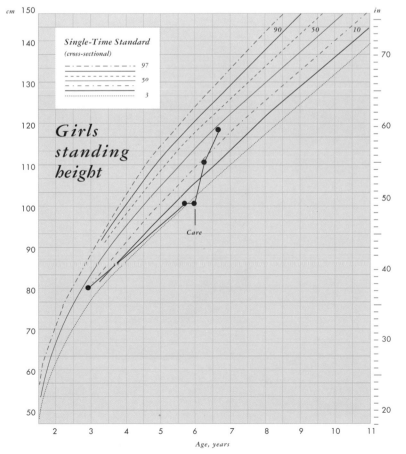

◀ **9.57**

Growth chart of older sibling of child in figs 9.52 and 9.53.

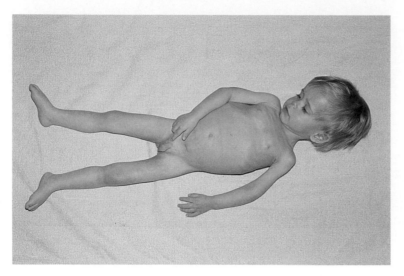

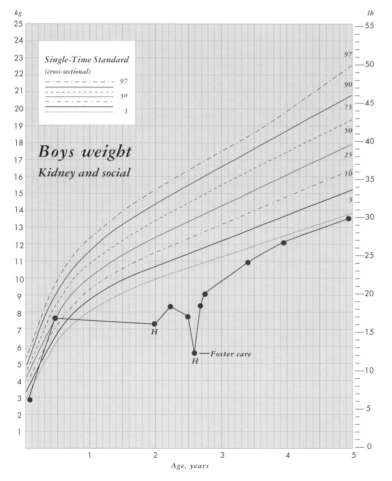

◄ ◄ ▼ 9.58–9.60 Male aged 2 years

Child was referred by the paediatric nephrologist who was caring for the boy because of renal insufficiency. A child welfare charity was also involved because of concerns about neglect at home. He was admitted to hospital after weight loss accelerated by dehydration. He was a passive child with gaze avoidance. A bruise is seen on his right forehead. He is seen to be emaciated with thin arms and legs, a protuberant abdomen, and unkempt hair. This child did well in alternative care, but initially had a very difficult feeding problem. The anorexia had been put down to renal disease; in reality this child failed to grow because of organic and non-organic causes. (Note: organic disease and child maltreatment may co-exist.)

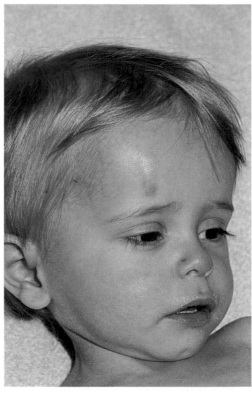

▶ 9.61, ▼ 9.62 Male aged 4 years

Child was referred to the paediatric out-patients by his doctor because of a cough, pallor and low weight. He was an emaciated pale child, with grossly carious teeth (Fig. 9.62) and a chest drain (he had a pneumococcal empyema secondary to pneumonia). He also had untreated hypospadias. This boy had been grossly neglected, and in spite of regular visits by the health visitor who said they were 'a nice family', this child's parlous state was not detected.

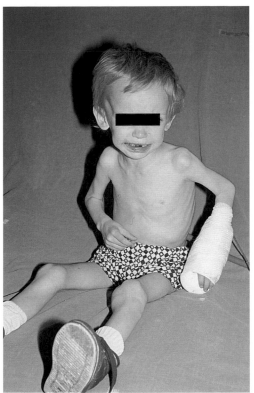

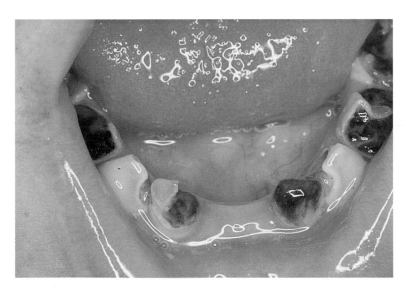

▶ 9.63 Female aged 5 years

She was known to the paediatrician over a long period whilst social services supported the family. The photograph shows a thin, watchful child with thin arms and legs. She showed repeated catch-up growth when with alternative carers. When she was allowed to remain in foster care for a longer period her growth rate accelerated and she reached the 50th centile (growth chart overleaf). There was severe emotional abuse in this family, and as a teenager the girl showed severe emotional damage.

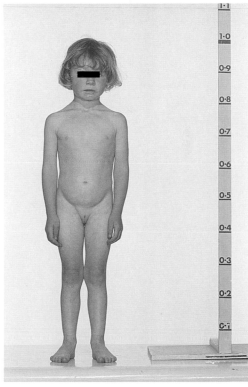

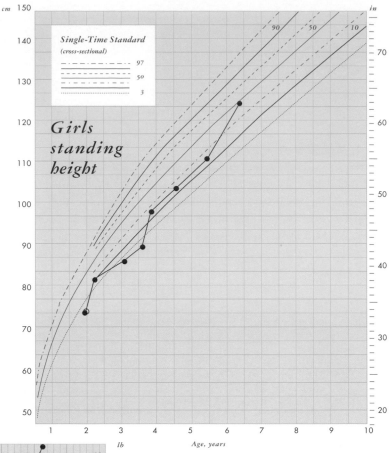

Fig 9.64 Female aged 5 years
Growth chart to 7 years of child in Fig 9.63.

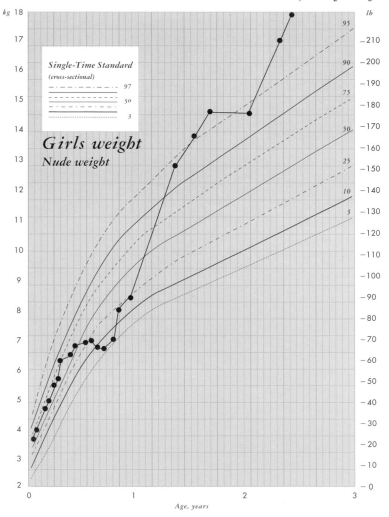

9.65 Female aged 3 years
Growth chart of a child who was referred initially because of failure to thrive, but was subsequently overfed and became obese. Failure to thrive and obesity may be part of the same attachment difficulty, which amounts to emotional abuse.

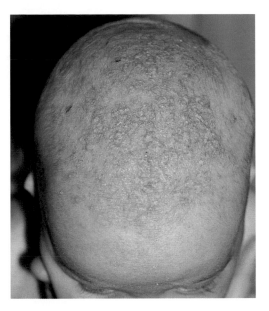

▶ 9.66 Male aged 6 months

He was referred from the infant welfare clinic because of a rash on the scalp, which was due to neglected seborrhoeic dermatitis. This is a treatable disorder; the mother's failure to gain medical advice and treatment reflects her lack of care.

▶ 9.67, ▼ 9.68 Male aged 6 months

He was seen in the paediatric out-patient clinic for possible physical abuse and this rash was noted. This is a typical rash of scabies.

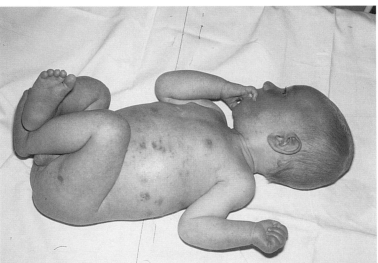

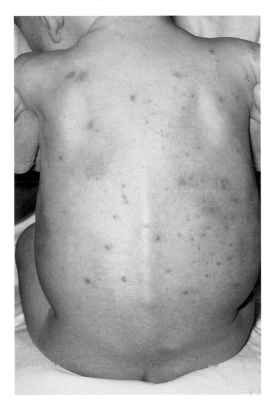

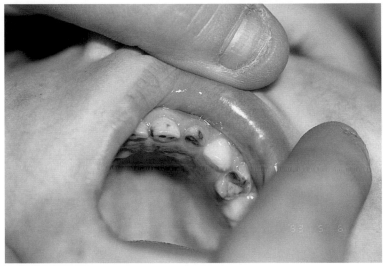

▲ 9.69 Male aged 4 years

He was referred by social services because of extensive bruising and was found to have 60 separate areas of bruising and scratches, and carious teeth. Untreated caries such as these are part of the picture of neglect.

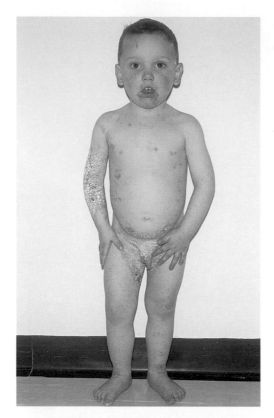

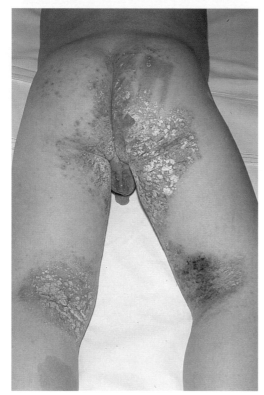

◄ ▼ ▼ 9.70–9.72 Male aged 3 years

The child was referred by the dermatology department to the paediatrician because of concerns about neglect. The mother was known to be a binge drinker and four older siblings were on the Child Protection Register because of neglect and emotional abuse. The photographs show a stunted boy with a healing scald of the right arm and extensive eczema affecting the face, nappy area and back of the knees. The skin lesions were inappropriately treated by the mother with calamine. Note the unusual shape on the right buttock, possibly another burn. This child's skin healed up completely within a week on the ward, but deteriorated again rapidly at home. This child had been neglected, which led to the accidental scald. He had eczema, but this was made much worse by being left in wet nappies, and his mother in spite of being given appropriate treatment used calamine.

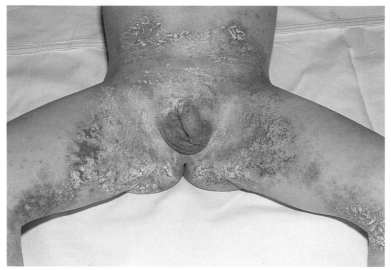

▼ 9.73 Male aged 3 months

Child was referred by his doctor because of worries about neglect. The child was suffering from frostbite. Note the gangrenous area on the great toe and fourth toe. Cold injuries of this degree only occur after prolonged periods of neglect.

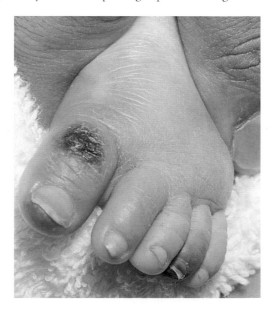

▼ 9.74 Female aged 6 weeks

The parents took the baby to the hospital emergency department complaining about her 'black toes'. This is a cold injury, including frostbite of both feet. This child has been submitted to prolonged neglect.

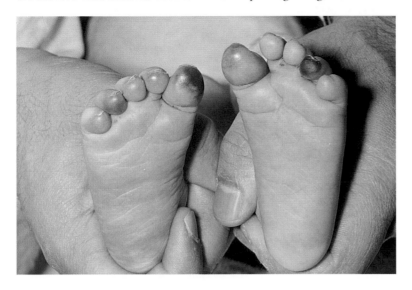

▶ 9.75, ▼ 9.76 Male aged 18 months

Child was left in the care of his 5-year-old sister, who tried to give him a bath, which resulted in severe scalds to both lower legs and feet. The child was in hospital for a long time, and the plastic surgeons referred the child to the paediatrician when the mother failed to visit the boy for weeks on end. It is very worrying, neglectful behaviour when adults leave children in the care of other young children.

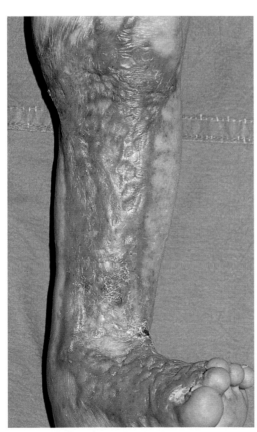

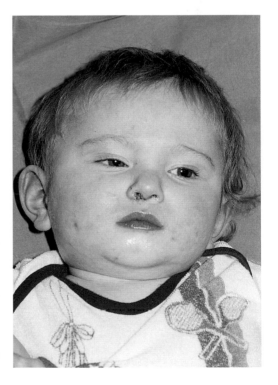

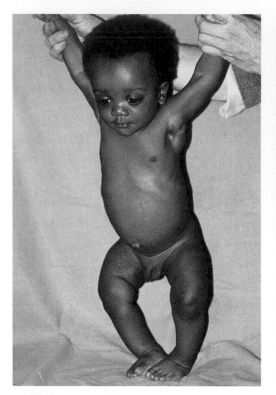

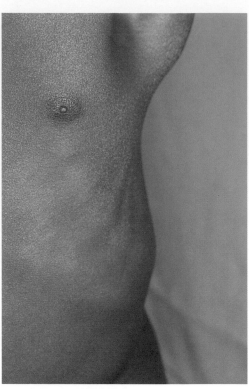

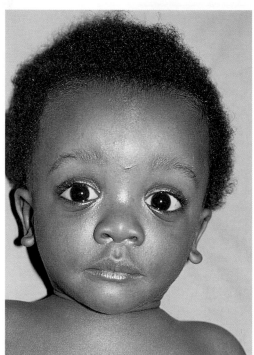

▲ ▲ ◄ ▼ **9.77–9.80 Male aged 12 months**

Child was referred to the paediatrician by his doctor because of poor growth. He was stunted, with weight and height under the 3rd centile, and florid rickets. Rickety rosary is seen, with frontal bossing (Fig. 9.80) and swollen wrists (Fig. 9.81). The X-ray (Fig. 9.82) confirms the diagnosis of rickets. This boy and his two older siblings were taken into care after they had been left alone in the house, which caught fire. They thrived in care.

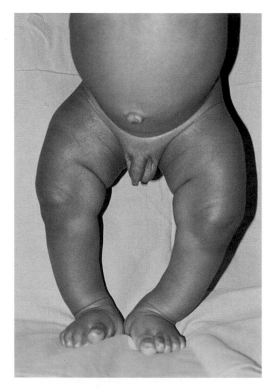

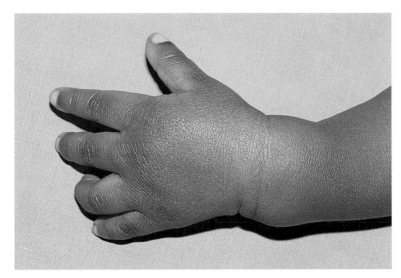

◀ **9.81**, ▼ **9.82**
(Caption opposite)

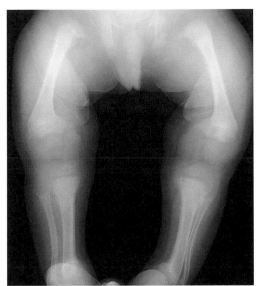

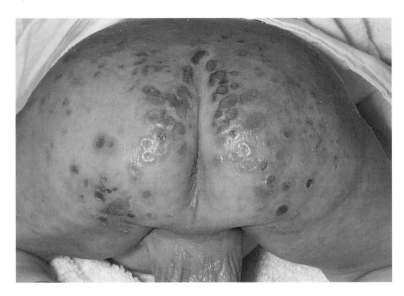

▲ 9.83 Male aged 6 months

He was referred by the health visitor because of concern about neglect and poor weight gain. Severe chronic ulcerated nappy rash is seen, with wasted buttocks. Nappy rash of this order is a consequence of prolonged poor physical care.

▶ 9.84 Female aged 3 years

She was known to the paediatrician because of a long history of neglect within the family. She has a left convergent squint. The family repeatedly failed to attend for appointments in the eye department. Non-attendance for necessary hospital treatment, commonly squints and hearing difficulty, are part of the wider picture of neglect

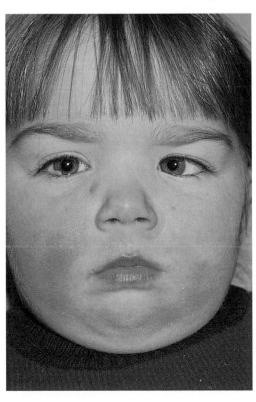

▶ 9.85 Female aged 4 years

Child was referred to the paediatrician by her doctor because her 'hair was falling out in lumps'. Very thin, sparse hair is seen over the crown. Thin, sparse hair is commonly seen in children who are neglected and emotionally deprived.

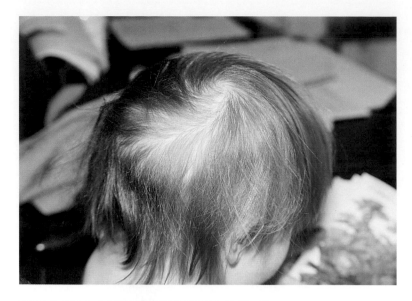

▼ 9.86, ▶ 9.87 Female aged 12 months

Child was referred by social services after she was found to be living in a house with several convicted child abusers. She is seen to be an alert child, with ingrained dirt particularly on the lower limbs. She giggled when her nappy was changed and the paediatrician then found signs consistent with sexual abuse. Fig. 9.87 shows a follow-up photograph taken 9 months later when the child had been in foster care. The child's whole demeanour has changed.

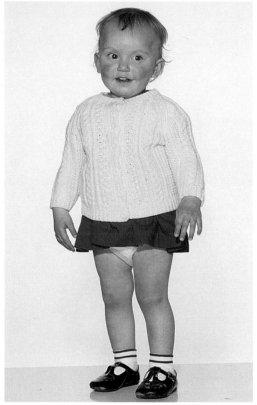

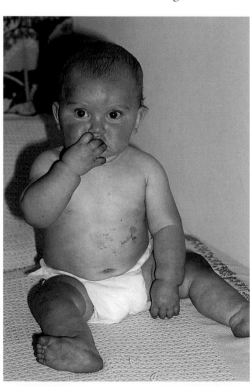

Chapter 10

Failure to thrive

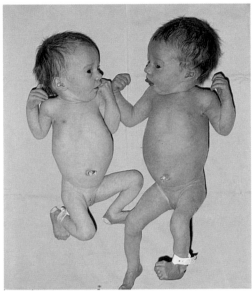

◀ **10.1**
Differences in growth during intra-uterine life reflect the state of nutrition of the foetus. This is well demonstrated in this slide of twins.

▼ **10.2 Male aged 3 months**
He had previously been seen because of a painful swollen leg due to a fracture of the fibula. He was seen again because of severe failure to thrive, with marked passivity, flexed posture, and signs of malnutrition.

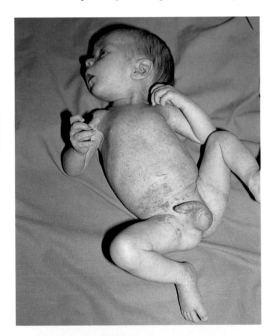

▶ **10.3, ▲ 10.4 Male aged 7 months**
He was referred from the infant welfare clinic because of poor weight gain. A thin, watchful baby is seen, with wasted buttocks and chronic nappy rash. There is minimal subcutaneous fat allowing the muscle pattern to be seen.

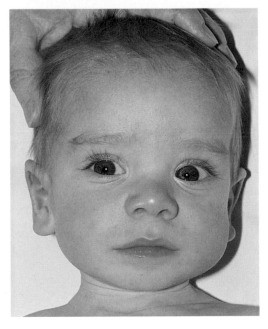

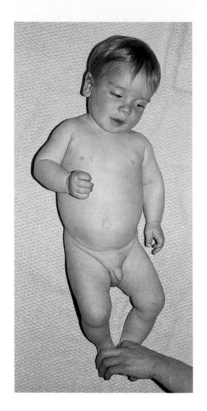

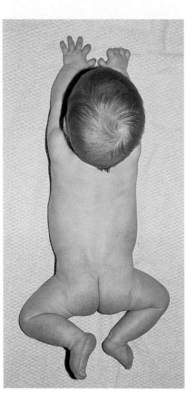

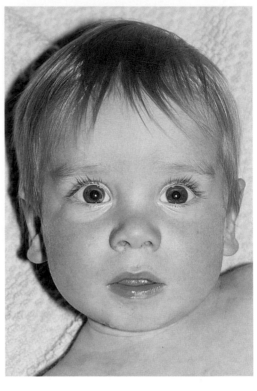

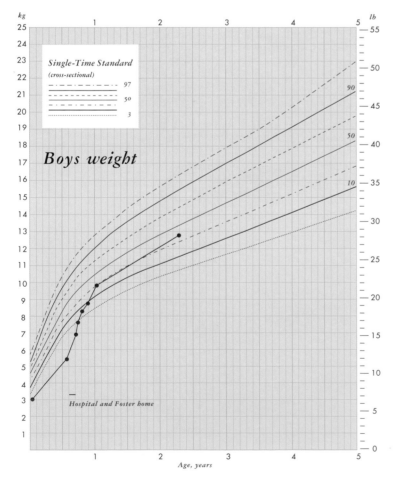

▲ ▲ ▲ ◀ **10.5–10.8 Male aged 1 year**

The same child as in Figs 10.3 and 10.4. He is visibly fatter with much thicker hair. He has an alert interested expression. Note the increase of subcutaneous fat. The growth chart (Fig. 10.8) shows falling away across the centiles during the first months of infancy, followed by dramatic acceleration in weight gain first in hospital and then foster care. Subsequently the weight gain begins to level off until reaching a position above the 25th centile.

▶ 10.9 Male twins aged 18 months

They were referred because both children were failing to thrive. One twin was markedly thinner than the other but both were underweight. In this case both twins grew much better in alternative care. This was post-natal non-organic failure to thrive.

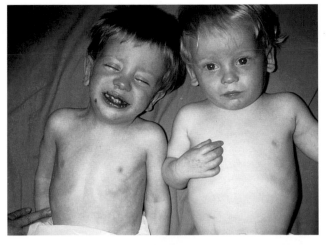

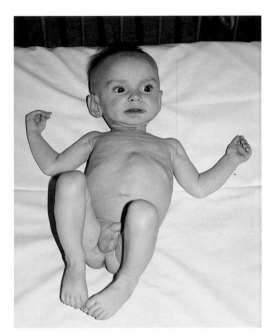

◀ 10.10 Male aged 8 months

He was referred because of persistent vomiting. He was an alert, watchful baby, seen to be emaciated with a flexed posture. Rumination was diagnosed on admission to hospital. There was a very poor interaction with his mother. Rumination is a rare manifestation of severe emotional deprivation.

▶ 10.11, ▼ 10.12 Male aged 15 months

The same child as in Fig. 10.10, in a child welfare charity nursery where his mother was receiving intensive help. The growth chart (Fig. 10.12) shows that the child grew along the 50th centile for the first couple of months of life before progressively falling across the centiles. It was difficult working with this child and mother and it was not until he was around a year old that he began to thrive consistently.

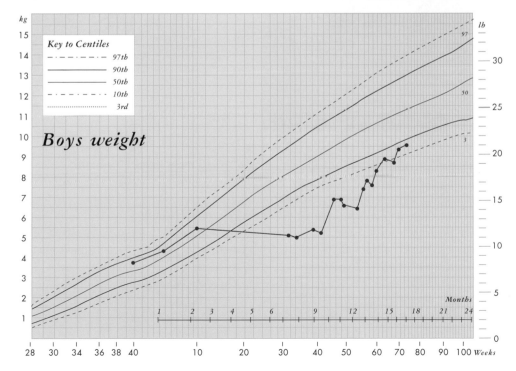

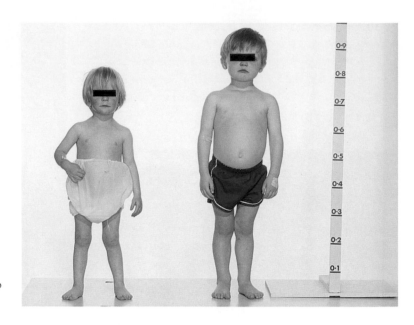

▶ 10.13 Two males both aged 4 years
The child on the left has severe growth retardation and malnutrition, and is not yet toilet trained. Severe emotional abuse has an association with failure to thrive and leads to stunting which may be permanent. (Note: late development of social skills and language are also seen in cases of emotional abuse.)

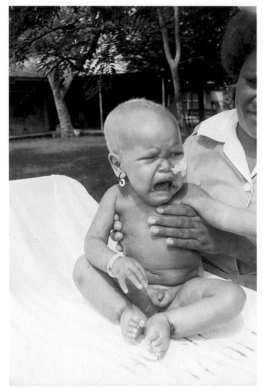

▲ 10.14 Male aged 2 years
He is an anxious-looking child with patchy depigmentation, and is grossly emaciated with a pot belly. The grandmother was caring for the child after his mother was murdered. She too is malnourished. This child was thin due to emotional deprivation and inadequate diet.

▲ 10.15 Male aged 12 months
He was referred because he was irritable and not growing. He has thin arms and swollen legs, sparse, pale hair, angular cheilosis and flexural dermatitis painted with gentian violet. The pattern of malnutrition here is of nutritional oedema (kwashiorkor). The aetiology of kwashiorkor is complex.

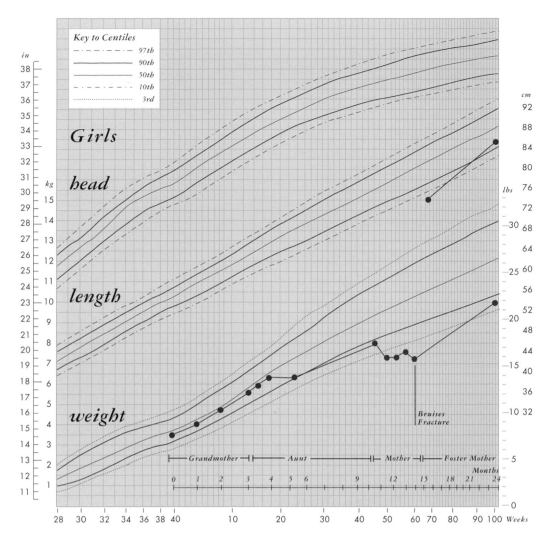

▶ 10.16, ▲ 10.17 Female aged 14 months

She was taken to the hospital emergency department because she was not moving her left arm. The history given was that she had fallen out of a highchair. She is a thin child, with bruises on the left outer thigh, and a treated fracture of the radius and ulna. The growth chart shows that this child thrived well in the care of her grandmother, less well when looked after by her aunt and badly when she was returned to her mother's care. She then showed catch-up growth in foster care. Although initially it was thought that the child had fallen out of the highchair her father subsequently admitted to swinging her round holding her by the wrist.

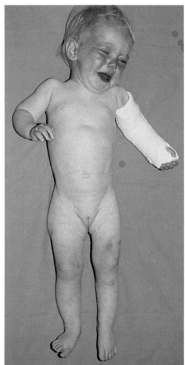

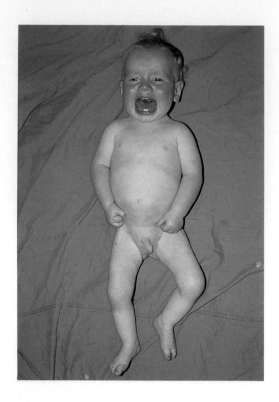

▲ 10.18 Male aged 15 months

He was referred because of poor weight gain. The child does not look badly nourished, although his thighs are thin. He weighed 6.6 kg (14.5 lbs), i.e. the weight of a child of 6 months and had the body proportions of a child of this age.

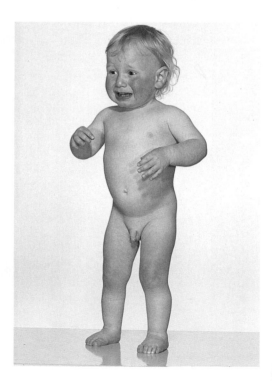

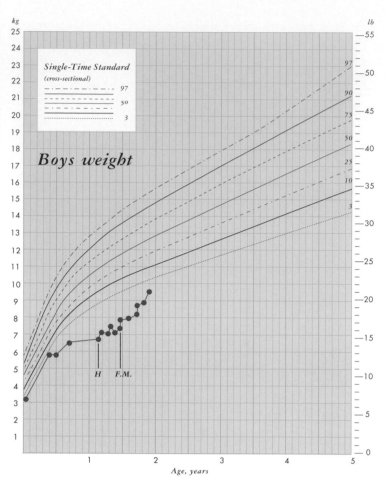

◄ 10.19, ▲ 10.20 Male aged 2 years

The same child as in Fig. 10.18. He still has infantile proportions but is better nourished. The growth chart shows that the failure to thrive started early on in infancy and the child did not start to thrive until in alternative care. (H = admission to hospital, FM = admission to foster care.)

▼ 10.21 Female aged 6 years

The child was referred from a district general hospital where she had been admitted with a swollen abdomen. The photograph shows a watchful, thin child with wasted upper arms and protuberant upper abdomen. Investigation showed pancreatitis and a pseudopancreatic cyst. Skeletal survey showed fractures of the spine, and a healing fracture of the humerus. The pancreatitis was thought to be secondary to a forceful blow in the abdomen, the spinal fractures due to a forced flexion injury and the fracture of the humerus was unexplained. This child was thin and part of her malnutrition was probably due to her intercurrent illness but she also had a history of failure to thrive. This therefore was a multiply abused child.

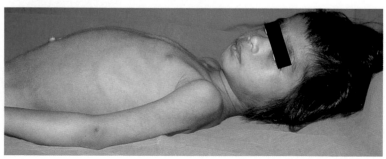

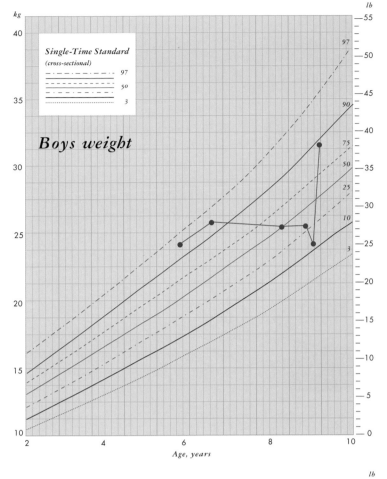

Boys weight

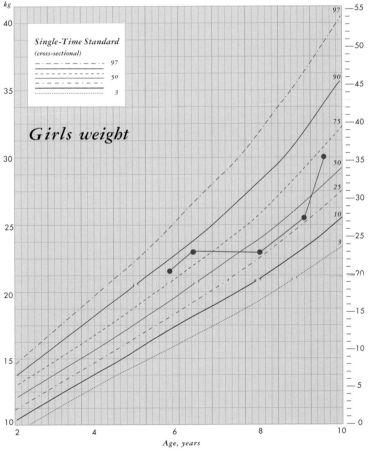

Girls weight

◀ ◀ ▼ **10.22–10.24**

When children are failing to thrive it is often useful to ask the carer to write down the food consumed over a two or three day period, i.e. keep a food diary. The foster mother who filled in this diary (Fig. 10.22) for a child of 3 years describes a diet adequate for two or three children. The growth chart (Fig. 10.23) shows the weight gain of another child in the foster home who had not been recognized as failing to thrive. He had put on weight well until the age of 6 years and then failed to thrive over the next 3 years because of emotional abuse and food deprivation. Fig. 10.24 is a growth chart for the twin sister of the previous child who has a similar growth pattern to her brother, in the same foster home.

It is important to assess all children in a family for failure to thrive if this condition has been recognized in one child.

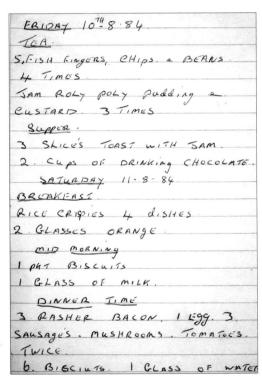

FRIDAY 10TH·8·84.
TEA.
S, FISH FINGERS, CHIPS & BEANS.
4 TIMES.
JAM ROLY POLY Pudding &
CUSTARD. 3 TIMES
Supper.
3 SLICE'S TOAST WITH JAM.
2. Cups OF DRINKING CHOCOLATE.
SATURDAY 11·8·84
BREAKFAST.
RICE CRISPIES 4 dISHES
2. GLASSES ORANGE.
MID MORNING
1 pkt BISCUITS
1 GLASS OF MILK.
DINNER TIME
3 RASHER BACON, 1 EGG. 3.
SAUSAGE'S. MUSHROOMS. TOMATOES.
TWICE.
6. BISCIUTS. 1 GLASS OF WATER

◄ 10.25

Mid upper arm circumference is a useful measurement in the assessment of nutrition. A non-stretch tape measure is looped around the arm firmly opposed to the skin without causing compression and measurement is taken from the 10 cm mark. In the example shown the arm circumference is 26 cm. This measurement is sensitive to changes in nutrition in terms of weeks, compared with, for example, height which often only accelerates slowly over months.

◄ 10.26 Female aged 3 years 2 months and her brother aged 1 year 9 months.
The boy had repeated admissions to hospital because of poor weight gain. Children in a family may show different growth patterns. This boy was emotionally deprived and failed to thrive.

▼ 10.27

The growth chart of a male who died at 3 months. The diagnosis was sudden infant death syndrome and a fractured rib. There is an increased mortality in children who fail to thrive.

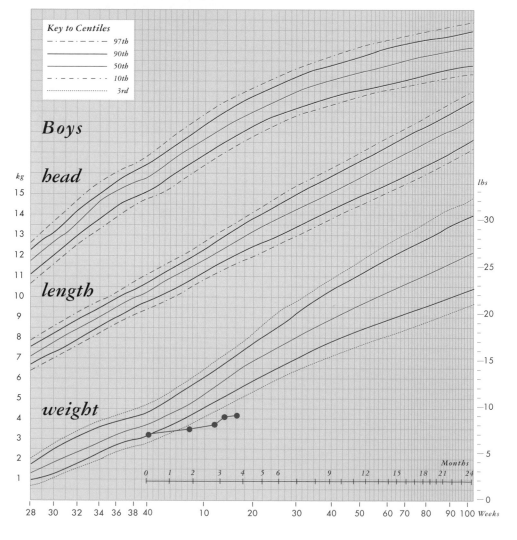

Key to Centiles
— · — · — · — 97th
———————— 90th
———————— 50th
— · — · — · — 10th
············· 3rd

Boys

head

length

weight

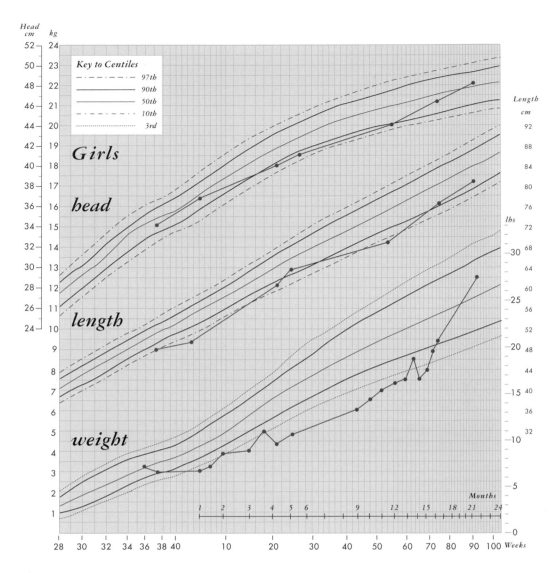

▲ **10.28**

This growth chart shows measurements for a child from birth until 2 years.
Early on in life she was repeatedly admitted to hospital with chest
infections but also failed to thrive. Her head circumference did not grow
optimally and neither did her length. She was admitted to the child welfare
charity day nursery where she initially began to thrive but then lost weight
and was admitted to foster care. This child has been followed up in the
paediatric clinic and now has a height measurement on the 25th centile,
which is matched with her weight.

▶ **10.29 Female aged 10 months**

She was referred to the clinic because of failure
to thrive. The photograph shows a miserable,
wasted, thin child.

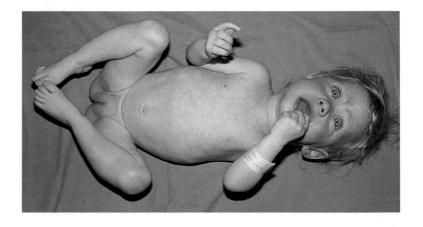

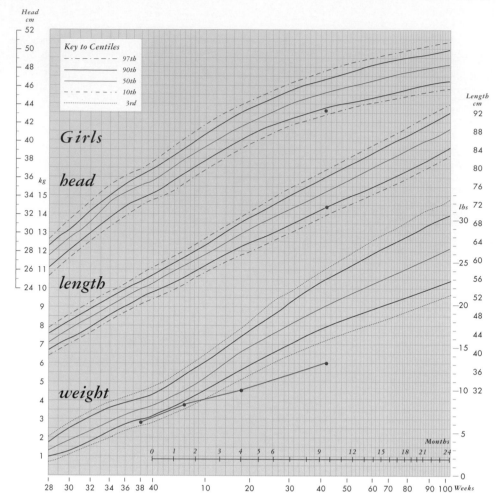

▲ **10.30 Female aged 10 months**

Same child as in Fig 10.29. The growth chart
shows marked discrepancy between length and
weight. Her weight gain was acceptable in the
first 6 weeks of life but then fell.

▶ **10.31**

This growth chart shows a boy born at 39 weeks
gestation who was light for dates with a birth
weight of 2.16 kg (4.76 lbs). He did not show
any catch-up growth and failed to thrive over
the first months of life. He was referred to a
child welfare charity and gained weight but was
then seen with a small facial bruise at 5 months.
He remained at home with his parents and put
on weight rapidly but at the age of 7 months was
seen with severe bruising on his face and
buttocks. The child went into foster care and at
the age of almost two had a height and weight
matched on the 10th centile.

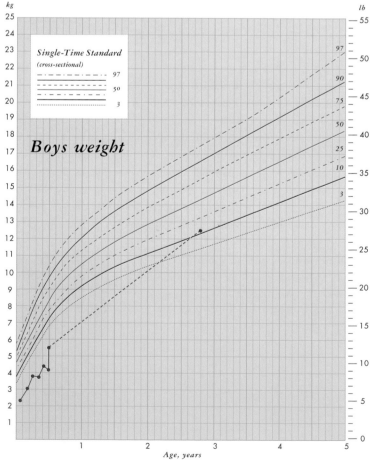

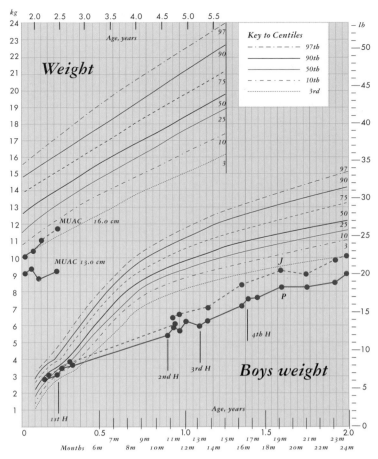

▲ 10.32, ▶ 10.33

These growth charts shows the weight and height gain of pre-term twins. Both twins severely failed to thrive, but showed they were able to put on weight more rapidly on admission to hospital. From the age of 21 months Twin J put on weight steadily and by the age of 2½ had a weight just below the 10th centile with a mid upper arm circumference (MUAC) of 16 cm. Twin P continued to fail to thrive. The chart recording the height measurements shows the same disparity, and Twin J has failed to catch up in terms of his height compared with his weight gain. (H = hospital admission.)

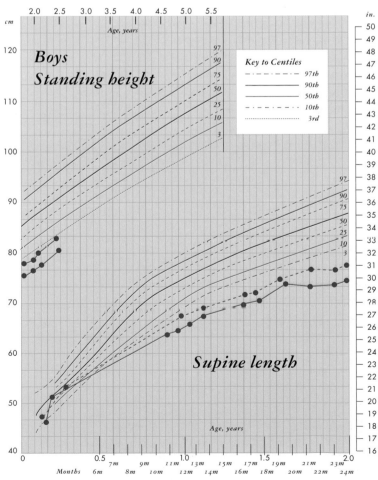

▶ **10.34**

This growth chart shows a child who failed to thrive from the age of about 3 months until she was taken into foster care and then put on weight very rapidly. Unfortunately she then had to change foster placement at about 3 years and immediately lost weight. The child was attached to the first foster mother and grieved on placement. Children who have failed to thrive previously tend to respond to stress by losing weight. (FM = admission to foster care.)

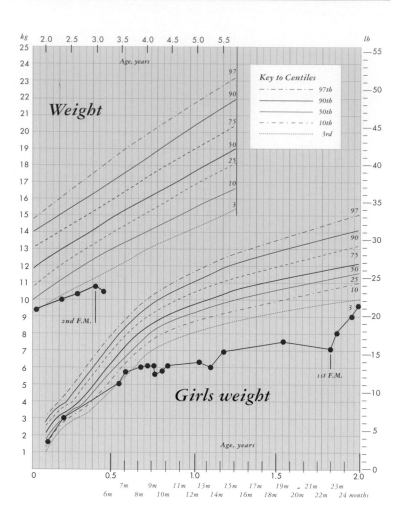

▼ **10.35**

This girl weighed 3 kg (6.6 lbs) at birth at 42 weeks gestation. She failed to thrive very early on and was admitted to hospital at 9 weeks, 11 weeks and 3 ½ months with bruising to the face. From 9 months to a year she lost weight and was placed with her grandparents on an interim care order. Once with her grandparents she began to thrive very quickly. When the child was 21 months old her grandmother broke a leg and the child went home rather precipitously. However, she continued to thrive and at the age of 2 had a weight on the 25th centile.

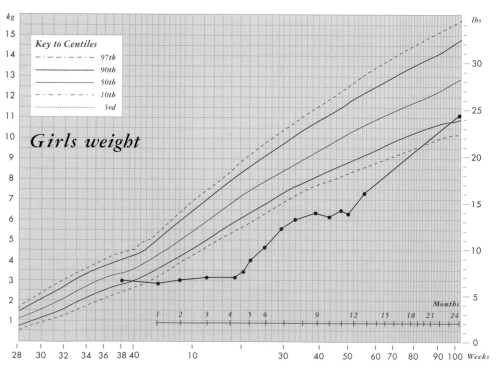

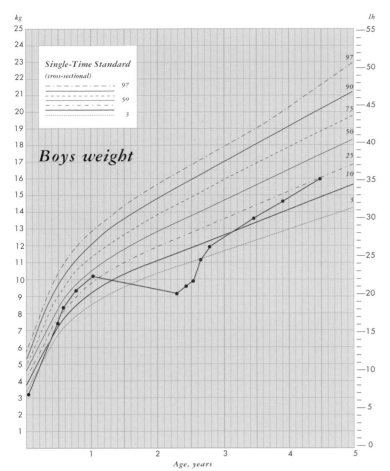

Boys weight

Single-Time Standard
(cross-sectional)

◀ **10.36**

This boy grew well at home but his mother asked for him to be received into care when he was around 6 months old. He continued to thrive until he moved to second foster parents at the age of 12 months. When he was having a medical before adoption it was realized that he had lost weight from the age of 1 until 2½. He had never been seen in the infant welfare clinic as the foster mother was very busy looking after 12 children. He was moved immediately to a third set of foster parents where he thrived well. He was subsequently adopted and at the age of 10 had a weight and height on the 50th centile.

▶ **10.37**

This boy had a weight appropriate for his gestation at 30 weeks. He thrived initially in hospital but his weight gain at home was always poor. He was fostered from the age of 6 months until he was rehabilitated with his mother after a period of 3 months in foster care. He then continued to thrive in his mother's care. (H = hospital admission, FM = admission to foster care.)

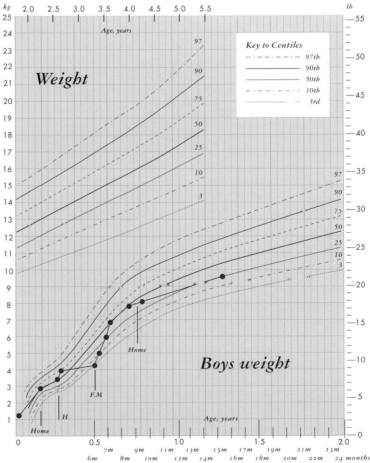

Weight

Key to Centiles

Boys weight

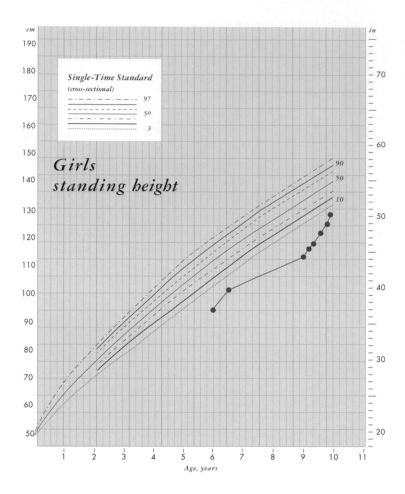

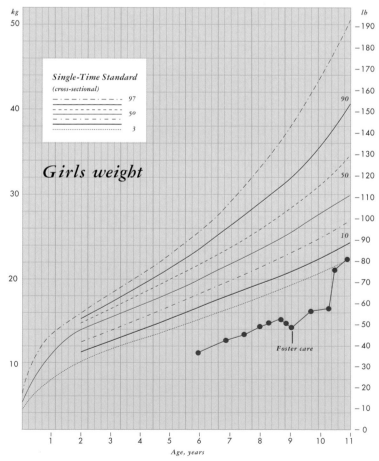

This girl of 9 years was known to be very small and underweight from the age of 5 years. At 9 years she was referred because of education failure; she was also wetting in the day and was mute. She was fostered and began to put on weight quite rapidly although her linear growth acceleration took longer. Although her growth pattern improved and she began to talk and stopped wetting, she did not catch up developmentally.

▶ **10.39**

When the child in Fig. 10.38 presented it was also realized that her sister was small and underweight and growth charts were constructed for her.

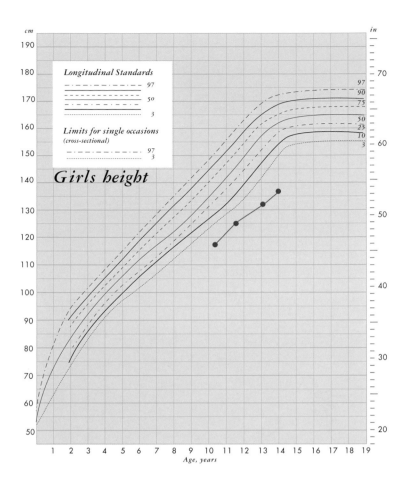

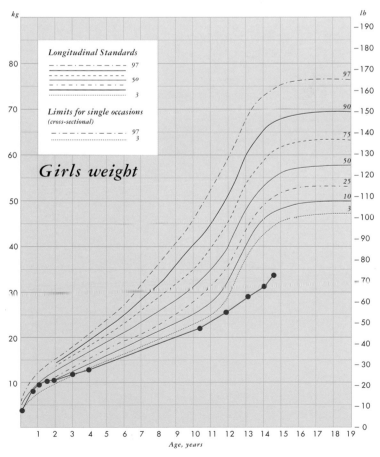

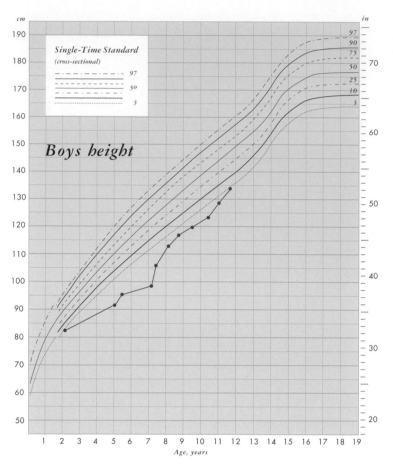

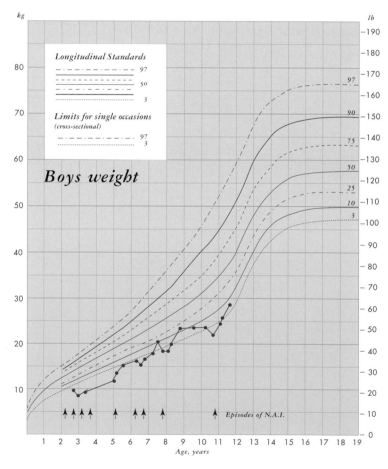

◀ 10.40, ▼ 10.41 This boy failed to thrive from early childhood and his weight gain was never really satisfactory, showing a sawtooth pattern before having a sustained weight gain when he was taken into care. He was emotionally abused and intermittently physically abused throughout this period. This child came from an ethnic minority group and alternative appropriate care was not available. After the supervision order was made there was improvement, which was not sustained.

▶ **10.42,** ▼ **10.43** The boy whose growth is shown in Fig. 10.42 was a twin born at 35 weeks gestation weighing 2 kg (4.4 lbs). He did well early in life but was then received into care at the age of 2. His carers had 'healthy eating practices'. His failure to thrive was severe and by the age of 5 years he weighed less than he had done when he was 2½ years. The foster parents were very angry when asked to change his diet but the child did put on weight initially. After a further weight loss he was transferred to a children's home. He gained weight very rapidly and started to grow. His sister showed a similar growth pattern (Fig. 10.43). The two children were adopted.

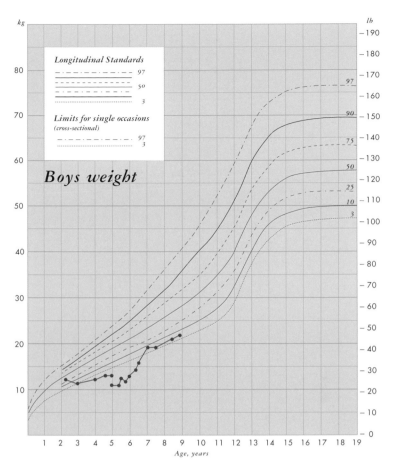

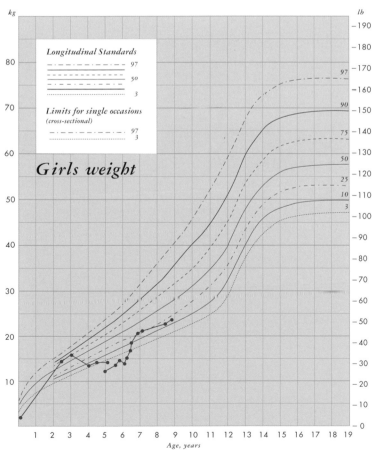

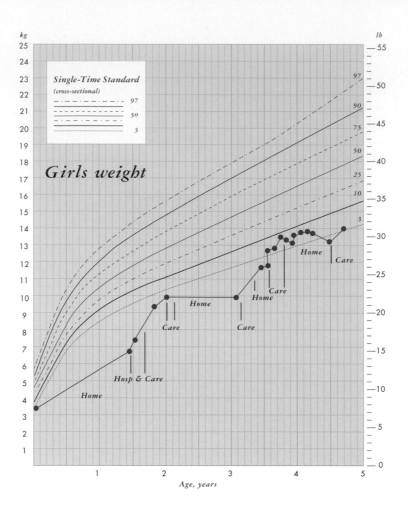

▲ 10.44, ▶ 10.45

This girl presented at the age of 18 months with physical injury (bites and bruises), failure to thrive and emotional deprivation. She showed catch-up growth in hospital and care and three attempts at rehabilitation were associated with failure to gain weight. The courts finally accepted that rehabilitation was not possible. As a teenager this girl has severe emotional problems.

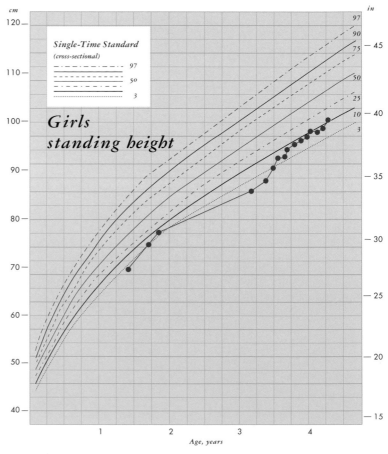

◀ 10.46

This growth chart shows a 'saw-tooth' pattern. In infancy this girl had gastro-oesophageal reflux, and repeated episodes of infection-induced wheezing, but the dips in weight related to periods of neglect when the marital relationship deteriorated. Her mother would leave home, the father took over the childcare and the child would begin to thrive.

▼ 10.47

This growth chart shows parallel poor centiles; this girl was physically neglected. Her mother described the huge meals she ate but the clinical diagnosis was that this child did not eat an adequate number of calories. Her height (not shown) grew along the 3rd centile and her weight gradually increased to a position just below the 3rd centile.

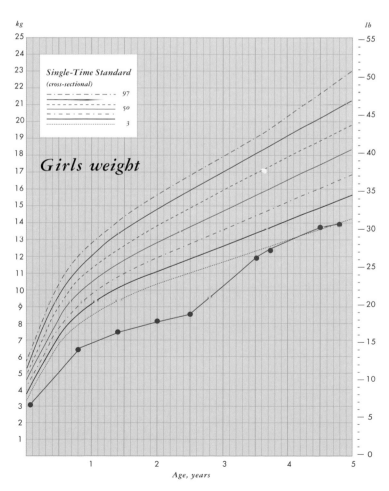

SECTION 4

SEXUAL ABUSE

Chapter 11

Associated non-sexual injuries

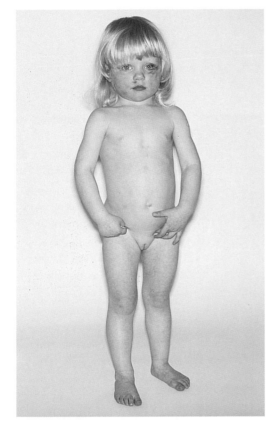

◀ ◀ ▼ ▼ 11.1–11.4 Female aged 3 years

The mother returned after an evening out to find the child with a badly bruised face. Her partner admitted to hitting the child. There is a recent hand slap across the right side of the face with bruising in one ear. There is also bruising on the mid and lower back, the left groin, and a faint bruise is also visible on the right lower abdomen. The other bruises were inflicted by gripping the child. The child disclosed sexual assault but there was no abnormality of genitalia or anus.

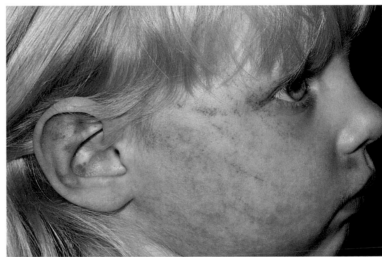

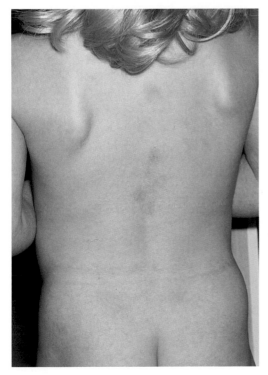

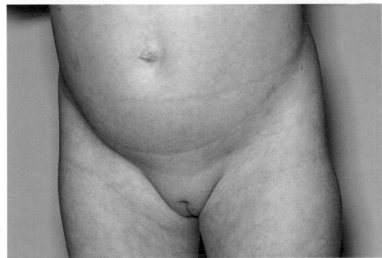

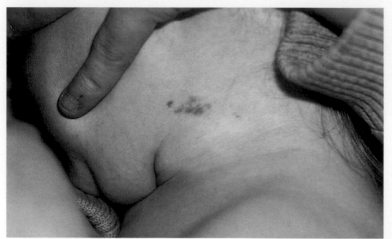

◀ 11.5 Female aged 3 years
The bruise on her neck was noticed in day nursery. The photograph shows a bruise on the left side of the neck, with the appearance of a 'love bite'. (Note: bruises such as these are highly correlated with sexual abuse.)

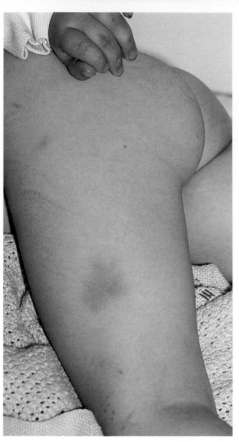

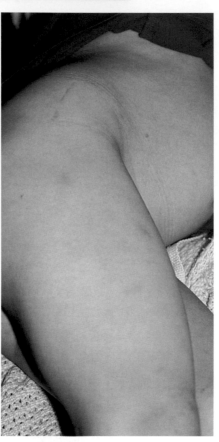

◀ ◀ 11.6, 11.7 Female aged 4 years
She was seen in the clinic because her older sister had disclosed sexual abuse. A large, roughly triangular bruise is seen on the posterior aspect of the left upper thigh, with a smaller bruise on the buttock. There were also scratches just above the knee and several further bruises on the outer aspect of the right thigh laterally. Examination of the genitalia and anus showed signs consistent with vaginal and anal penetration. (Note: if one child in the family has disclosed sexual abuse, it is usual practice to examine all the other siblings. Whilst these injuries are non-specific they are worrying in their distribution, i.e. thigh, and the smaller round bruises may be fingertip bruising.)

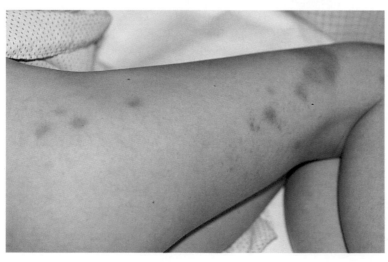

◀ 11.8 Female aged 7 years
She was referred by a school nurse who noticed bruising on her thigh. There are multiple round bruises on the outer aspect of the right upper thigh and a larger triangular shaped bruise on the lower thigh. The father admitted to sexually abusing this child, and also hitting her with a belt.

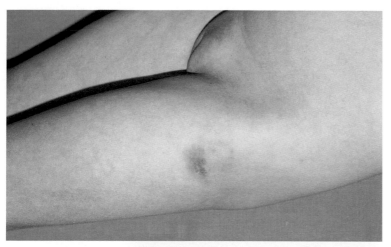

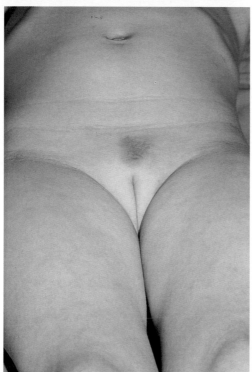

◀ ◀ ◀ ▼ **11.9–11.12 Female aged 5 years**
Initially the child was taken to the hospital
emergency department by her parents who
alleged that the girl's older cousin had sexually
assaulted her. Investigations revealed a recent
bruise on the symphysis pubis. Approximately a
year later the child was brought back to the
emergency department by her parents because of
serious vaginal bleeding. Again bruising was seen
on the symphysis pubis and both outer thighs.
Further investigation revealed profuse bleeding
from the genitalia with a large clot at introitus,
and a tear was seen to extend from the posterior
vaginal wall onto the perineum. The genital signs
were of vaginal rape and the bruising associated
with this.

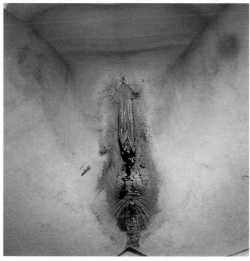

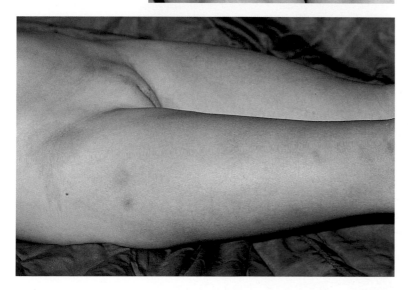

▶ ▶ ▼ **11.13–11.15 Male aged 4 years**
Social services referred the child after sexually explicit play was seen at nursery school. The photographs show linear bruises on the posterior aspect of both upper thighs proximally, bruising of the proximal phalanx of the fourth and fifth fingers of the left hand and old healed scratches on the outer aspect of the thigh and buttock. Abnormal anal findings consistent with penetration were also seen. These are unusual injuries, all unexplained, combined with abnormal anal findings, and later the child disclosed abuse by his father and grandfather.

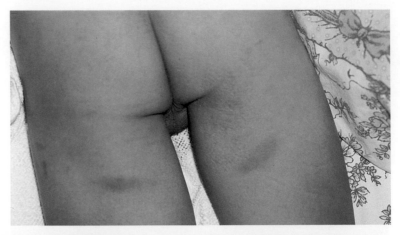

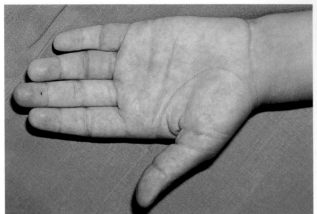

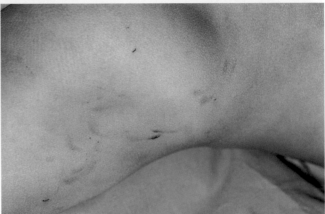

◀ **11.16 Female aged 2 years**
The mother moved into a friend's house, and shortly afterwards the child complained of a sore bottom. The doctor examined her and found an acute anal fissure and referred her to the paediatrician. The photograph shows an irregular recent bruise on the outer aspect of the right upper thigh. Examination of the anus showed an acute fissure, dilated veins, and perianal oedema. (Note: a diagnosis of anal abuse was made in this child and the older children in the household were subsequently taken into care because of multiple abuse, including physical abuse, due to Munchausen's syndrome by proxy.)

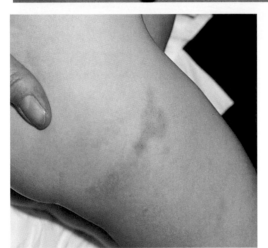

▶ **11.17 Male aged 2 years**
The child's father took him to the hospital emergency department saying that 24 hours earlier the child had fallen and hurt his arm. X-ray showed a metaphyseal humeral fracture and the child was also noted to have multiple facial bruising and an abnormal anus. The child was returned to the care of the father and step-mother and re-referred by his nursery with new injuries. Linear scratches are seen on the anterior and medial aspect of the right thigh. A small bruise on dorsal aspect of penis is also seen. The scratches are consistent with nail marks and the bruise with a nip to the penis.

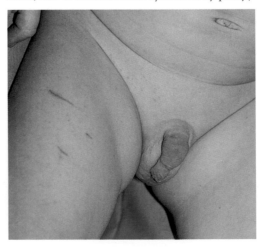

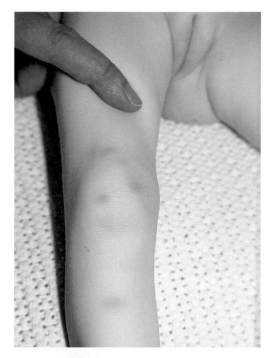

▶ **11.18 Female aged 15 months**
She was admitted to hospital following an emergency call claiming she had 'drowned in the bath'. Multiple circular bruises are seen on the right knee. Signs of sexual abuse, physical abuse and failure to thrive were all identified. (See also Figs. 7.18-7.21.)

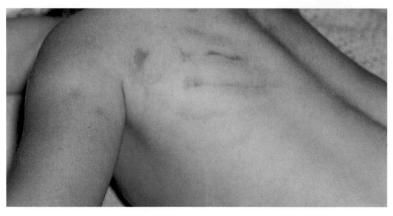 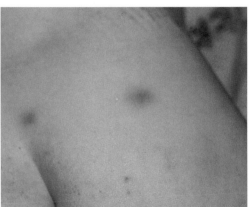

▲ **11.19, ▲ 11.20 Female aged 3 years**
The family was under supervision of the social services because of concern about Munchausen's syndrome by proxy. The mother told a social worker that the child had injured her back when she slipped in the bath. There is a clear adult hand print across the right upper back and three round bruises on the right buttock. The child made a very clear disclosure of sexual abuse following physical examination.

▶ **11.21 Female aged 14 months**
The mother took the child to the doctor because of 'soreness'. Social services were involved because of contact with a known child abuser. There is multiple bruising of different ages over the abdomen and left groin. There was also associated nappy rash and the genitalia were abnormal. This is very unusual bruising; abdominal bruising is frequently associated with sexual abuse.

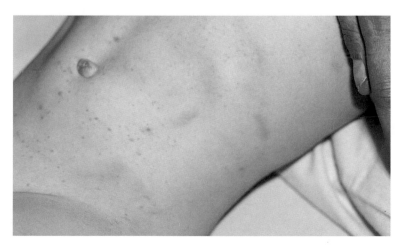

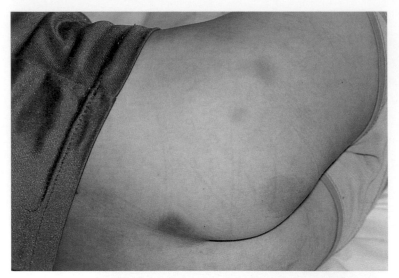

◄ 11.22 Male aged 7 years

He told his parents that a man had tried to touch his bottom in the street. A large bruise is seen on the superior aspect of the natal cleft, purple in colour with brown edges, and two more bruises are seen on the lateral aspect of the right buttock. The bruise in the natal cleft is particularly unusual, but the bruises on the buttock are also relevant given the history. Abnormal anal signs were present too.

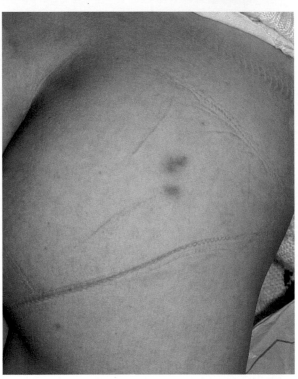

◄ 11.23 Female aged 5 years

She was examined because her older sibling had been sexually abused. A pinch mark is seen on the right buttock. Pinch marks on the buttocks are always of great concern, and particularly in view of the family history in this case.

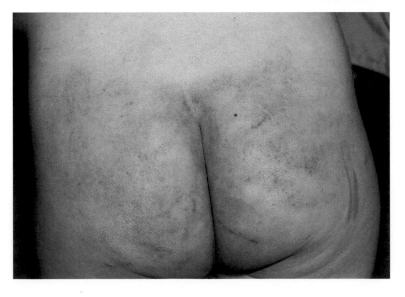

◄ 11.24 Male aged 12 months

The mother complained to the social services that following an access visit to his father the child had a badly bruised bottom. There is extensive bruising over both buttocks, and finger marks are visible within the mass of bruising. This is a severe beating in a very young child. There was evidence of sexual abuse in an older sibling. 'Spanking' may have sexual connotations.

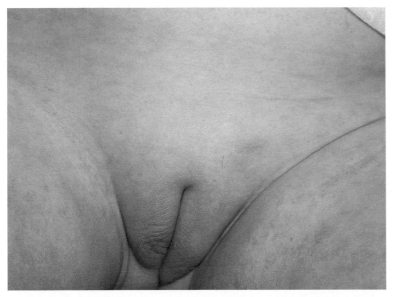

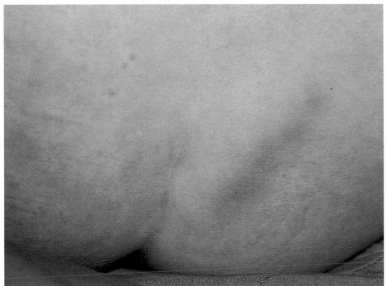

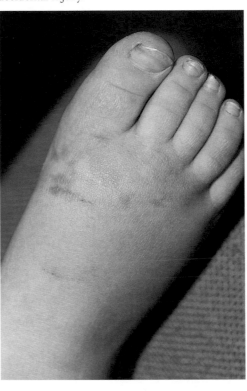

◀ ◀ ▼ 11.25–11.27 Female aged 2 years

Social services referred her when bruises had been seen at day nursery. Bruising is seen in the left pubic area; there was also bruising on the buttocks and dorsum of the right foot. Further examination showed anal findings consistent with sexual abuse. Bruising in the pubic area is always very worrying, and is unusual in accidental injury.

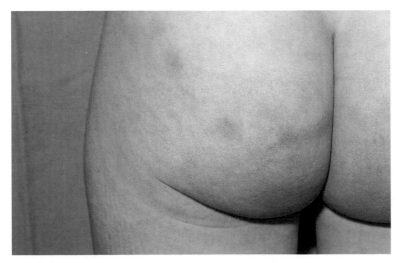

◀ 11.28 Female aged 4 years

She attended a routine paediatric follow-up appointment, having been previously physically abused, and also possibly emotionally abused with an over-involved father and very anxious stepmother. There is fingertip bruising of the left buttock. Bruising of this nature is always of great concern and raises a strong possibility of sexual abuse.

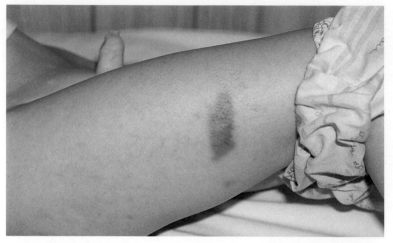

◀ 11.29 Male aged 6 years

He was referred by the family service unit after it had been discovered that his older sister had been sexually abused by their father. A large bruise is seen on the outer aspect of the right upper thigh, but also note several small fingertip bruises too. The bruise on the outer thigh is non-specific but may have been caused by a kick; the small fingertip bruising in this location is worrying. (Note the sustained erection, this is a very worrying sign in small boys.) Several other children in this family had evidence of sexual abuse.

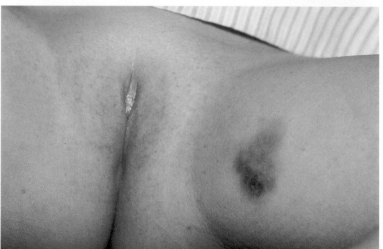

◀ 11.30 Female aged 5 years

During a games lesson when the child was sitting cross-legged the teacher noticed a bruise on the inner thigh, and also a similar bruise on the outer thigh. She remembered that some 2 weeks earlier the child had complained of having a sore bottom. There is a large irregular bruise on the inner aspect of the left thigh. The findings were consistent with anal and genital abuse. The child subsequently gave a very clear disclosure of genital and anal abuse by her father.

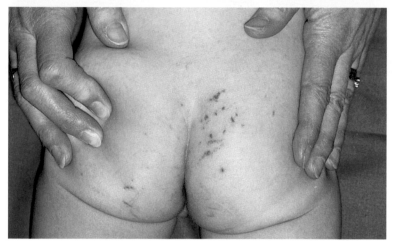

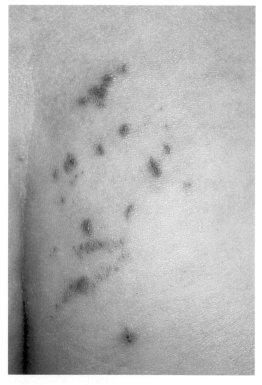

▲ 11.31, ▶ 11.32 Female aged 2 years

Child was previously known to the paediatric department because of extreme clinging, sore vulva, and a very anxious mother. She had been admitted to the local fever hospital when this 'unexplained' rash was seen. Scratch marks can be seen on both buttocks with linear scratch marks and small areas of skin loss. The child also had multiple anal fissures. These scratches are fingernail marks in a child who had also been sexually abused.

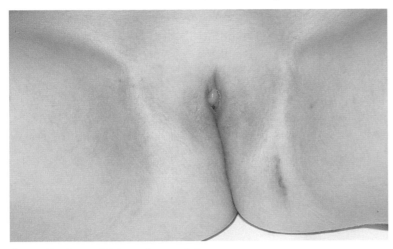

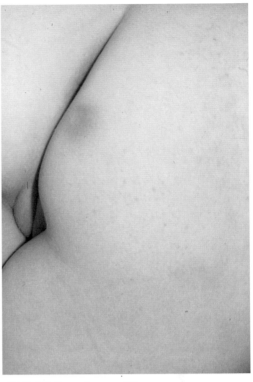

▲ 11.33, ▶ 11.34 Female aged 6 years

Over the previous months she had returned from access to her father with bruising about the face, but her grandmother was very anxious when she found bruising on the buttocks and in the groin and informed social services. The photographs show a linear bruise on the left groin and a bruise on the right buttock at the natal cleft. Examination showed signs consistent with anal abuse. The girl gave a very clear disclosure of physical and sexual abuse by her father occurring on access visits.

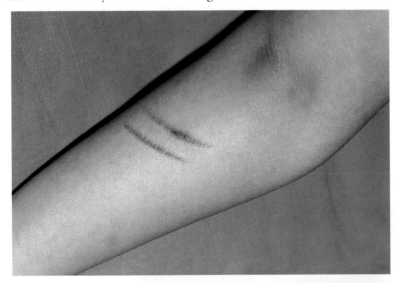

◀ 11.35 Female aged 7 years

She told a neighbour that her father had been hurting her. Social services were contacted. There is an unexplained burn on the outer aspect of the left forearm; also note the small brown bruise just above the wrist. Examination of the genital area showed marked reddening. Both the burn and the reddening were unexplained, and it was some months before this child could be protected when care from her mother deteriorated to even more unacceptable levels.

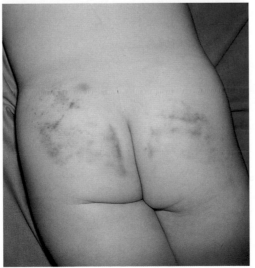

◀ 11.36 Male aged 4 years

He had been recently seen in the hospital emergency department with a fractured clavicle which had been accepted as being due to an accident. A second medical was requested by social services after it was realized that his father was a convicted child abuser. The photograph shows severely beaten buttocks. No abnormality was seen of the genitalia or anus. There is clearly serious non-accidental injury, and the possibility of sexual abuse remains.

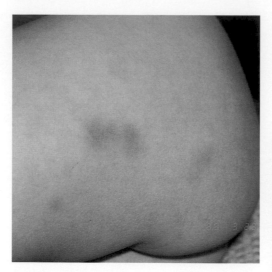

◀ 11.37, ▼ 11.38 Female aged 24 months
She was examined because her younger half-brother had severely beaten buttocks (Fig. 11.24). Grip marks are seen on the outer aspect of the left upper thigh/buttocks, and there is a scratch on the pubis. These are genital signs consistent with sexual abuse.

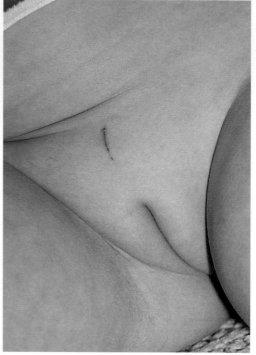

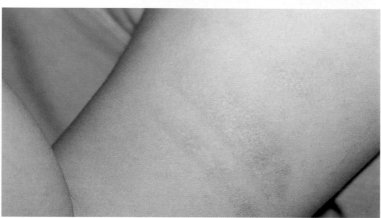

▲ 11.39 Female aged 3 years
She was seen in the paediatric clinic because her older brother had disclosed that his parents had sexually abused him, after he had been received into foster care. This girl was mute. There are healing linear burns on the posterior aspect of the right upper thigh. There was also a severe degree of labial fusion and abnormal anus. Unexplained burns are always of great concern. Burns are related to sadistic abuse and in particular sexual abuse. There is also an association between mutism and sexual abuse.

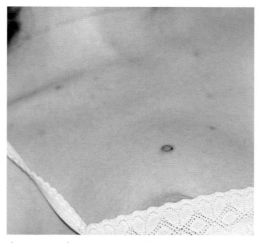

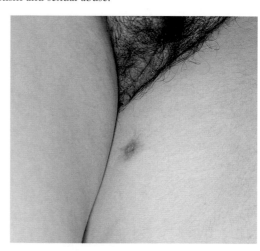

▲ 11.40, ▲ 11.41 Female aged 16 years
Child told her social worker that she had been sexually abused (again). She lived between the Safe House and a violent family. The photographs show a cigarette burn on the right breast and inner aspect of the left thigh. On further examination she had a total of 16 burns. These were caused by an unidentified assailant, and not thought to be self-inflicted. This was a severely damaged girl caught up in a violent relationship.

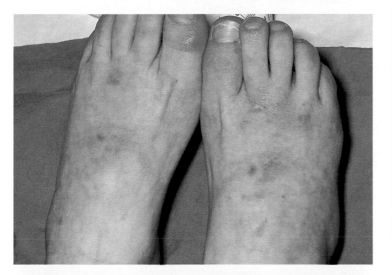

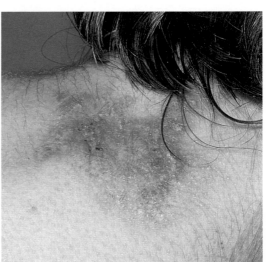

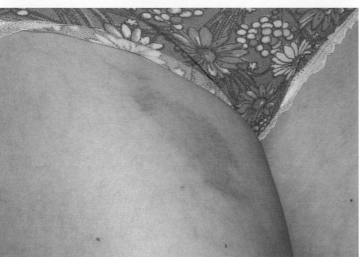

◀ ◀ ◀ ▼ **11.42–11.45 Female aged 11 years**
She was referred by her special school when bruising about the face was noted. The photographs show a healing burn on the back of the neck, an almost healed burn on the dorsum of the right hand across the knuckles, bruises on the dorsum of both feet and a large bruise on the inner aspect of the right thigh. There were signs consistent with genital and anal abuse. These were inflicted burns on the back of the neck and on the back of the hand. The injury to the feet is consistent with stamping, and of the inner thigh with a kick (see Chapter 5). The child subsequently disclosed sexual abuse by the stepmother. The younger stepbrother had been encouraged to stamp on the girl's feet. These injuries were seen in the context of sadistic abuse, which also included the child having a polythene bag put over her head.

▼ 11.46 Male aged 11 years

The social services requested that the child be seen in the paediatric clinic after he had been seen visiting a known child abuser. There is an unexplained circular bruise on the inner aspect of the right upper thigh, and a probable pinch mark. Further examination showed a markedly abnormal anus. The circular bruise is unexplained, but is in a worrying site as are the pinch marks. The boy later disclosed sexual abuse by the known child abuser.

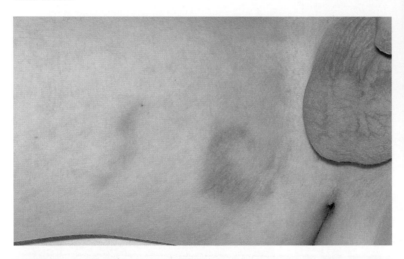

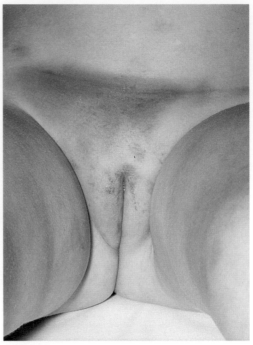

▲ 11.47 Female aged 10 months

The mother took the child to the hospital emergency department because of concern about bruising on her abdomen. There is extensive bruising in the pubic area and lower abdomen. This is an old photograph from the early 1970s; sexual assault was questioned but not confirmed.

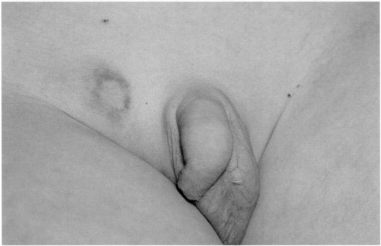

▲ 11.48 Male aged 4 years

The mother sought help from social services after separation from her husband. The oldest daughter had nightmares, and profuse vaginal discharge. Examination of her sister revealed signs consistent with abuse. All the children were examined. The boy showed a circular bruise on the right pubic area. He also had an abnormal anus. The child initially said the injury was due to handle bars on his bicycle. He later went on to disclose sexual abuse by his father. This is an unexplained bruise in an unusual site, and may be a suction bruise.

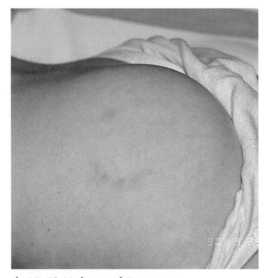

▲ 11.49 Male aged 5 years

He was seen in the clinic after it had been found that his younger sister, who had been admitted to hospital because of severe physical abuse, had been sexually abused. The father asked the boy to say that he had bruised his buttocks after having fallen off a gate. Investigation revealed an incomplete circular bruise consistent with a bite, there were also abnormal anal signs. It was felt that this was an adult bite, but the opinion of the forensic orthodontologist was not sought.

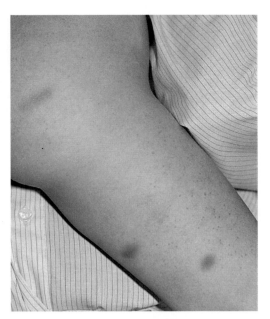

◄ 11.50 Female aged 3 years

Child told her mother that her mother's partner had rubbed her tuppence. There is a linear bruise on the right buttock, and linear and circular bruises on the lateral aspect and posteriorly on the right thigh. The genitalia were reddened. The bruises are suggestive of fingertip bruising, and the reddening is consistent with rubbing.

▼ 11.51–11.58 Female aged 18 months (continued overleaf)

She was seen for routine follow-up in the failure to thrive clinic when bruising was noticed. The photographs show multiple pinches and fingertip bruising on the abdomen, a probable bite on the left lower leg, a linear bruise on the left calf posterio-laterally, scratches about the right knee with a bruise on the front of the knee, a bruise on the outer aspect of the right upper arm and right chest, a bruise on the outer aspect of the right lower arm, a laceration on the lateral border of the left foot and recent and healed scratches on the face. Further examination showed genital and anal abnormality. These are multiple bruises and fingernail scratches in a child already known because of failure to thrive. These injuries are consistent with repeated physical abuse in association with sexual abuse.

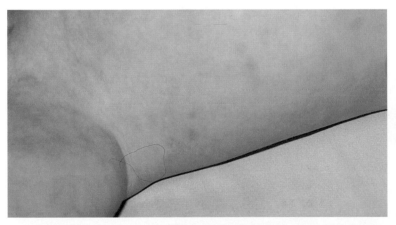

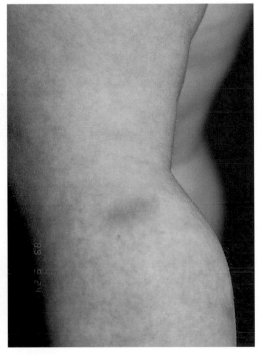

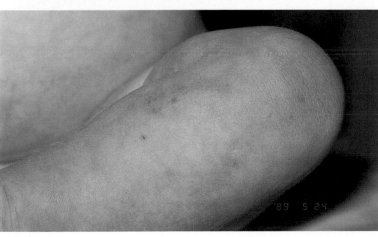

▼ **11.51–11.58 Female aged 18 months** (continued)

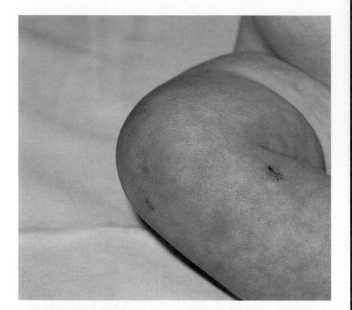

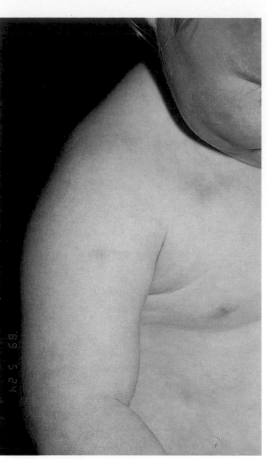

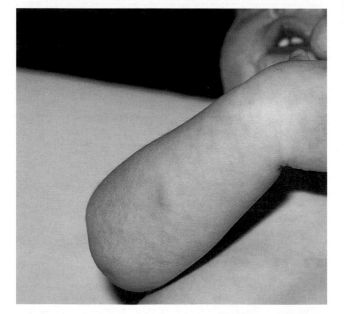

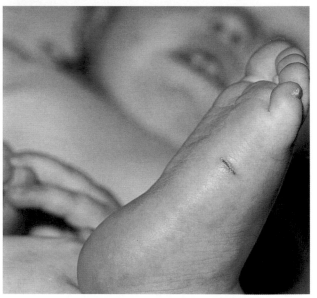

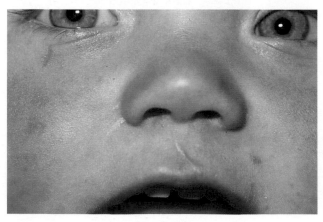

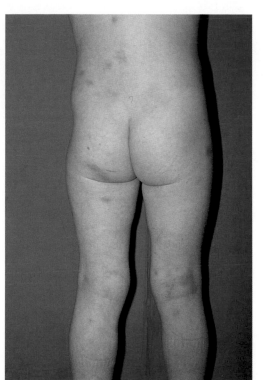

◀ **11.59 Female aged 3 years**

She was seen for examination after it was disclosed to the girl's mother that her 12-year-old sister was abusing her. Multiple, fingertip bruising of the left lower back, the left buttock, the posterior aspect of the left thigh and the right outer thigh can be seen. Her genitalia were normal. This child had far too many bruises suggestive of fingertip bruising. She was seen again 3 months later with grossly abnormal genitalia and anus where she had been sexually abused by an adult.

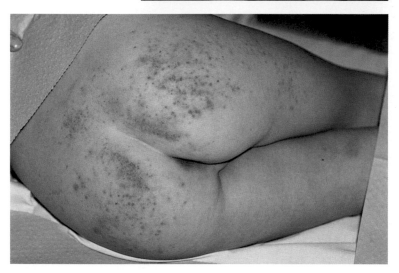

◀ **11.60 Female aged 5 years**

The child returned home with a rash on her buttocks after a contact with her father. Her mother took her to the doctor who referred her to hospital. Extensive bruising and petechial haemorrhages can be seen over both buttocks. The anus was abnormal. The signs are consistent with a beating of the buttocks and sexual abuse.

Chapter 12

Normal anogenital findings

Normal genitalia and variants

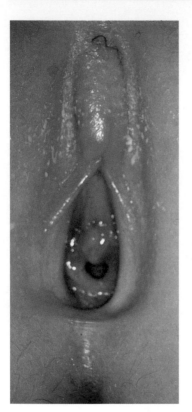

◀ **12.1**

A crescentic opening in a fleshy hymen.

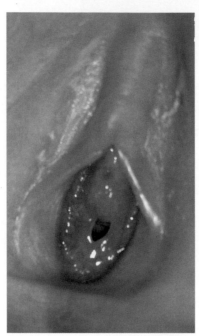

◀ **12.2**

A crescentic hymen and semi-transparent smooth margin with no disruption of blood vessels.

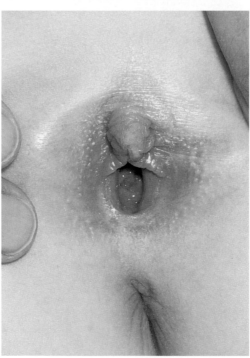

▲ **12.3**

A fleshy hymen with a redundant free edge and normal anus in a 2 year old.

◀ **12.4**

A closed fleshy hymen in a 2 year old.

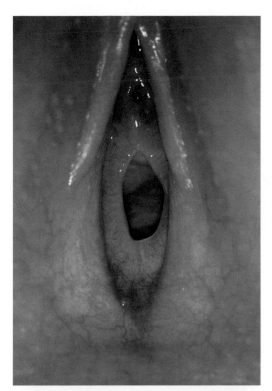

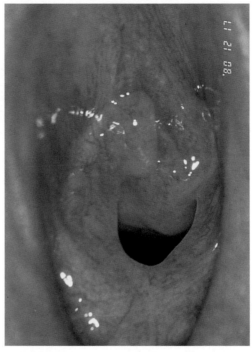

◀ 12.5
A high magnification view which gives the appearance of a gaping but smooth semi-translucent free edge and an undisturbed vascular pattern. Annular hymen.

▲ 12.6
A high magnification view of a crescentic hymen.

◀ 12.7
A high magnification view of an annular hymen.

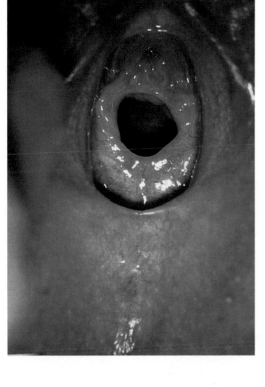

▶ 12.8
Annular hymen in a 3 year old. The hymen is still infantile and fleshy. Note again the clear vascular pattern.

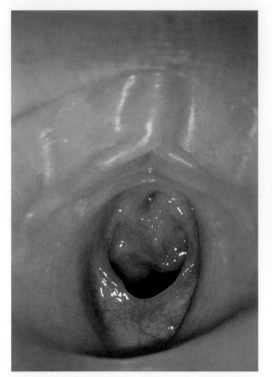

◀ **12.9**
A high magnification view of a crescentic hymen in a 6 year old. Note the thin posterior rim which is almost translucent with clearly visible blood vessels. There is little hymenal tissue anteriorly.

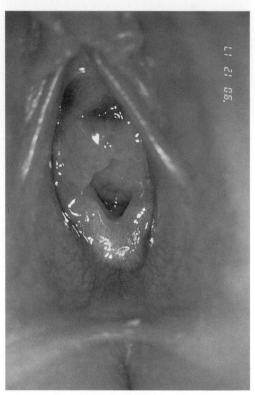

▲ **12.10**
A high magnification view of the fleshy redundant hymen of infancy leading to a distorted view of the hymenal opening.

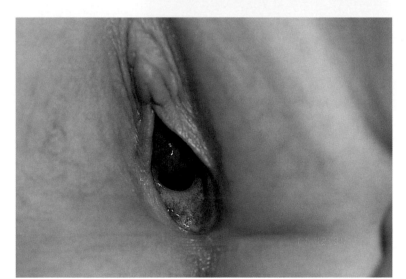

◀ **12.11**
A normal crescentic hymen in a child with vulvitis.

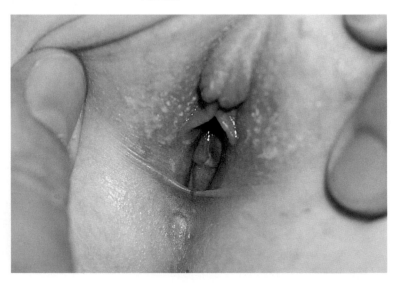

▶ **12.12**
Mild vulvovaginitis but fleshy hymen of infancy.

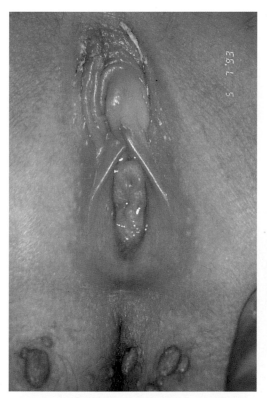

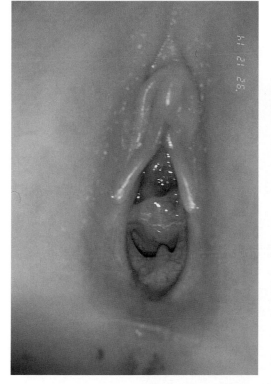

◀ **12.13**

Fleshy redundant hymen of infancy. The perianal warts need to be investigated as a possibly sexually transmitted disease.

▼ **12.14**

Infantile hymen with fleshy tag.

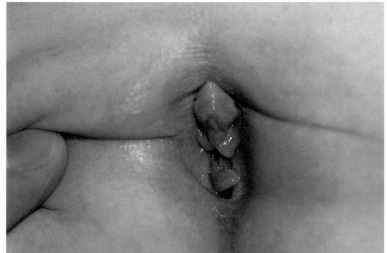

◀ **12.15**

Septal remnant at 6 o'clock seen in a normal crescentic hymen.

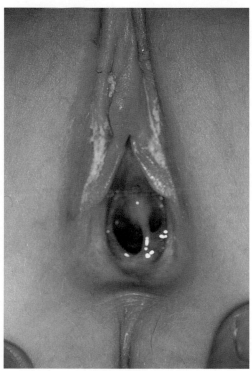

▶ **12.16**

Septate hymen.

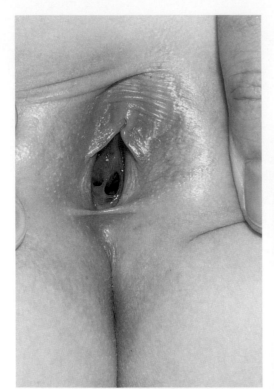

Multiperforate hymen.

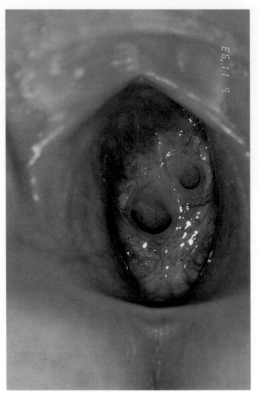

▲ **12.18**
High magnification of a septate hymen.

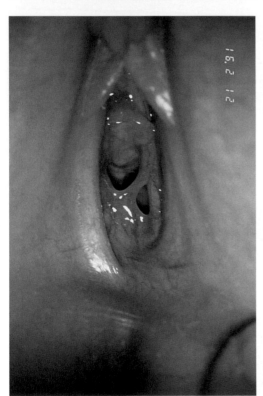

▲ **12.19**
Septate hymen.

▶ **12.20**
Unusual appearance with a 'flap of hymen' forming across the hymenal opening. This may be a normal variant.

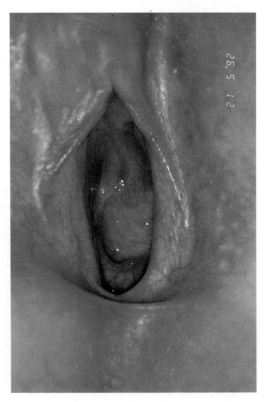

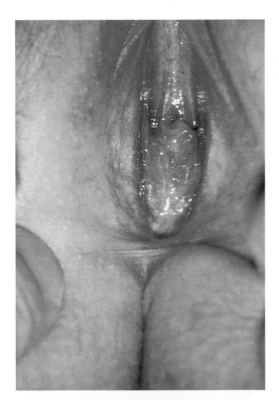

 12.21

The effect of oestrogen on the hymen at puberty – note thickened, pale tissue, and vasculature less evident.

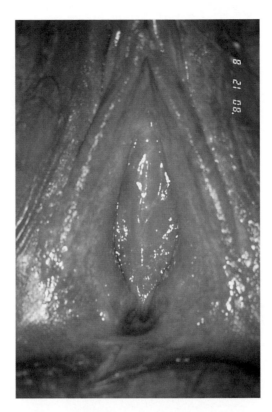

▲ **12.22,** ▼ **12.23**

Normal oestrogenized hymen in a 12 year old.

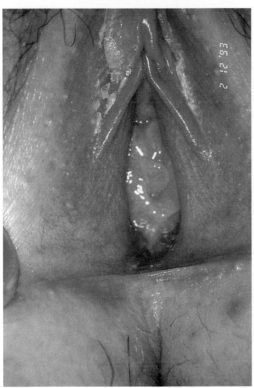

▲ **12.24**

An oestrogenized hymen in a 12 year old – the hymen requires further examination to reveal if there is any abnormality.

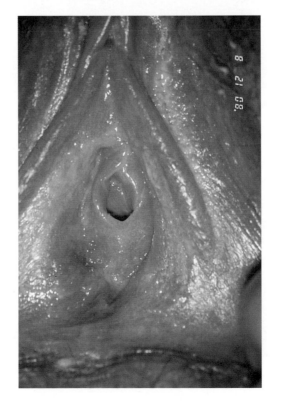

Normal anal findings

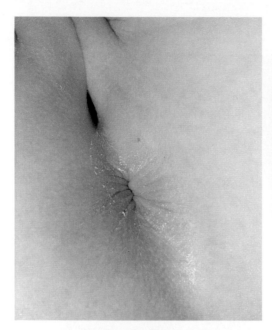

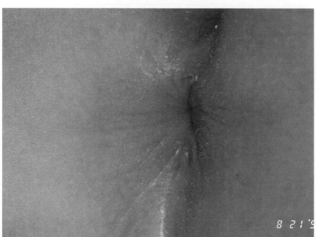

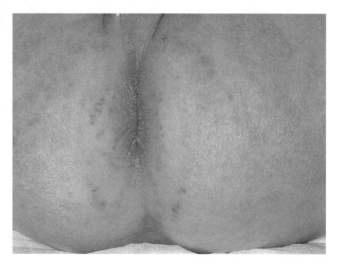

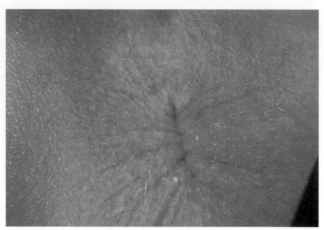

◀ **12.25**
A normal anal sphincter.

▲ **12.26**
A normal anal sphincter in pigmented skin.

◀ **12.27**
A normal anal sphincter, but note there are often rather shiny areas at 6 and 12 o'clock which superficially look like scars.

▲ **12.28**
Slight perianal reddening and mild nappy rash. Some perianal reddening is common in babies still in nappies.

◀ **12.29**
Prominent raphe.

Chapter 13

Genital findings in sexually abused boys

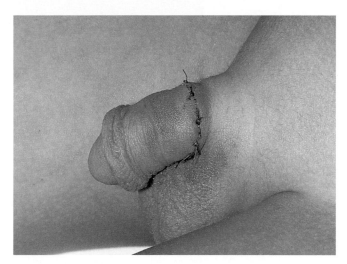

◀ 13.1 Male aged 4 years

He was brought to the hospital emergency department by his parents. History was later provided that he must have caught his penis on a tile sticking out from the wall. There is a circumferential skin-deep laceration of the base of the penis. The diagnosis is an unexplained severe injury. Note blood tracking down into the scrotum.

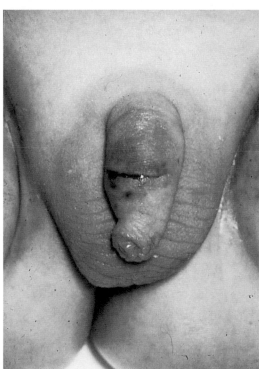

◀ 13.2 Male aged 5 years

He was brought to the hospital emergency department by his mother after a female babysitter aged 13 years had sawn the penis with a bread knife after warning the child to stop masturbating in front of the television. There is a deep incision of the penis. The babysitter was later found to have been repeatedly sexually abused for the previous 6 years.

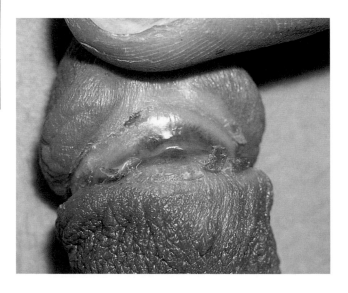

▶ 13.3 Male aged 5 years

He was taken to the doctor by his parents who referred him on to the hospital. The photograph shows marked swelling at distal end of the penis. Hairs were removed from around the coronal sulcus. There are signs of an early infection. No satisfactory history was available.

▶ 13.4 Male aged 2 years

The child had developmental delay. He was noticed to have burns on his thigh and penis at day nursery. A healing triangular burn is seen on the dorsum of the penis. The mother admitted to burning the child.

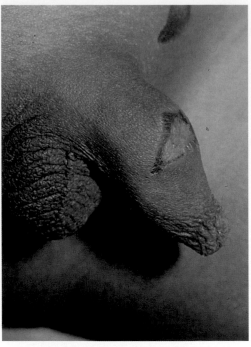

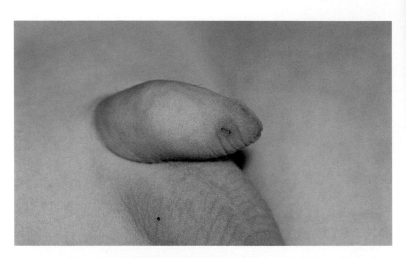

◀ 13.5 Male aged 3 years

He was seen in the follow-up paediatric clinic because of previous sexual abuse. A small laceration is seen at the distal end of the penis. This is probably a fingernail scratch.

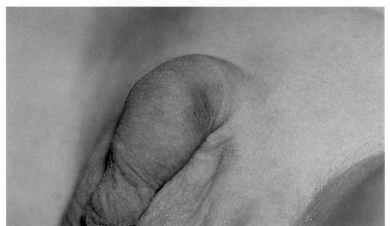

◀ 13.6 Male aged 3 years

Day nursery referred the child because of scratches on his thigh and a bruised penis. There was a past history of repeated physical and sexual abuse. Clear bruising is evident at the base of the penis. This is probably due to pinching.

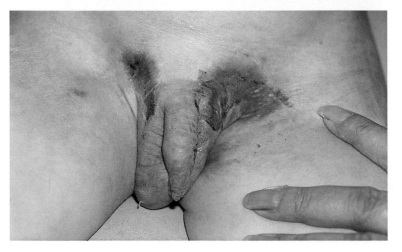

◀ 13.7 Male aged 6 years

He was sent to the local infectious diseases hospital by his doctor because of bloody diarrhoea. The child told a nurse that his father had poured a jug of hot water over him. There is a scald in the groin with signs of early healing. There were also marked anal signs. The diagnosis is inflicted scald in association with anal abuse.

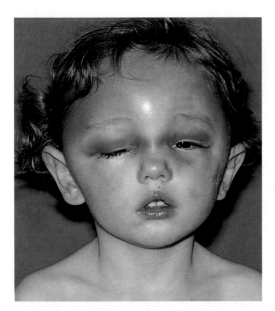

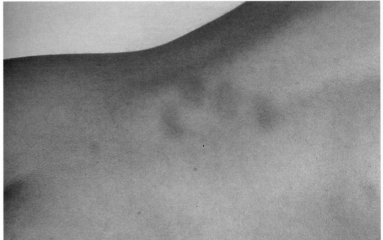

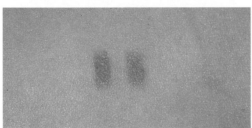

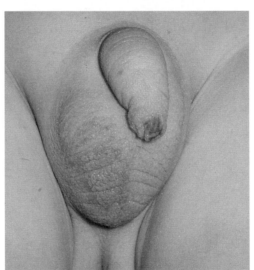

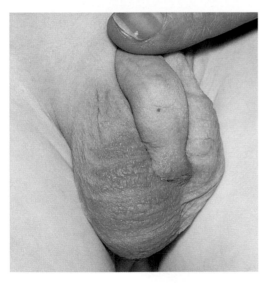

◀ ◀ ◀ ▼ ▼ **13.8–13.12 Male aged 3 years**

He returned home from access with his father with severe facial bruising. The photographs show a tense, swollen forehead with bruising to the orbit and nose. There is an additional bruise on the cheek, fingertip bruising in the right loin, paired contact burns on the thigh, a swollen blistered scrotum and petechiae on the penis. A photograph of the scrotum 24 hours later shows swelling settling but a blister is evident as well as bruising of the foreskin. This was a severe physical and sexual assault. Note the complex contact burns; he had several pairs of burns on his abdomen and legs as well as on the genitalia.

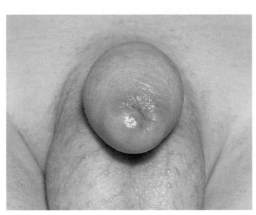

◀ **13.13 Male aged 3 years**

He was referred by his day nursery to social services after he complained about a 'sore willy' and drew what looked like sexualized pictures. The photograph shows a swollen smooth distal end of the penis. It was not possible to retract the foreskin. The diagnosis is xeroderma obliterans, the male equivalent of lichen sclerosus.

Chapter 14

Genital findings in sexually abused girls

Prepubertal females

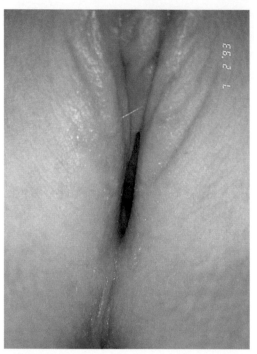

◄ 14.1 Female aged 1 year
Markedly wrinkled, flattened labia majora. Note the gaping hymenal opening. The midline raphe is probably normal.
Signs: flattened labia, gaping hymenal opening.

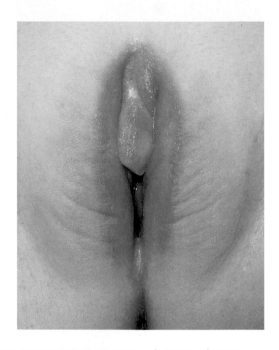

▲ 14.2, ◄ 14.3 Female aged 3 years
Flattened, wrinkled labia majora with tramline reddening. A smooth posterior fourchette is seen. There is marked oedema with vulvitis and discharge.
Signs: reddening, swelling.

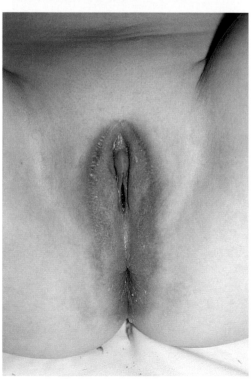

◄ 14.4 Female aged 5 years
Flattened labia, with marked reddening extending from the genitalia across the perineum and peri-anally.
Signs: flattened labia, symmetrical reddening.

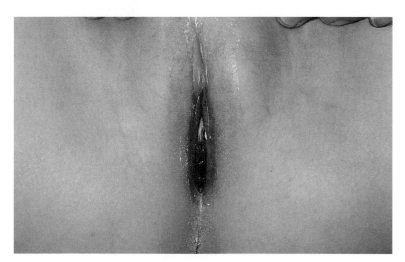

◀ **14.5 Female aged 5 years**
Marked reddening and oedema of the labia minora and hymen.
Signs: reddening, swelling.

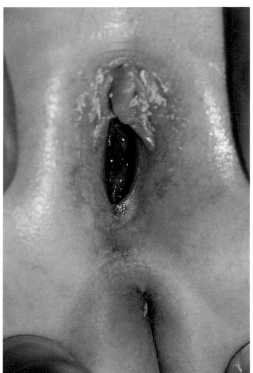

▶ **14.6 Female aged 4 years**
Marked reddening and swelling of the hymen and perihymenal tissues.
Signs: reddening, swelling.

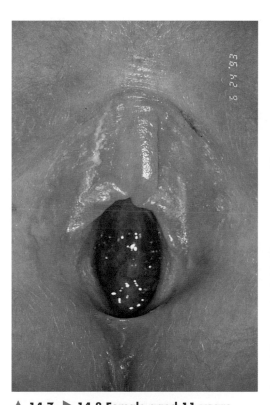

▲ **14.7,** ▶ **14.8 Female aged 11 years**
Marked swelling and reddening of the hymen and perihymenal tissues. An asymmetrical hymenal opening is also seen.
Signs: reddening, swelling, asymmetrical hymenal opening.

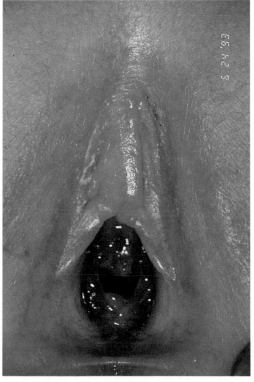

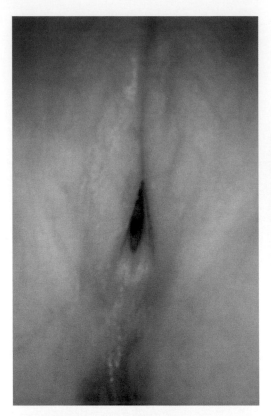

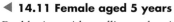

◀ 14.9 Female aged 5 years
Flattened labia majora with a scooped out
appearance posteriorly. Labial fusion is also seen.
Note the gaping hymenal opening.
Signs: flattened labia, labial fusion.

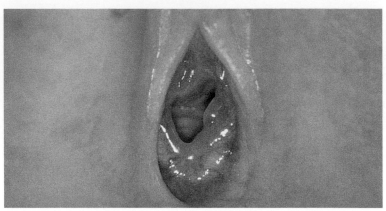

▲ 14.10 Female aged 8 years
Reddened, swollen and markedly asymmetrical hymenal opening with
notch at 2 o'clock and a bump at 3 o'clock.
Signs: reddening, swelling, notch in hymen at 2 o'clock.

◀ 14.11 Female aged 5 years
Reddening with swelling and an irregular
hymenal opening.
Signs: reddening, swelling, gaping, irregular
hymenal opening.

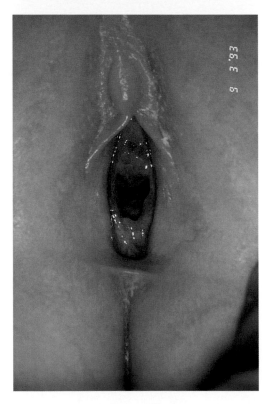

▶ 14.12 Female aged 6 years
The photograph shows reddening with a gaping
dilated hymenal opening, attenuated hymen, and
some rolling of hymenal edge. Note the vaginal
ridge adjacent to the hymen at 5 o'clock.
Signs: reddening, gaping and dilated hymenal
opening, attenuated hymen.

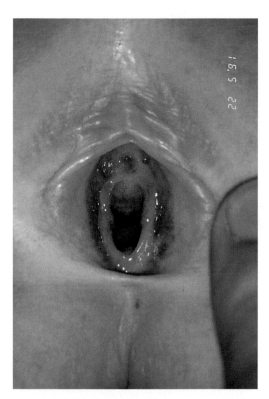

▶ 14.14 Female aged 7 years

A gaping hymenal opening is seen with attenuation of the hymen and a recent tear at 5 o'clock.

Signs: gaping hymenal opening, attenuation, tear at 5 o'clock in hymen.

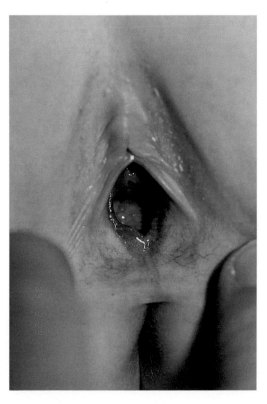

◀ 14.13 Female aged 5 years

There is uniform perihymenal reddening with a gaping, dilated hymenal opening, with little hymen persisting posteriorly. Note vaginal ridges at 3, 6 and 9 o'clock.

Signs: reddening, gaping, dilated hymenal opening, attenuation.

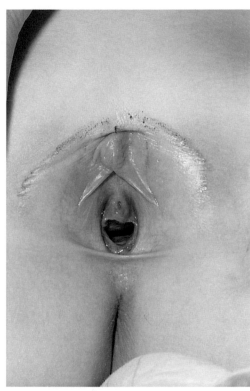

◀ 14.15 Female aged 6 years

There is a gaping hymenal opening with a notch at 6 o'clock and a bump at 7 o'clock, and a rolled edge to the hymen.

Signs: gaping hymenal opening, notch in hymen, bump, rolled edge to hymen.

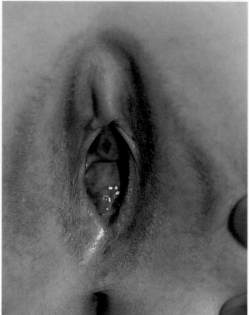

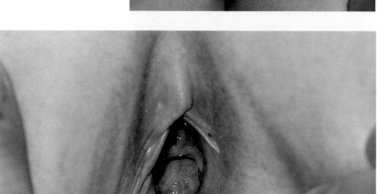

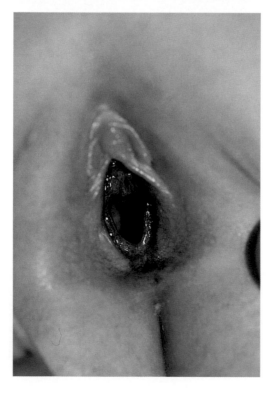

◀ ◀ ▼ 14.16–14.18 Female aged 9 years

The photographs show dry reddened skin and a gaping vagina with only remnants of hymen left posteriorly. An old scar is visible on the posterior vaginal wall between remnants of the hymen. Note the smooth posterior vaginal walls. The angled view (below) shows friability at the posterior fourchette with localized disruption and scarring.

Signs: reddening, gaping vagina, scar, friability at fourchette, remnants of hymen.

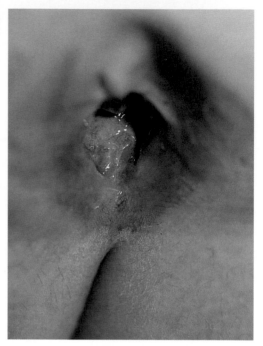

◀ 14.19 Female aged 5 years

There is a dilated, gaping hymenal opening with reddish/purple adjacent tissues. The hymen is attenuated, persisting as a thin rim. The fourchette skin is friable with surface bleeding.

Signs: reddening/purple, dilated, gaping hymenal opening, attenuated, friable posterior fourchette.

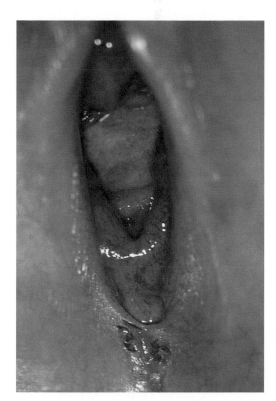

◀ 14.20 Female aged 4 years

The posterior fourchette is friable and bleeds when the labia are separated. There is a deep notch in the hymen at 6 o'clock.

Signs: friable posterior fourchette, notch in hymen.

▼ 14.21 Female aged 8 years

There is marked reddening of the labia and perineum with labial fusion traumatically separated. A gaping hymen is visible.

Signs: reddening, labial fusion, gaping hymenal opening.

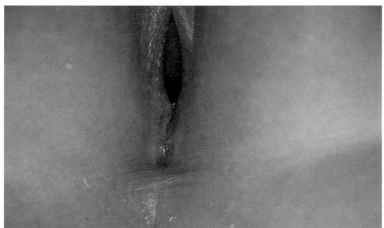

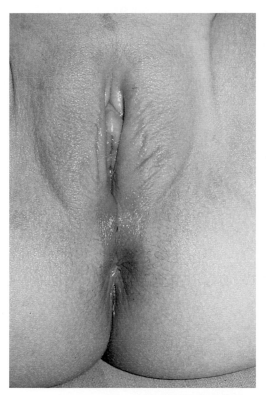

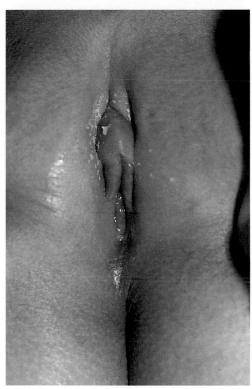

▲ 14.22, ▲ 14.23 Female aged 1 year

Fig. 14.22 shows flattened, wrinkled labia. A midline tear can be seen extending posteriorly. The resulting scar is seen in Fig. 14.23.

Signs: flattened labia, tear, scar.

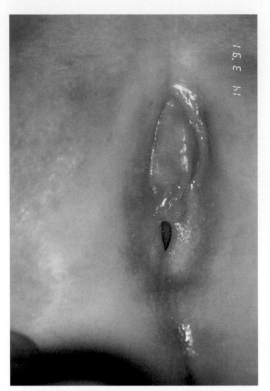

◀ **14.24 Female aged 9 years**
A very unusual appearance due to extensive
posterior labial fusion.
Signs: labial fusion.

▼ **14.25 Female aged 2 years**
There is labial fusion with a visible line of fusion.
Signs: labial fusion.

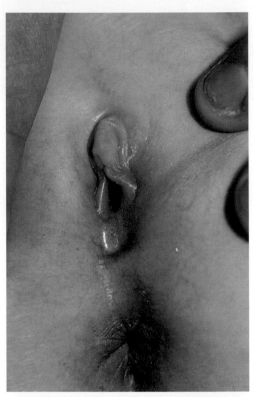

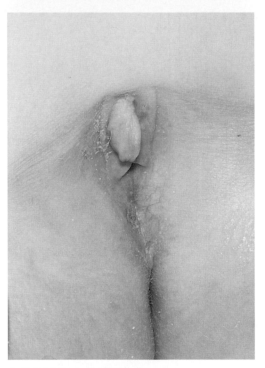

▲ **14.26 Female aged 9 years**
Very extensive, thick posterior labial fusion is
seen in an older child.
Signs: labial fusion.

▶ **14.27 Female aged 2 years**
Extensive thick posterior labial fusion.
Signs: labial fusion.

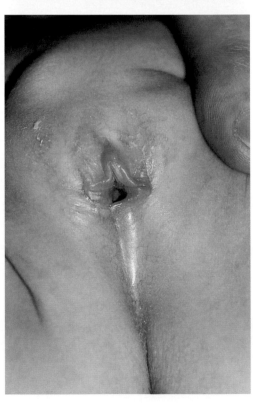

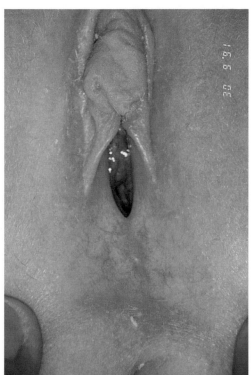

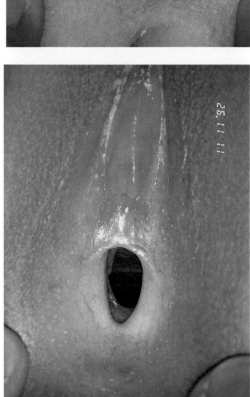

◀ 14.28 Female aged 3 years
Posterior labial fusion, with a gaping, elongated hymen.
Signs: labial fusion, gaping hymen.

▼ 14.29 Female aged 3 years
Posterior labial fusion.
Signs: labial fusion.

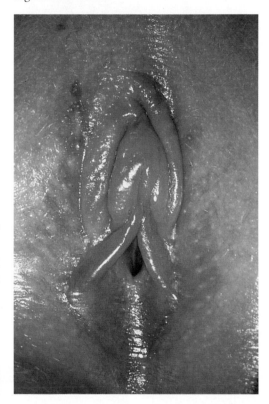

◀ 14.30 Female aged 6 years
Anterior and posterior fusion of the labia. Note the gaping hymenal opening, with a notch at 9 o'clock.
Signs: labial fusion, notch in hymen.

Girls who have been raped

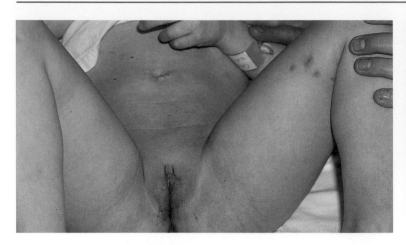

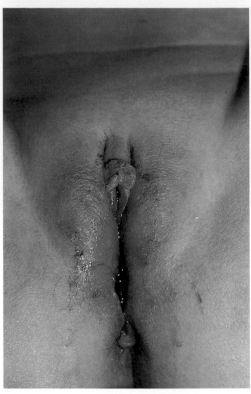

▲ ▶ ▼ 14.31–14.33 Female aged 4 years

The photographs show scratch marks on the inner thigh, and reddening
and bruising to the labia. The labia are seen to be swollen and bruised.
There is a blood clot at the introitus with a midline tear. An anterior anal
haematoma is seen at the posterior end of the tear. The tear extends
through the posterior vaginal wall, posterior fourchette and across the
perineum to the anterior margin of the anal sphincter. The anal sphincter
is intact.

Signs: reddening, scratching, swelling of labia, tear, haematoma, tag.

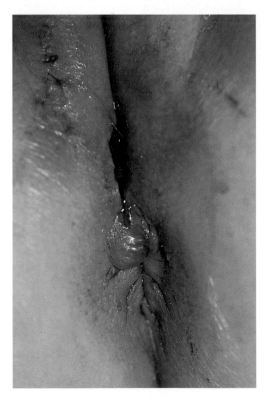

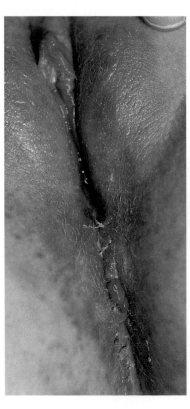

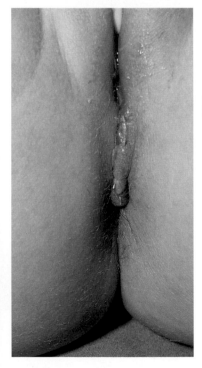

**◀ 14.34 ▲ 14.35 Female aged
4 years**

Same child as in figs 14.31–14.33.
These photographs were taken 4
weeks later at follow-up and show
healing.

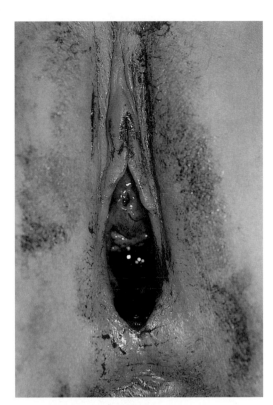

◀ **14.36 Female aged 5 years**

An extensive blood clot is visible with a gaping, but largely deficient, hymenal opening and a tear through the posterior vaginal wall and posterior fourchette onto the perineum.

Signs: tear, gaping hymen.

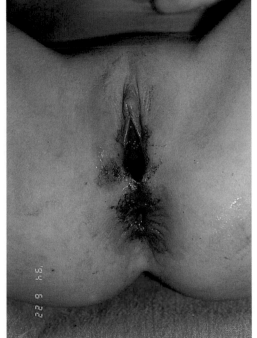

▶ ▶ ▼ **14.37–14.39 Female aged 5 years**

The photographs show a bruise to the right of the labia, dilated hymenal opening, disrupted hymen and a torn posterior fourchette. There is a gaping anus, with anterior abrasion, and red and swollen anal margin.

Signs: bruise, reddening, disrupted dilated hymen, torn posterior fourchette, gaping anus, abrasion.

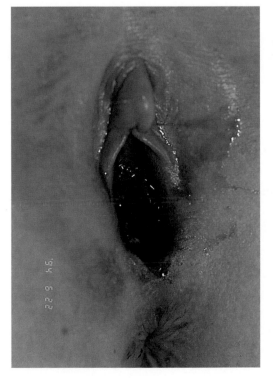

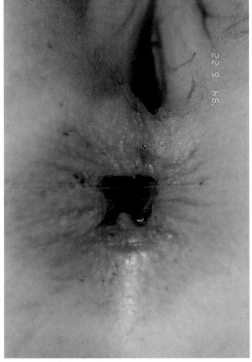

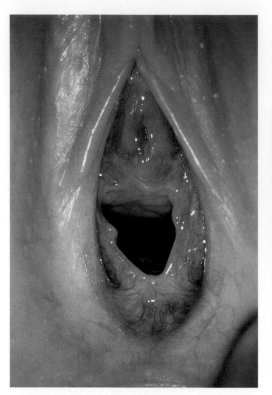

◀ **14.40 Female aged 8 years**
Dilated hymenal opening with bumps at 3 and 9 o'clock, and a deep rounded notch posteriorly.
Signs: dilated hymenal opening, bumps, notch.

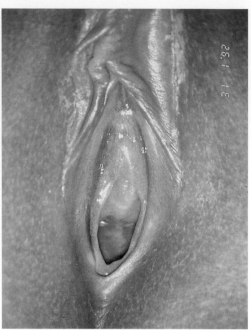

▲ **14.41,** ◀ **14.42 Female aged 9 years**
Fig. 14.41 shows the shape of the hymenal opening with labial separation, and Fig. 14.42 with labial traction. A dilated hymenal opening is seen, and attenuation of the hymen, with a small notch at 7 o'clock.
Signs: dilated hymenal opening, attenuated hymen, notch.

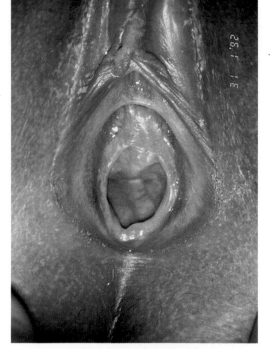

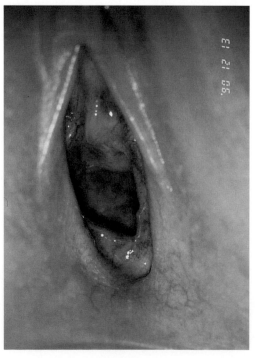

▶ **14.43 Female aged 6 years**
There is reddening of the hymen and vaginal wall with a dilated hymenal opening which is asymmetrical with notches at 3 and 5 o'clock.
Signs: reddening, dilated hymenal opening, notch.

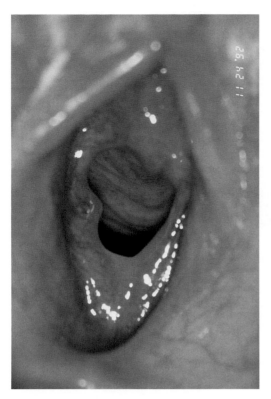

▶ **14.45,** ▶ **14.46 Female aged 4 years**

Reddening with vertical elongation of the hymenal opening is seen in Fig. 14.45. There is a rolled edge to the hymen, a bump at 9 o'clock, and a friable fourchette. Fig. 14.46 is a follow-up photograph taken 2 years later. This picture is taken with greater magnification but shows a markedly dilated hymenal opening, with attenuation, particularly laterally. There is little hymen anteriorly. A prominent vaginal ridge is seen.

Signs: reddening, dilated hymenal opening, rolled edge to hymen, friable fourchette, vaginal ridge.

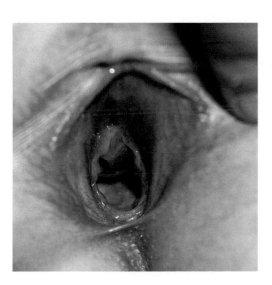

◀ **14.44 Female aged 6 years**

A reddened, dilated hymenal opening is seen with marked asymmetry giving a 'ballooned effect' (notch) at 10–11 o'clock. There is still hymen present circumferentially with a bump at 9 o'clock.

Signs: reddening, dilated hymenal opening, notch.

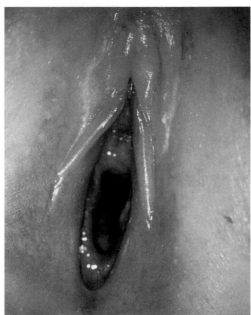

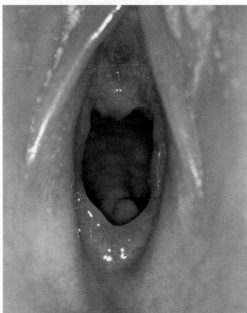

◀ **14.47 Female aged 10 years**

There is reddening with a dilated gaping hymenal opening. An asymmetrical shape is seen with little hymen remaining (attenuated). There are bumps at 3 and 9 o'clock and a notch at 12 o'clock.

Signs: reddening, dilated hymenal opening, attenuated hymen, notch, bumps.

▶ 14.48 Female aged 8 years

There is some reddening with a gaping, dilated hymenal opening. A vaginal ridge is shown clearly at 3 o'clock and there is a bump at 2 o'clock where the ridge joins the hymen. The hymenal edge is rolled and attenuated.
Signs: reddening, dilated hymenal opening, attenuation of hymen, vaginal ridge.

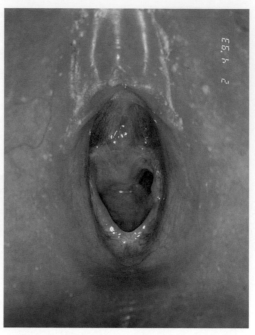

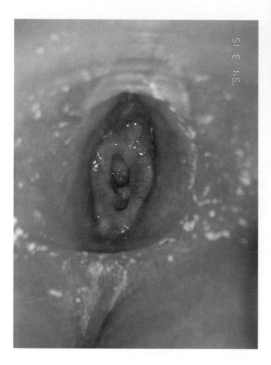

◀ 14.49 Female aged 6 years

There is reddening with an unusual shaped hymenal opening with a deep, wide notch at 6 o'clock and adjacent hymenal remnant.
Signs: reddening, notch, hymenal remnant.

▶ 14.50 Female aged 6 years

The hymenal opening looks to be dilated but a clear view is not obtainable because of the posterior labial fusion.
Signs: gaping hymenal opening, labial fusion.

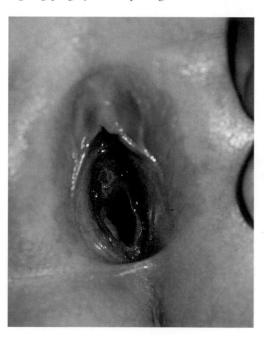

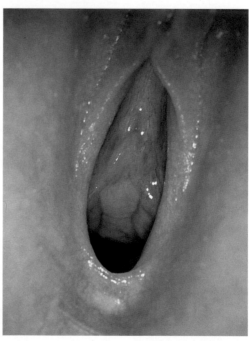

◀ 14.51 Female aged 7 years

A markedly red introitus is seen. The surface area was very friable and bled on contact. The hymenal opening is gaping, dilated, irregular, and attenuated with recent tear at 6 o'clock.
Signs: reddening, friable, dilated, attenuated hymenal opening, tear.

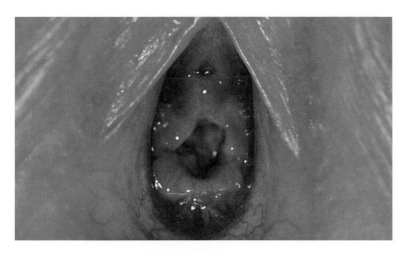

▲ **14.52 Female aged 4 years**
A reddening, fleshy hymen is seen with
transsection at 9 o'clock.
Signs: reddening, transsection.

▶ **14.53 Female aged 8 years**
There is reddening, with a dilated, gaping
hymenal opening with fixed shape. The hymenal
edge has a rolled appearance. The urethra is
prominent.
Signs: reddening, dilated hymenal opening,
rolled edge to hymen.

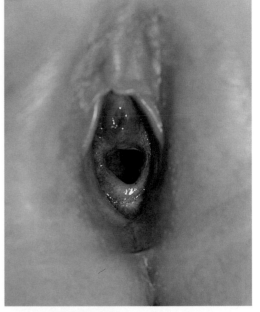

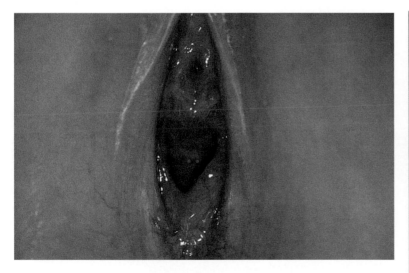

▲ **14.54 Female aged 6 years**
Reddening is seen, with a triangular shaped
dilated hymen with fixed shape. There is a deep
notch at 6 o'clock. Vascular hyperaemia is visible
at the posterior fourchette.
Signs: reddening, dilated, fixed hymenal
opening, notch.

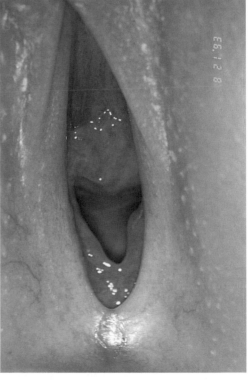

▲ **14.55 Female aged 10 years**
Asymmetrical hymenal opening with a deep
notch at 6 o'clock.
Signs: asymmetry of hymenal opening, notch.

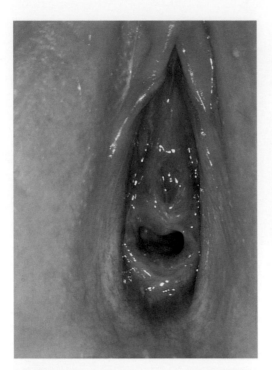

◀ **14.56 Female aged 5 years**

A thickened hymen is seen with constant shape, not dilated.

Signs: thickened hymen.

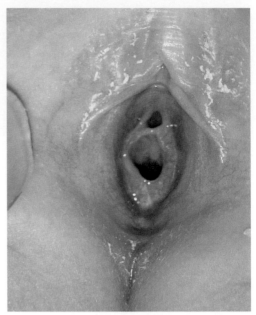

▲ **14.57 Female aged 4 years**

There is localized reddening with a markedly dilated urethral opening. The hymen is also gaping with little hymen persisting between 9 and 12 o'clock (attenuated).

Signs: reddening, urethral dilatation, gaping hymenal opening, attenuated hymen.

▶ **14.58 Female aged 3 years**

There is generalized reddening with marked dilatation of the urethral opening. A minimal amount of hymen is present anteriorly. The hymenal opening is dilated.

Signs: reddening, dilated urethral opening, dilated hymenal opening.

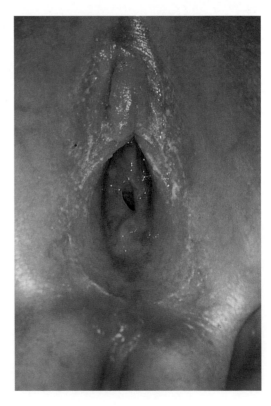

▶ **14.59 Female aged 3 years**

A distorted asymmetrical hymenal opening is seen with thickened scarred tissues posteriorly at 7 o'clock.

Signs: distorted hymenal opening, scar.

▶ 14.60 Female aged 9 years
A disorganized fleshy hymen is seen.
Sign: obliterated hymen.

▼ 14.61 Female aged 11 years
Reddening is seen with a gaping dilated hymenal opening. There is marked asymmetry anteriorly with a notch at 1 o'clock, and a bump at 9 o'clock.
Signs: reddening, gaping dilated hymenal opening, bump.

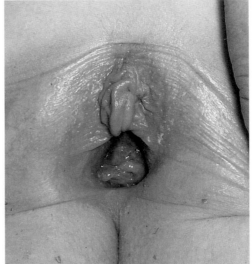

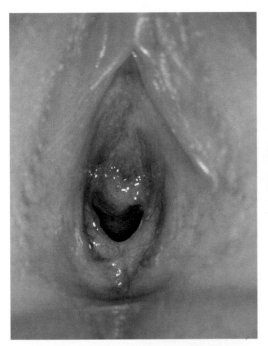

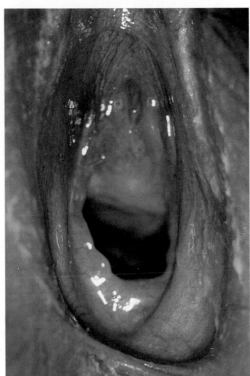

◀ 14.62 Female aged 8 years
She was referred after a foreign body (a coil of cotton) had been removed from her vagina. A dilated gaping hymenal opening with an irregular thickened margin. Children who insert foreign bodies have almost always been sexually abused.
Signs: gaping hymenal opening, thickened margin.

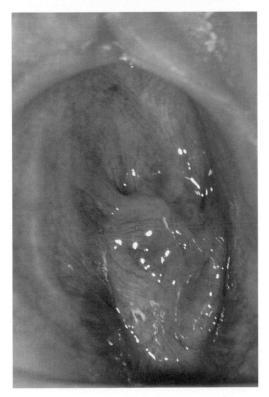

◀ 14.63 Female aged 3 years.
Hymenal opening is obliterated.
Sign: obliterated hymenal opening.

Pubertal females

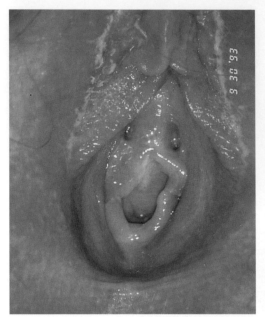

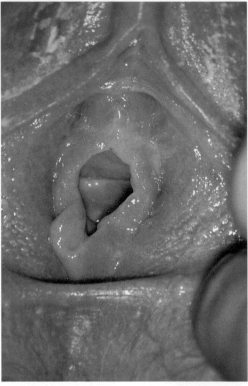

◀ 14.64 Female aged 13 years
An oestrogenized hymen with an irregular margin is seen. These are inconclusive findings.

◀ 14.65 Female aged 10 years
oestrogenized hymen is seen with a notched appearance at 6 o'clock; normal physiological discharge.

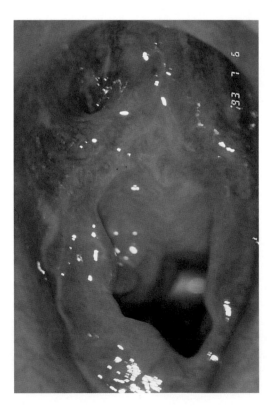

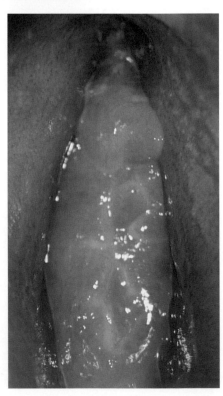

◀ 14.66, ▶ 14.67 Female aged 9 years
Fig. 14.66 is a high magnification view showing vulvitis and some early oestrogen change. The shape of the hymen is irregular posteriorly. Fig. 14.67, taken 12 months later, shows a marked oestrogen effect with a physiological discharge. On this occasion the hymen was closed and appeared to be secondarily obliterated.

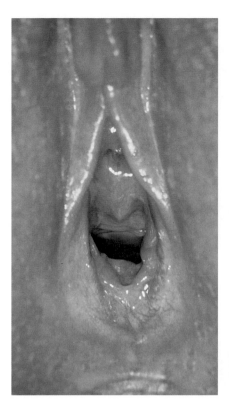

◄ ▼ ▼ 14.68–14.70 Female aged 10 years

Child seen after a straddle injury. Note the change in shape of the hymen due to earlier abuse. There are abrasions periurethrally and on the labia minora. Early oestrogen changes are apparent. Note the dramatic effect that oestrogen has had on this hymen which is now redundant, pale and appears to have a deep notch posteriorly still.

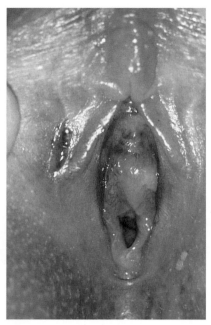

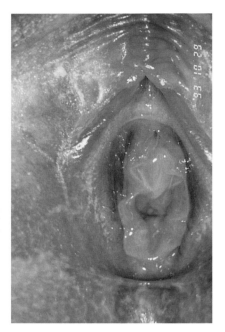

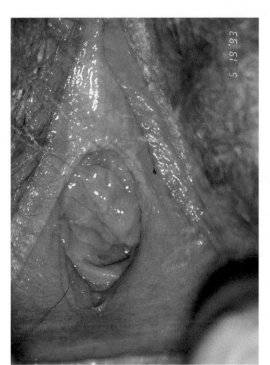

◄ 14.71 Female aged 15 years

A redundant oestrogenized hymen is visible anteriorly but with little hymen persisting posteriorly. Vaginal examination admitted two fingers with ease demonstrating the deceptive width of this hymen on inspection.

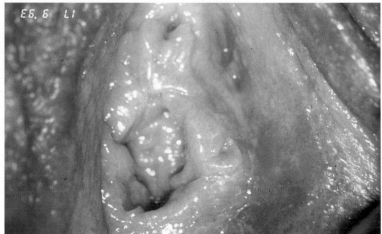

▲ 14.72 Female aged 15 years

An oestrogenized hymen is seen, pale and thickened but very irregular and with only remnants persisting laterally and inferiorly. Vaginal examination admitted two fingers with ease.

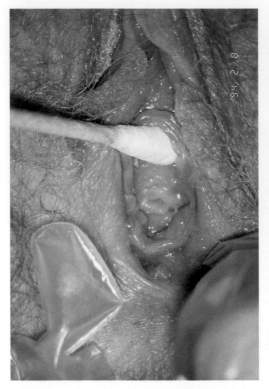

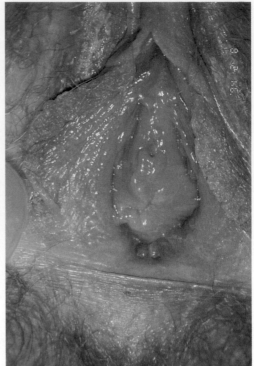

▲ ▲ ▶ **14.73–14.75 Female aged 14 years**
The photographs show an oestrogenized hymen with two warts visible inferiorly. The hymenal margin is demonstrated by use of a cotton wool bud and showing transsection at 3 o'clock. The warts are well illustrated inferiorly.

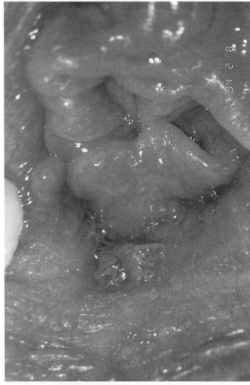

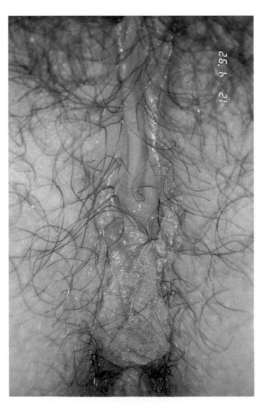

◀ **14.76 Female aged 15 years**
Thickened, redundant pigmented perineal skin is seen.

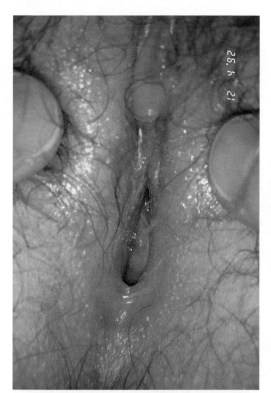

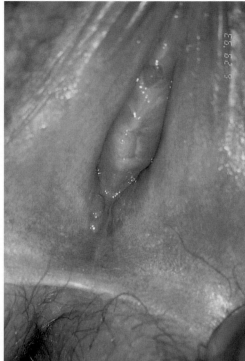

◄ 14.77 Female aged 13 years

An oestrogenized hymen is seen associated with labial fusion.

◄ 14.78 Female aged 10 years

The oestrogenized hymen admitted the tip of a little finger. There is an unusual nodular appearance at the posterior fourchette.

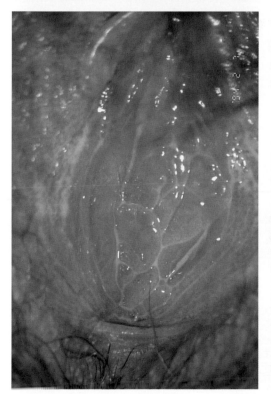

▲ 14.79 Female aged 16 years

Note the oestrogenized appearance of the hymen with physiological discharge. Note also the appearance of the hymen in a consensually sexually active teenager.

▲ 14.80 Female aged 14 years

An oestrogenized but deficient hymen.

Chapter 15

Anal findings in sexually abused children

▶ **15.1 Male aged 9 years**

Perianal reddening is seen, and a dilated vein at 6 o'clock with some irregular skin folds at 7 o'clock and more irregular skin folds adjacent. This boy was handicapped, and therefore at greater risk of abuse of all types.

Signs: reddening, irregular folds, veins.

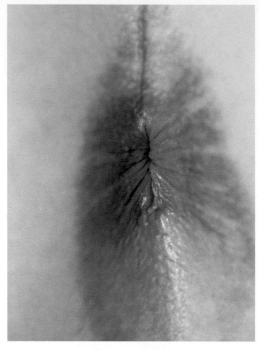

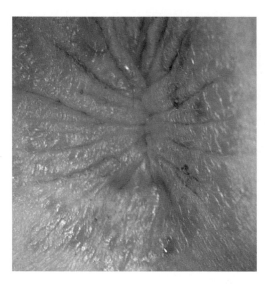

◀ **15.2 Male aged 3 years**

Perianal reddening is seen with superficial small abrasions.

Signs: reddening, abrasions.

▶ **15.3 Male aged 3 years**

There is perianal reddening with swelling and scattered dilated veins and a deep fold at 9 o'clock. A reddened, prominent midline raphe is seen.

Signs: reddening, veins, midline raphe, deep fold.

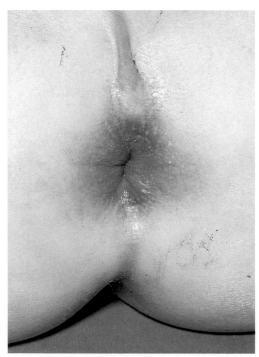

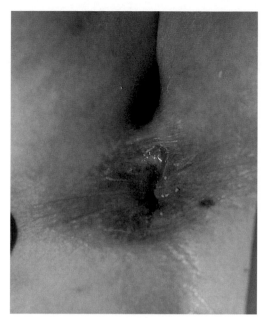

◀ 15.4, ▼ 15.5 Female aged 5 years

Fig. 15.4 shows perianal reddening with a recent fissure at 12 o'clock extending across the anal margin. There is a possible healing fissure at 1 o'clock. Irregular skin folds are seen, with dilated veins in an arc. Fig. 15.5 shows healing 1 month later – see anterior fissure.

Signs: reddening, veins, acute fissure, healing fissure.

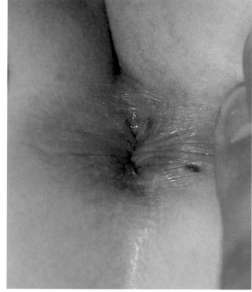

◀ 15.6 Male aged 12 years

Perianal reddening is seen with increased pigmentation. There are recent fissures at 1, 4, 6, 7 and 11 o'clock with scattered distended perianal veins at 5, 7, 8 and 10 o'clock and smooth areas at 6 and 12 o'clock.

Signs: reddening, increased pigmentation, veins, acute fissures.

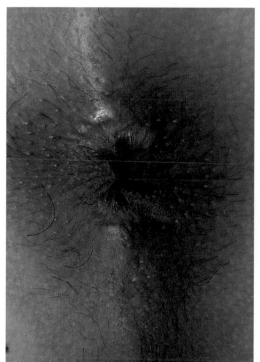

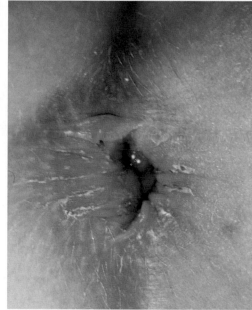

▶ 15.7 Female aged 2 years

There is perianal reddening with an anterior fissure at 12 o'clock running to a skin tag, a healing fissure at 7 o'clock and adjacent thickened fold/small tag. The anus is gaping and the rectal mucosa is visible.

Signs: reddening, tag, healing fissures, gaping sphincter, visible mucosa.

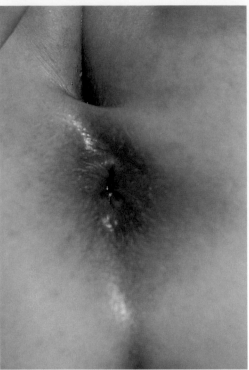

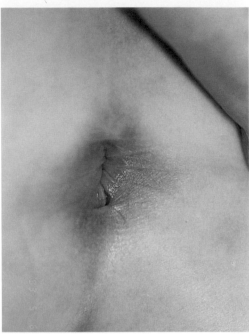

◀ 15.8 Female aged 15 months
Perianal reddening is seen with swelling and venous congestion. There is a disrupted fold pattern to the anus, and a healing fissure at 6 o'clock.

Signs: reddening and swelling, venous congestion, folds, fissure.

▶ 15.9 Male aged 3 years
There is some perianal reddening with an almost complete ring of dilated veins. A recent fissure is seen at 5 o'clock, along the fold.

Signs: reddening, veins, fissure.

◀ 15.10 Female aged 3 years
There is some perianal reddening with scattered dilated veins and a recent fissure at 1 o'clock with a clear deficit in anal margin at 9 o'clock.

Signs: reddening, veins, fissure, deficit.

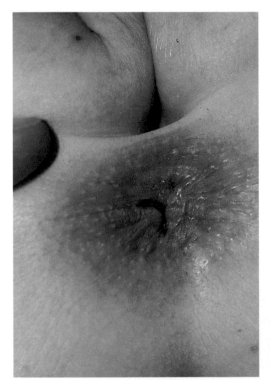

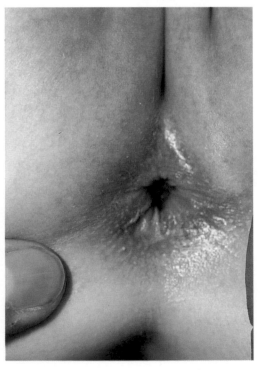

▶ 15.11 Female aged 2 years
Some perianal reddening is seen with scattered dilated veins. There is anal laxity and a healing fissure at 6 o'clock.

Signs: reddening, veins, anal laxity, fissure.

▶ **15.12,** ▼ **15.13 Male aged 8 years**
There is some perianal reddening with venous congestion. A skin tag is seen at 12 o'clock. There is a linear scar extending from just inferior to the anal margin anteriorly across the perineum, due to previous knife wound.
Signs: reddening, venous congestion, tag, scar.

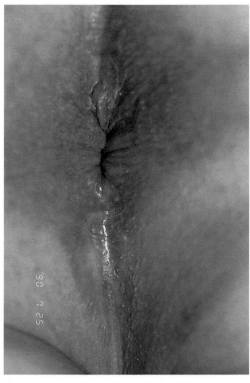

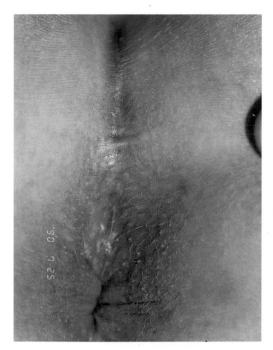

▶ **15.14 Female aged 12 months**
There is perianal reddening, with swelling and halo of veins, and recent stellate fissures.
Signs: reddening and swelling, veins, acute fissures.

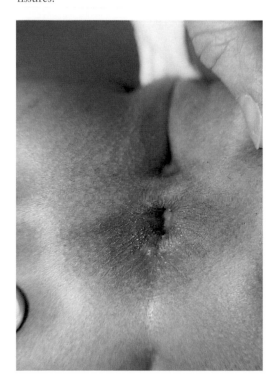

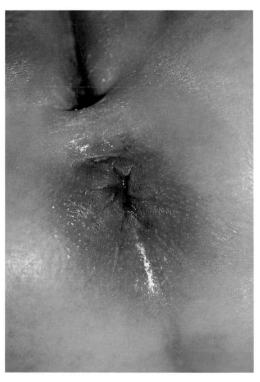

◀ **15.15 Female aged 2 years**
Tyre sign and lax dilating anus are seen. A dilated vein is visible at 7 o'clock.
Signs: tyre sign, veins, laxity, dilating anus.

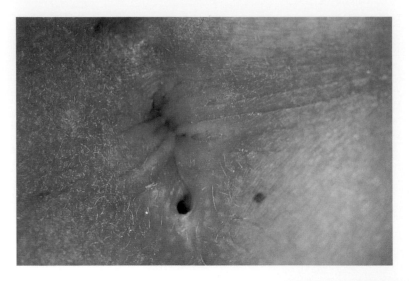

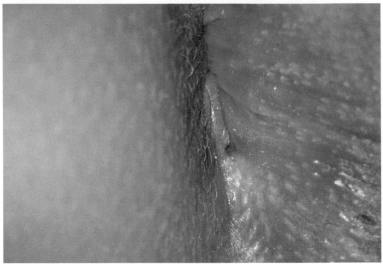

◀ 15.16, ▼ 15.17 Female aged 2 years
Fig. 15.16 shows minimal perianal reddening, with irregular folds and an unhealed posterior fissure. The follow-up photograph after surgery (Fig. 15.17) shows a long posterior skin fold. The fissure has not completely healed distally.
Signs: reddening, irregular folds, fissure, scar.

▼ ▼ 15.18 Female aged 18 months
Some perianal reddening and a gaping anus are seen in Fig. 15.18a. Healing has occurred 1 week later (Fig. 15.18b).
Signs: reddening, gaping, healing.

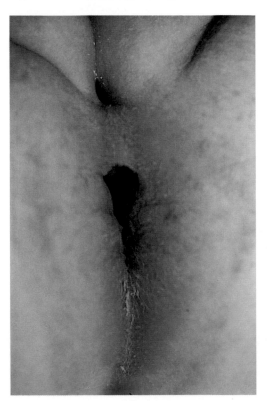

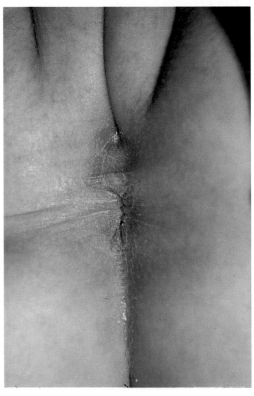

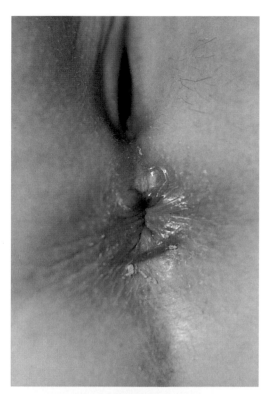

▼ 15.19 Female aged 8 years

Minimal reddening is seen with an almost complete arc of dilated veins. There is a recent tear at 12 o'clock extending across the anal margin (Fig. 15.19a). Healing is seen 3 months later with irregular folds anteriorly (Fig. 15.19b). Signs: reddening, veins, recent fissure, healing.

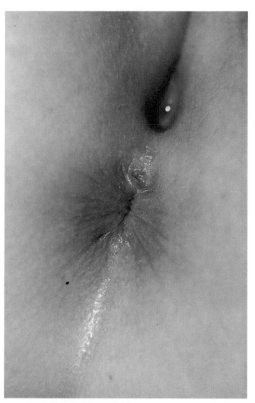

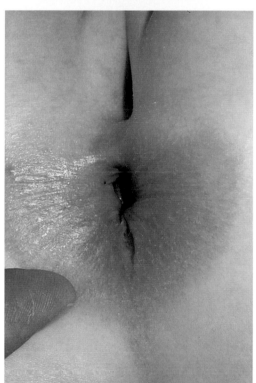

◀ 15.21 Male aged 9 years

Minimal perianal reddening is seen and an anal verge haematoma at 5 o'clock.
Signs: reddening, anal verge haematoma.

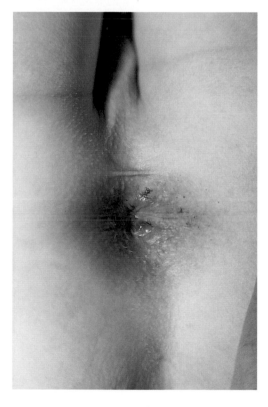

▲ 15.20 Female aged 5 years

Perianal reddening is seen with a recent extensive fissure extending across the anal margin. The anus is gaping and stool is visible. Signs: reddening, gaping anus (not dilation), acute fissure.

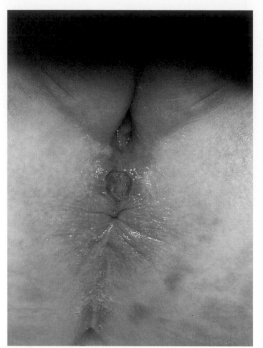

◀ 15.22 Female aged 15 months
Some perianal reddening is visible, with an extensive tear anteriorly.
Signs: reddening, acute fissure.

▼ 15.23 Male aged 9 years
Smooth shiny perianal skin is seen and dilated veins are present. There is a gaping anus with a deep chronic posterior fissure.
Signs: smooth shiny skin, veins, chronic fissure.

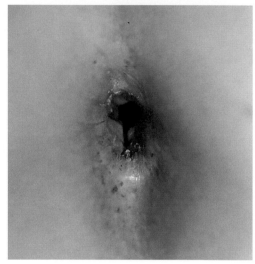

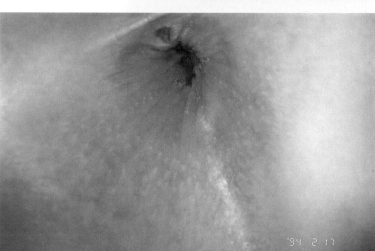

◀ 15.24 Female aged 4 years
Pink, smooth skin is seen perianally with a healing fissure at 12 o'clock with a prominent fold. The anus is gaping.
Signs: smooth shiny skin, fold, fissure, gaping.

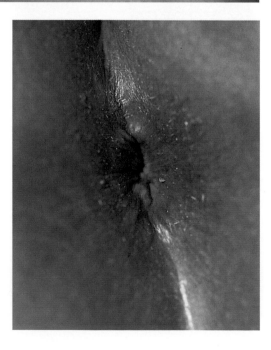

◀ 15.25 Female aged 9 years
An irregular anal margin is shown with a pale scar at 1 o'clock and a skin tag at 7 o'clock with an adjacent dilated vein. The perianal skin is pigmented.
Signs: pigmented skin, tag, vein, scar.

▶ 15.26 Male aged 7 years
There is marked perianal reddening with a swollen anal verge, i.e. the tyre sign, and some laxity of the anus.
Signs: reddening, swelling, laxity.

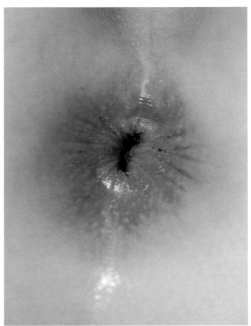

▼ 15.27 Female aged 5 years
Large skin tags are seen at 6 and 12 o'clock.
Signs: tags.

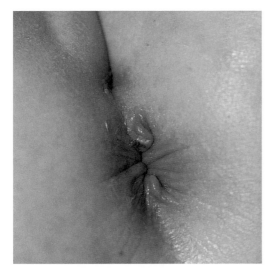

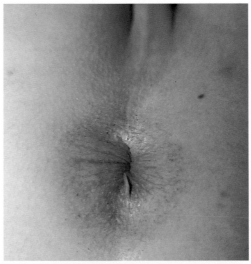

▶ 15.28 Male aged 10 years
There are dilated veins and a skin tag at 5 o'clock.
Signs: veins, tag.

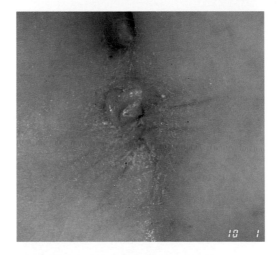

▲ 15.29 Female aged 5 years
Irregular anal skin folds are seen with a large skin tag at 12 o'clock.
Signs: folds, tag.

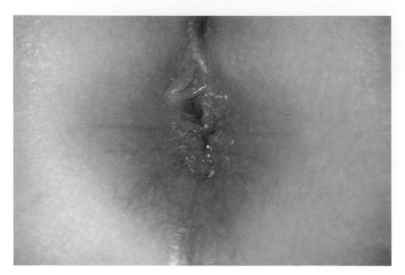

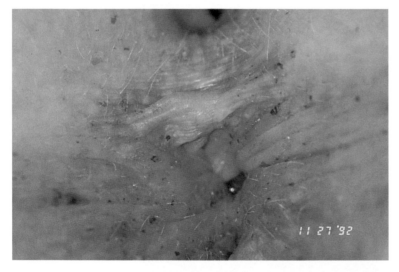

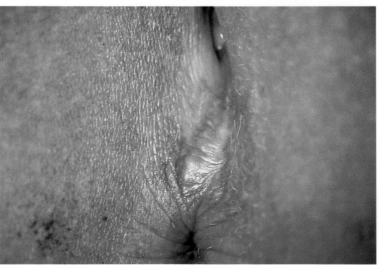

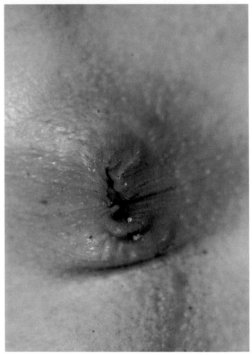

◄ 15.30 Female aged 2 years
An irregular anal margin is seen with a skin tag and linear scar extending anteriorly.
Signs: folds, tag, scar.

▼ 15.31 Male aged 9 years
A funnelled anus is seen with a disorganized fold pattern and deficit with a prominent fold at 1 o'clock. The anus is lax.
Signs: funnelled, folds, deficity, laxity.

◄ 15.32 Female aged 6 years
A distorted anal margin is visible with a large anterior scar. The anus is lax.
Signs: scar, laxity.

◄ 15.33 Female aged 8 years
There is a large vertical anterior scar extending from the anal margin across the perineum.
Signs: scar.

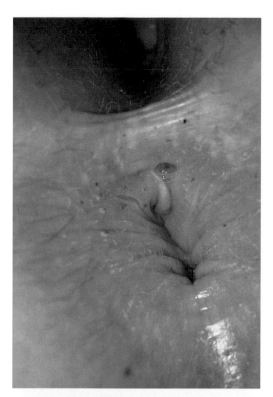

◀ **15.34 Female aged 7 years**
A highly magnified view of the anal margin showing a linear scar at 12 o'clock extending across the anal margin.
Signs: scar.

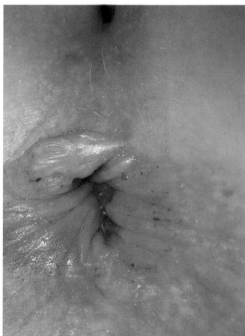

◀ **15.35 Female aged 7 years**
Perianal reddening is seen with a lax anus, irregular skin folds and a large anterior skin tag.
Signs: reddening, folds, tag, laxity.

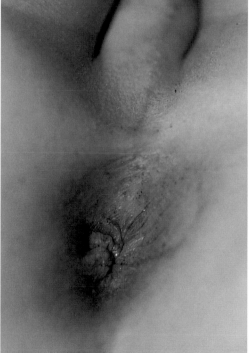

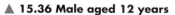

▲ **15.36 Male aged 12 years**
A funnelled anus is shown with swelling and irregular skin folds, and scattered veins.
Signs: funnelling, folds, veins.

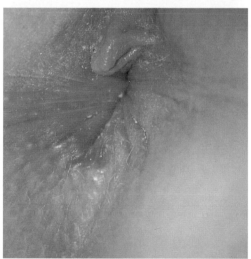

▲ **15.37 Female aged 3 years**
Perianal reddening is seen with a large anterior skin tag. Superficial fissures and venous congestion are seen at 5-6 o'clock.
Signs: reddening, tag, fissure, venous congestion.

▼ 15.38 Female aged 4 years

There is perianal reddening with dilated veins, and a very unusual and complex series of skin folds extending anteriorly and across the perineum.

Sign: reddening, veins, folds.

▼ 15.39 Male aged 7 years

Some perianal reddening is seen with veins particularly marked between 6 and 9 o'clock. There is a normal raphe across the perineum.

Signs: reddening, veins, raphe.

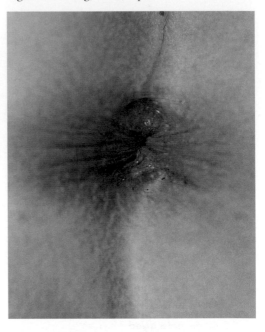

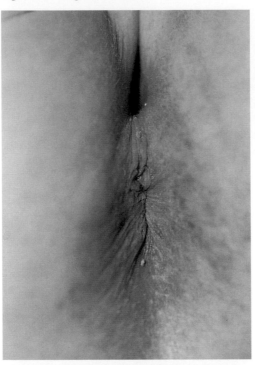

▼ 15.40 Male aged 3 years

Perianal reddening is seen with an irregular anal margin and deficits at 3, 6 and 9 o'clock, with some laxity. There is a skin tag at 12 o'clock. A medium raphe is seen anteriorly. (This child coincidentally has dystrophia myotonica. Organic disease does not exclude the possibility of additional abuse. A normal sister had genital and anal signs consistent with sexual abuse.)

Signs: reddening, tag, raphe.

▶ 15.41 Female aged 4 years

There is reddening perianally with dilated veins and a distorted anal margin.

Signs: reddening, veins, distorted anal margin.

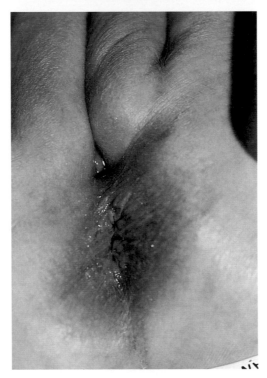

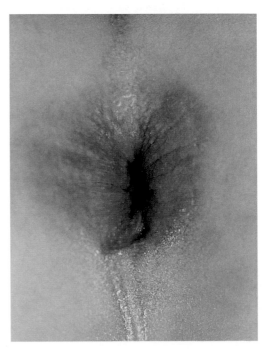

▼ **15.42 Female aged 12 years**

A disorganized anal margin is seen with an unhealed fissure at 6 o'clock and a large skin tag anteriorly; in addition small skin tags are seen at 3 and 4 o'clock.

Signs: fissure, tags.

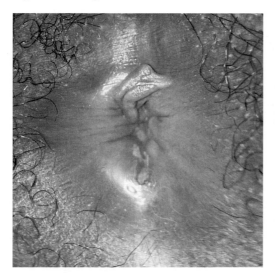

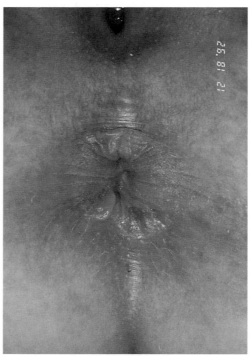

▶ **15.43 Female aged 18 months**

Dilated veins are seen, with skin tags at 7, 11 and 12 o'clock, and an irregular margin.

Signs: veins, tag, irregular margin.

▶ **15.44 Female aged 6 years**

There is an irregular anal margin with some laxity and a large anterior skin tag. This child had Down's syndrome; anal laxity is not part of this syndrome. Signs: laxity, tag.

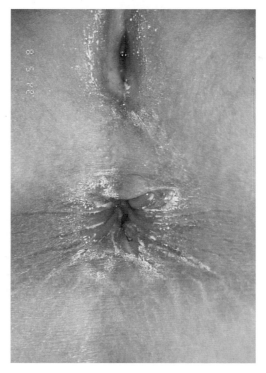

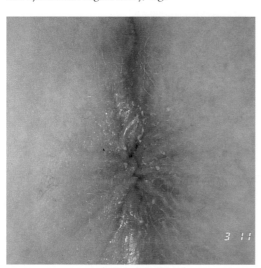

▲ **15.45 Female aged 3 years**

An almost complete ring of dilated veins is seen perianally and unusual skin folds at 7 and 11–12 o'clock.

Signs: veins, folds.

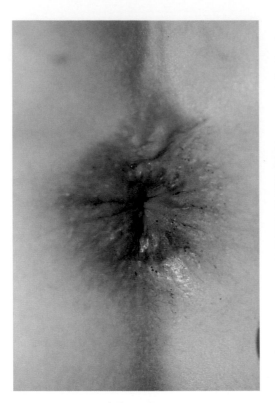

◀ **15.46 Male aged 5 years**
There is perianal reddening with a complete ring of markedly dilated veins and a scar anteriorly.
Signs: reddening, veins, scar.

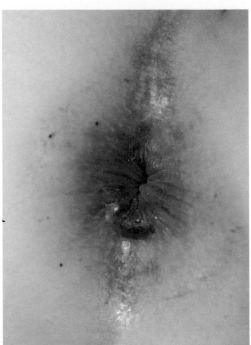

▶ **15.47 Male aged 8 years**
Perianal reddening is seen with an arc of dilated veins at 5-7 o'clock.
Signs: reddening, veins.

◀ **15.48 Male aged 8 years**
Increased perianal pigmentation is seen with a small dilated vein at 12 o'clock and a halo of venous congestion.
Signs: pigmentation, veins.

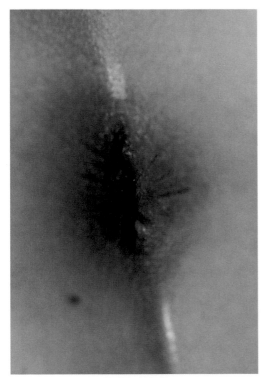

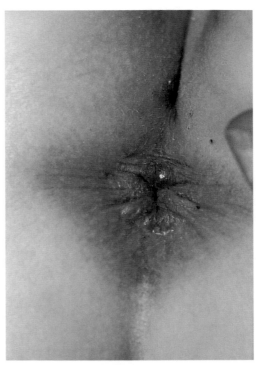

▶ **15.49 Female aged 3 years**
There is perianal reddening, a swollen margin and a ring of dilated veins.
Signs: reddening, swollen, veins.

▶ 15.50 Male aged 8 years

Perianal reddening is seen with swelling of the anal margin giving an irregular appearance to folds with dilated veins. There is a smooth area at 12 o'clock.

Signs: reddening, swollen, veins.

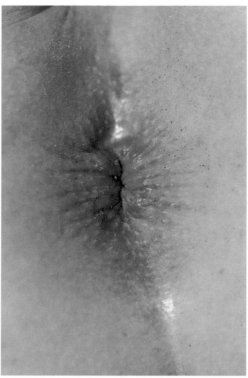

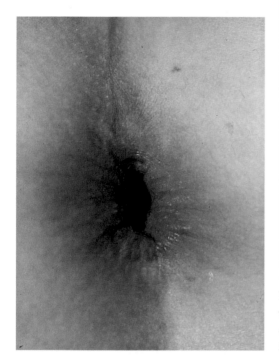

◀ 15.51 Male aged 5 years

Perianal reddening is seen, with reflex anal dilatation. There are dilated veins posteriorly and deficits in the anal margin at 5 and 7 o'clock. (The child had a rectal polyp diagnosed on proctoscopy.)

Signs: reddening, veins, reflex anal dilatation.

▶ 15.52 Male aged 4 years

There is increased perianal pigmentation and a complete ring of veins.

Signs: pigmentation, veins.

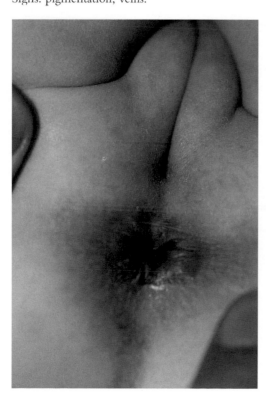

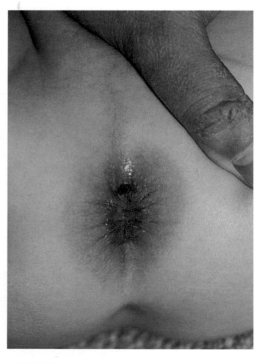

◀ 15.53 Female aged 2 years

Perianal redness is seen, with perianal swelling. There is an irregular anal margin with a skin tag at 12 o'clock and a prominent fold at 7 o'clock, and dilated veins anteriorly and posteriorly.

Signs: reddening, swollen, tag, veins.

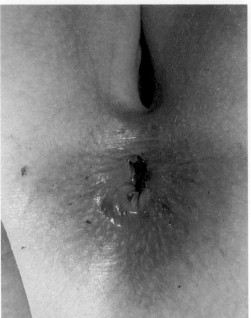

◀ **15.54 Female aged 7 years**
Perianal reddening is seen with a halo of dilated veins laterally and posteriorly. The anus is gaping with heaped up skin folds posteriorly.
Signs: reddening, veins, folds, gaping.

▼ 15.55 Female aged 3 years
Very congested perianal skin is seen with prominent veins and a distorted anal margin. The rectal mucosa is visible and the anus is lax.
Signs: veins, rectal mucosa, laxity.

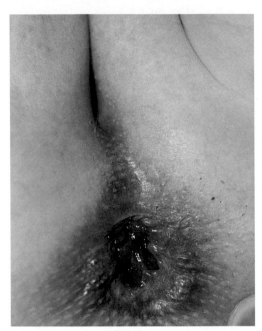

▶ 15.56 Female aged 12 months
There is marked venous congestion and stellate appearance of the lax anal sphincter with rectal mucosa visible.
Signs: veins, laxity, rectal mucosa.

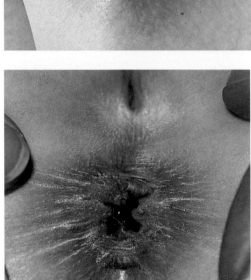

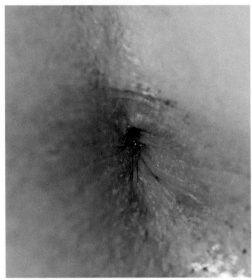

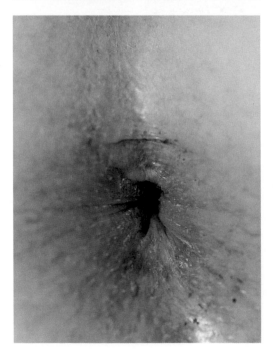

▲ 15.57, ◀ 15.58 Male aged 10 years
Fig. 15.57 shows perianal reddening with scattered dilated veins and irregular anal skin folds. The anus is dilated in Fig. 15.58 to show reflex anal dilatation and deficits in the anal margin at 5, 7 and 9 o'clock.
Signs: reddening, veins, folds, deficits.

▶ **15.59 Female aged 15 months**

Perianal reddening is seen with dilated veins and the rectal mucosa prolapsing to a disorganized, lax anal sphincter.

Signs: reddening, veins, laxity, rectal mucosa.

▼ **15.60 Female aged 2 years**

There is perianal reddening with venous congestion and swelling of the anal margin. The anal sphincter is lax and distorted with rectal mucosa visible.

Signs: reddening, swollen, veins, laxity, irregular folds, rectal mucosa.

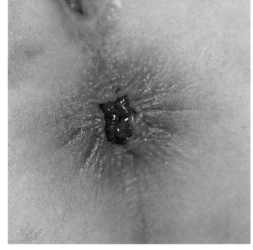

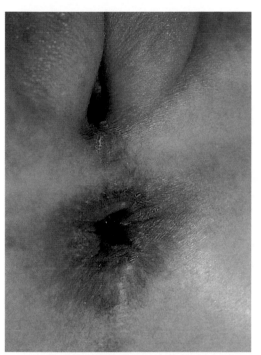

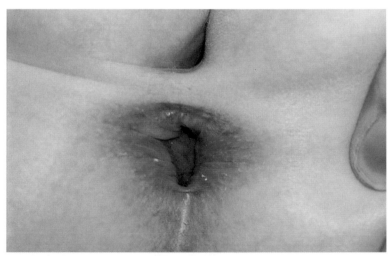

▲ **15.61 Female aged 4 years**

Perianal reddening is seen with a lax anal sphincter with visible rectal mucosa and dilated veins anteriorly.

Signs: reddening, veins, laxity.

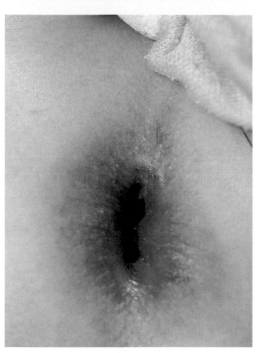

◀ **15.62 Male aged 3 years**

There is perianal reddening and smoothing of the skin perianally. Rectal mucosa is visible, and the sphincter is lax.

Signs: reddening, smooth skin, laxity.

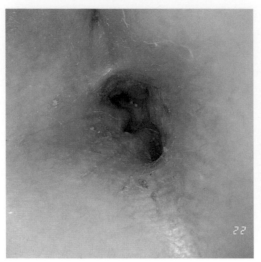

◀ 15.63 Female aged 4 years
Roughened, thickened, perianal skin is seen with loss of skin folds. The anus is gaping with rectal mucosa visible.
Signs: thickened skin, gaping, rectal mucosa.

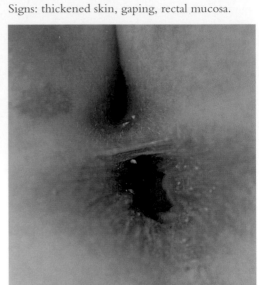

▶ 15.64 Female aged 3 years
Perianal reddening is seen with scattered dilated veins, a reddened anal margin with loss of usual skin folds and anal dilatation.
Signs: reddening, veins, anal dilatation.

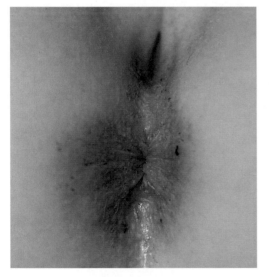

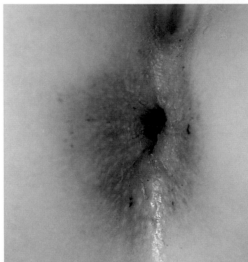

◀ 15.65–15.68 Female aged 5 years
The photographs show perianal reddening with marked anal dilatation of increasing magnitude across the four slides. There is an irregular margin with a few small veins visible.
Signs: reddening, veins, dilatation.

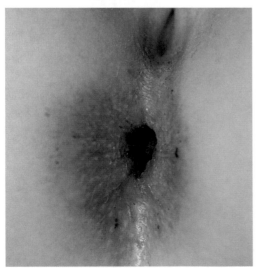

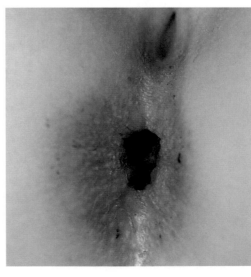

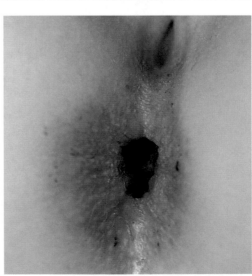

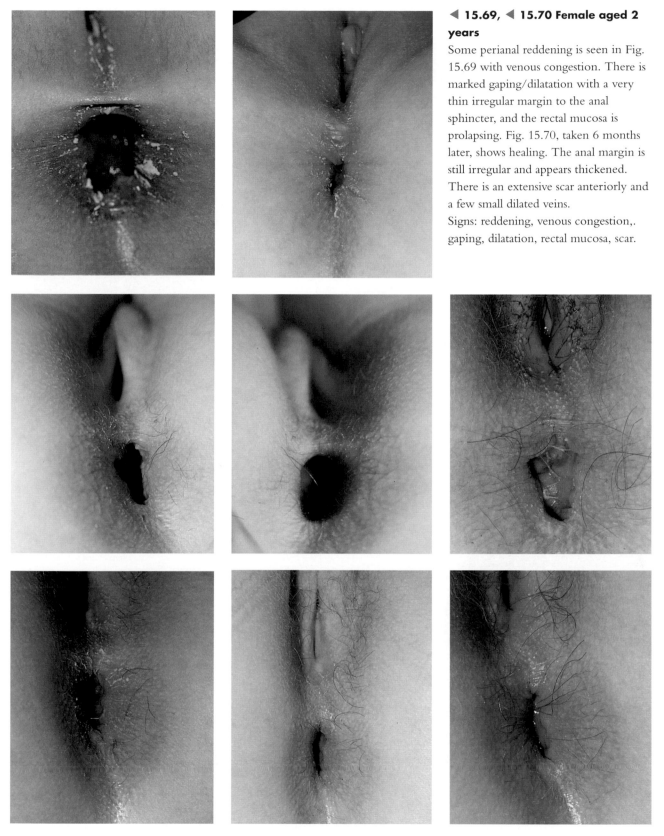

◀ 15.69, ◀ 15.70 Female aged 2 years

Some perianal reddening is seen in Fig. 15.69 with venous congestion. There is marked gaping/dilatation with a very thin irregular margin to the anal sphincter, and the rectal mucosa is prolapsing. Fig. 15.70, taken 6 months later, shows healing. The anal margin is still irregular and appears thickened. There is an extensive scar anteriorly and a few small dilated veins.

Signs: reddening, venous congestion,. gaping, dilatation, rectal mucosa, scar.

▲ 15.71–15.76 Female aged 12 years

Fig. 15.71 (top left) shows perianal reddening, thickened perianal skin and dilatation; in Fig. 15.72 (top centre) there is stool clearly visible in the rectum. These two photographs were taken at the first examination. Fig. 15.73 (top right) was taken 6 weeks later, Fig. 15.74 (bottom left) 3 months after that, Fig. 15.75 (bottom centre) 3 months later, and Fig. 15.76 (bottom right) 3 months later. These show that over the next year the anal sphincter gradually developed increased tone.

Signs: reddening, thickened skin, reflex anal dilatation.

▶ **15.77 Male aged 2 years**

There is marked perianal and anal reddening; the anus is widely gaping with rectal mucosa visible. The examination was carried out under sedation the effect of which is not clearly established.
Signs: reddening, gaping, rectal mucosa.

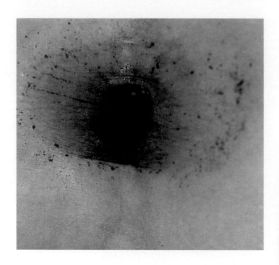

▶ **15.78 Male aged 17 years**

There is marked reflex anal dilatation. The posterior margin of the anus is very irregular and probably the site of previous fissures. Smooth perianal skin is seen, and stool is present in the rectum. (Note: if during the examination a child wishes to have his or her bowels opened it is better to re-examine the child again some time later. However, the presence of stool in the rectum does not invalidate the physical signs.)

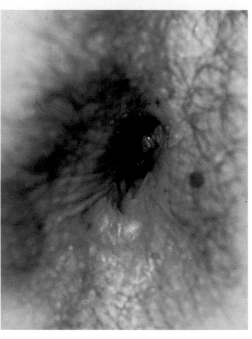

◀ **15.79 Female aged 4 years**

There is markedly red and swollen perianal skin with a lack of folds, marked anal dilatation with an irregular margin and stool present in the rectum.
Signs: reddening, swollen, reflex anal dilatation.

▼ **15.80 Female aged 6 years**

The perianal skin is smooth with new folds. Marked dilatation is seen with an irregular anal sphincter.
Signs: smooth skin, reflex anal dilatation.

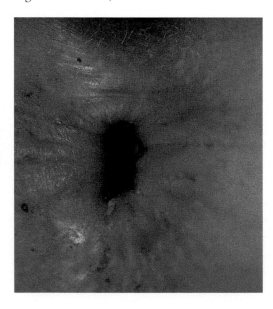

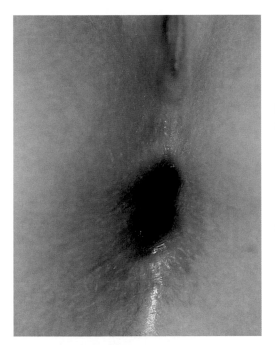

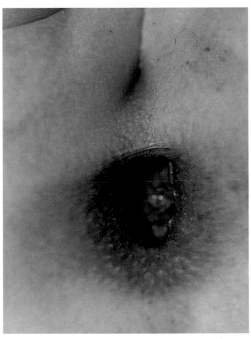

◀ **15.81 Female aged 5 years**

There is a marked perianal rim with reddening smooth skin, loss of anal folds and marked anal dilatation.

Signs: reddening, smooth skin, reflex anal dilatation.

▼ **15.83 Male aged 11 years**

A dilating anus is seen with some smoothing of the skin and pigmentation with small scattered veins.

Signs: pigmented skin, veins, smooth skin, reflex anal dilatation.

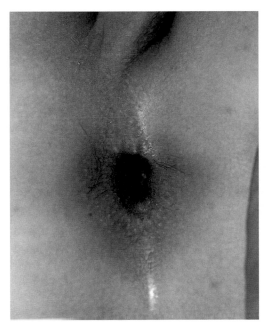

▲ **15.82 Female aged 5 years**

Perianal reddening is seen with loss of skin folds and marked anal dilatation. This child was markedly constipated and soiled. Her symptoms settled and the signs regressed as soon as she was admitted to foster care. She then disclosed sexual abuse within the family. This clinical picture demonstrates reflex anal dilatation, not the 'visibly relaxed' anus described in very severe chronic constipation where stools are protruding from the anus and the anal sphincter is therefore stretched about them.

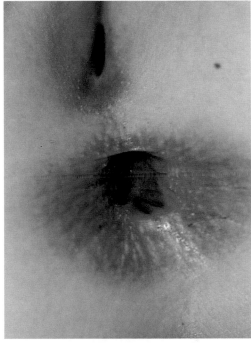

▶ **15.84 Female aged 5 years**

There is marked perianal reddening with some increased pigmentation, a markedly dilated anal sphincter with irregular margin and rectal mucosa prolapsing. The brother of this child had myotonic dystrophy.

Signs: reddening, pigmentation, reflex anal dilatation, mucosa prolapsing.

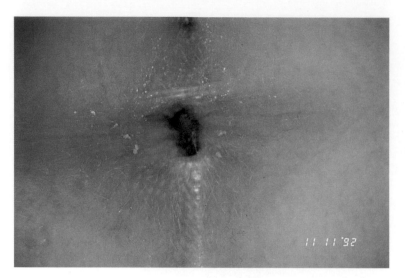

◀ **15.85 Female aged 5 years**
Thick and shiny perianal skin is seen with loss of skin folds, an irregular margin with a deficit at 10 o'clock and a lax anus.
Signs: shiny skin, folds, deficit.

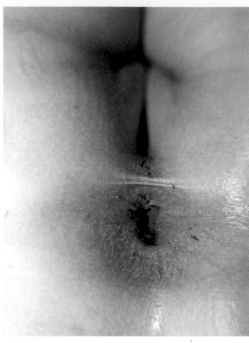

▶ **15.86 Female aged 4 years**
There is perianal reddening with an irregular anal margin and reflex anal dilatation. The perianal skin is thickened with loss of the usual skin folds, and rectal mucosa is visible.
Signs: reddening, thickened skin, reflex anal dilatation, rectal mucosa prolapsing.

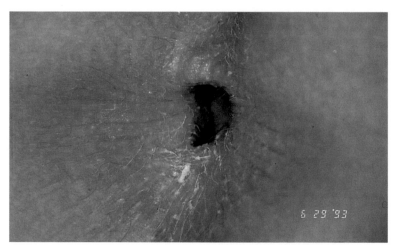

◀ **15.87 Female aged 13 years**
A thickened, smooth, pink anal verge is seen, with a dilated anus.
Signs: skin changes, reflex anal dilatation.

◀ **15.88 Female aged 9 months**
The perianal skin is red and swollen. There is an abraded anal canal and lax sphincter with visible mucosa.
Signs: skin changes, laxity, abrasion anal canal.

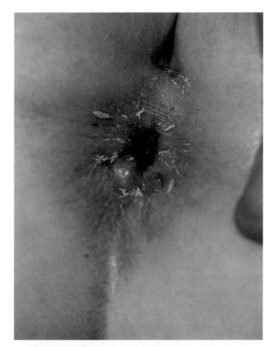

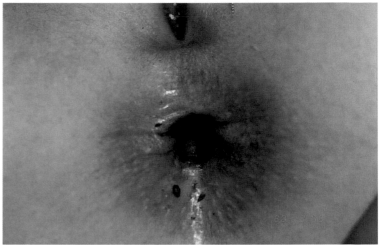

▲ 15.89 Female aged 4 years
Thickened, smooth, red, shiny skin is seen, with swelling of the anal verge. There is reflex anal dilatation, and the anus has deep folds at 2, 4, 8 and 10 o'clock.
Signs: skin changes, reflex anal dilatation, deep folds.

◀ 15.90 Female aged 3 years
Perianal reddening is seen with a large dilated vein at 6 o'clock and smaller veins at 4 and 5 o'clock. There is reflex anal dilatation with rectal mucosa visible.
Signs: reddening, veins, reflex anal dilatation.

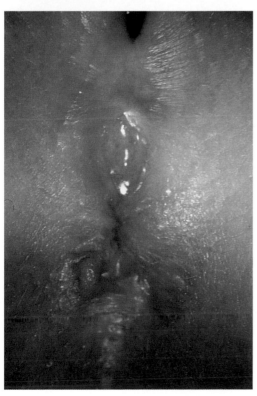

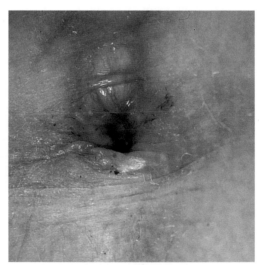

▲ 15.91, ◀ 15.92 Female aged 10 years
Red, swollen anal margin and wide anterior fissure, with reflex anal dilatation and an unusual fold posteriorly. One month later (Fig. 15.92) the anterior fissure has not healed. There is no anal dilatation. Skin tags are seen posteriorly at 5, 6 and 7 o'clock, and unusual skin changes are seen posteriorly.
Signs: reddening, swollen, fissure, reflex anal dilatation, tags.

▼ 15.93 Female aged 9 years

Perianal reddening and a gaping anus are seen. The examination was carried out under general anaesthetic the effect of which is not clear.
Signs: reddening, gaping.

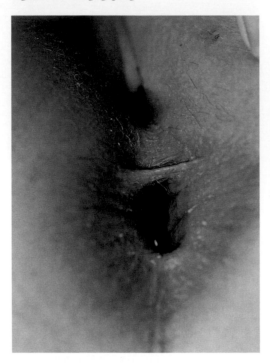

▼ 15.95 Male aged 10 years

Perianal reddening, smooth skin and loss of folds are seen, with reflex anal dilatation and funnelled anus.
Signs: reddening, skin changes, reflex anal dilatation, funnelled.

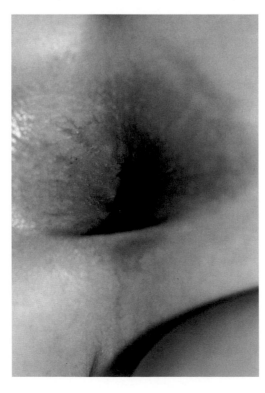

▼ 15.94 Female aged 3 years

There is perianal reddening and the skin is shiny and smooth. Venous congestion is seen, with reflex anal dilatation and prolapsed mucosa.
Signs: reddening, venous congestion, skin changes, rectal mucosa, reflex anal dilatation.

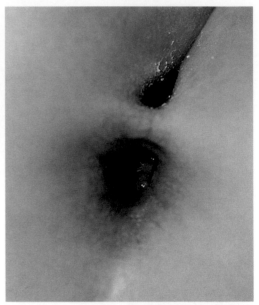

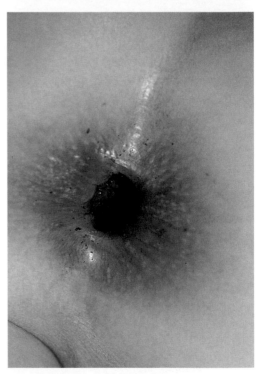

▲ 15.96 Male aged 3 years

Perianal reddening, smooth skin, dilating sphincter with mucosa prolapsing and venous congestion are seen.
Signs: reddening, skin changes, venous congestion, reflex anal dilatation, rectal mucosa.

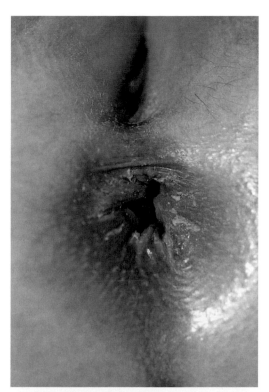

◀ 15.97 Female aged 3 years

Perianal reddening, venous congestion, an irregular margin and a lax sphincter are seen. There are healing fissures at 5, 9 and 11 o'clock.

Signs: perianal reddening, venous congestion, laxity, fissures.

▼ 15.98 Female aged 5 years

There is perianal reddening which continues into the anal canal, swelling perianally, marked venous congestion with a dilated arc of veins anteriorly and a stellate line of anal closure.

Signs: reddening, venous congestion, dilated veins, swelling, stellate line of closure.

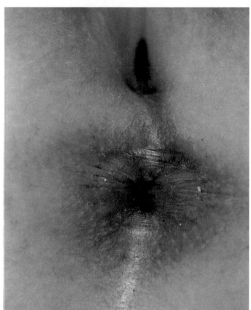

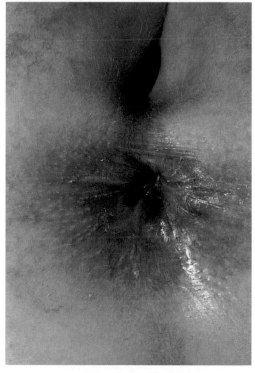

◀ 15.100 Female aged 6 years

There is perianal reddening and swelling, with venous congestion, laxity of the anal sphincter, a superficial fissure at 2 o'clock and abrasions at 5 o'clock.

Signs: reddening, swollen, venous congestion, laxity, fissure, abrasions.

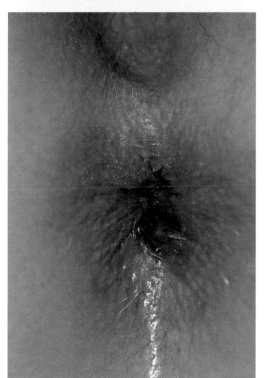

▲ 15.99 Female aged 11 years

Perianal reddening is seen, with a disrupted anal sphincter and an acute fissure at 6 o'clock. Rectal mucosa is visible, and there is a tag at 5 o'clock.

Signs: reddening, fissure, disrupted anal sphincter, rectal mucosa.

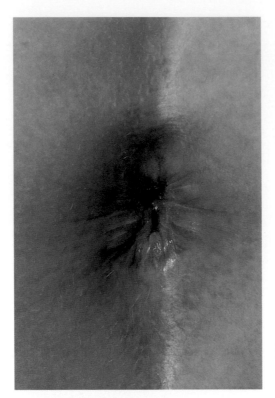

◀ **15.101 Male aged 10 years**
A distorted anal margin is visible with a definite scar posteriorly and possible scar anteriorly. There is venous congestion.

Signs: distorted anal margin, scars, venous congestion.

Note: This photograph was taken 6 months after the photograph in Fig. 15.23 to show healing.

▼ **15.102 Female aged 4 years**
Perianal reddening is seen, with venous congestion, an anal verge deficit at 3 o'clock and a lax anal sphincter with rectal mucosa visible.

Signs: perianal reddening, venous congestion, deficit in anal margin, laxity, rectal mucosa.

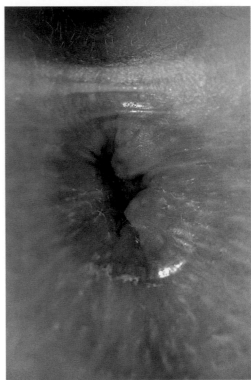

▶ **15.103 Male aged 2 years**
There is perianal reddening, shiny, smooth skin, venous congestion and a gaping, lax sphincter with a deficit in the anal margin at 9 o'clock. Stool is visible.

Signs: perianal reddening, skin changes, venous congestion, stool.

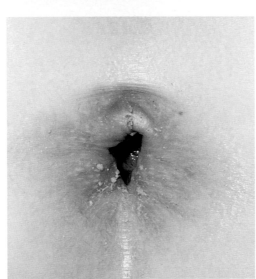

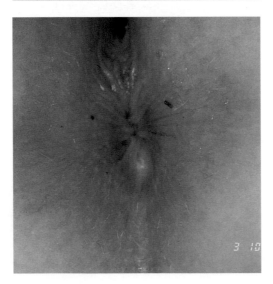

◀ **15.104 Female aged 5 years**
There is perianal pigmentation and a disorganized fold pattern. A scar is seen at 6 o'clock. There are irregular folds anteriorly.

Signs: pigmentation, scar, folds.

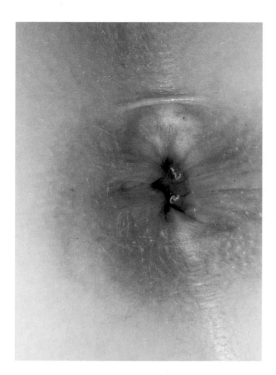

◀ 15.105 Male aged 5 years

Perianal reddening is seen with thick and shiny skin. There is a fan-shaped anterior scar and probable posterior scar, an irregular anal margin, deficits at 5, 7 and 9 o'clock and a lax anus with threadworms visible.

Signs: reddening, skin changes, deficits in anal margin, laxity, scars, threadworms.

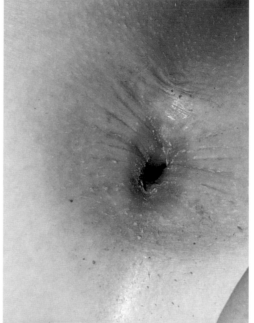

▼ ▶ ▶ 15.106–15.108 Male aged 8 years

The perianal skin is red and smooth, with irregular folds. There is reflex anal dilatation in two phases.

Signs: skin changes, folds, reflex anal dilatation.

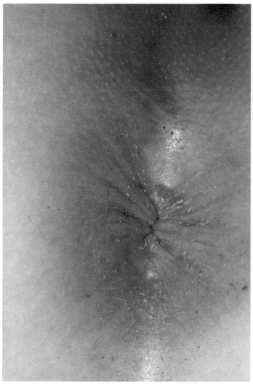

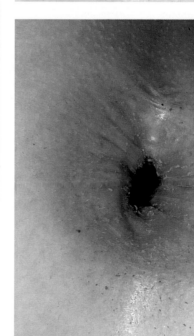

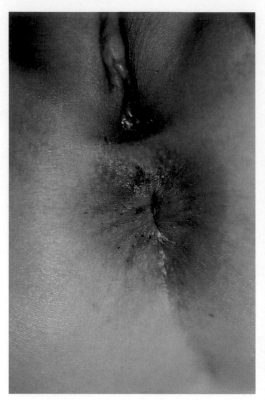

◀ **15.109 Female aged 2 years**
Marked perianal congestion is seen, with swelling. (Note: there was a history of recurrent rectal prolapse and anal abuse.)
Signs: venous congestion.

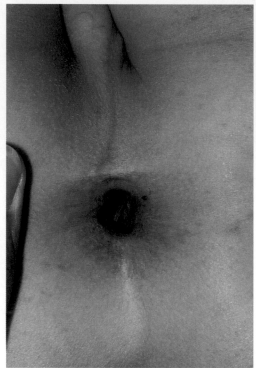

▶ **15.110 Male aged 7 years**
The perianal skin is red and smooth. There is an irregular anal margin, and reflex anal dilatation with stool visible in the rectum.

▶ **15.111 Male aged 9 years**
The perianal skin is red and smooth. There is an irregular anal margin, and reflex anal dilatation.
Signs: skin changes, irregular margin, reflex anal dilatation, stool.
(Note: the boys in Figs. 15.110 and 15.111 were brothers and both gave clear disclosures of anal abuse. Stool in the rectum does not invalidate the signs here.)

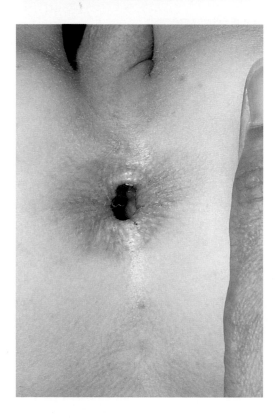

Chapter 16

Sexually Transmitted Diseases

▶ 16.1 Female aged 13 months

She presented to her doctor with unexplained lesions. Small scattered warts are seen across the flattened labia, and irregular skin is seen on the perineum. None of the carers of this child admitted to having a wart infection. A 9-year-old uncle was known to have been involved in inappropriate sexual play. The diagnosis is an unexplained wart infection.

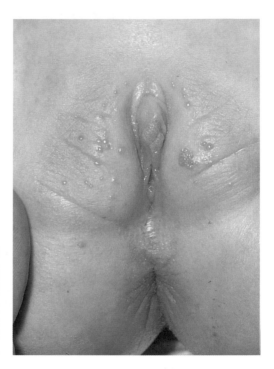

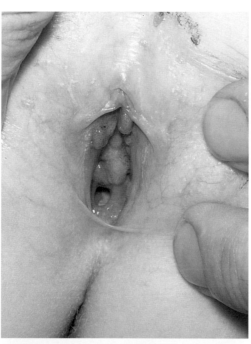

◀ 16.2 Female aged 5 years

The mother took her child to the doctor because of vaginal bleeding. The father was known to have penile warts. There are numerous vulval warts, mainly at the anterior introitus. A normal hymen is visible.

◀ 16.3 Female aged 3 years

She was taken to the doctor by her parents who were having difficulty in cleaning her bottom. There are unexplained perineal warts

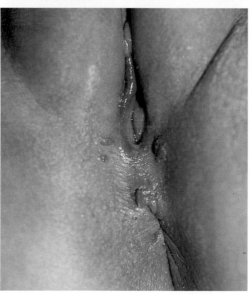

▼ 16.4, ▶ 16.5 Male aged 11 months

He was taken to the doctor for advice. Subsequently it was discovered that both of the separated parents had warts. Gross perianal warts are seen with a few seeded on the scrotum. The mode of transmission of these warts was uncertain.

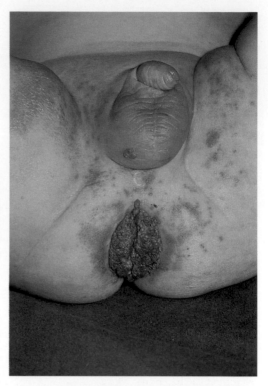

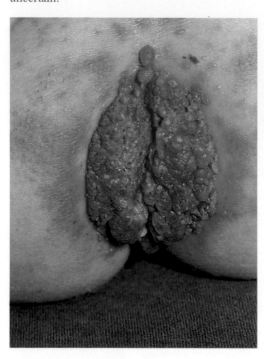

▼ 16.6 Male aged 18 months

The mother asked the health visitor for advice. A large number of genital warts are seen, with co-existing nappy rash. The mode of transmission of these warts was uncertain

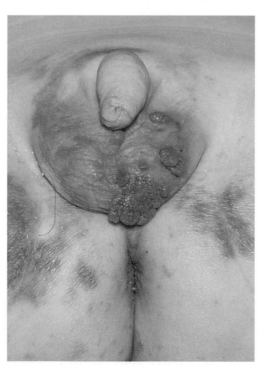

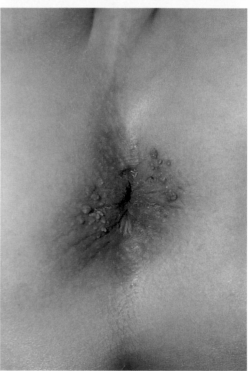

▲ 16.7 Male aged 6 years

The mother took the child to the doctor for advice about the warts. Perianal warts are seen, with venous congestion and irregular folds with a posterior scar. This boy later alleged sexual abuse by his father.

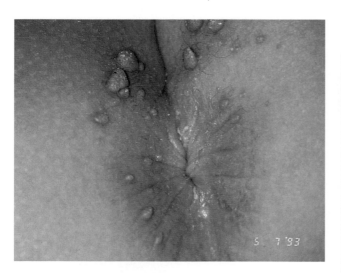

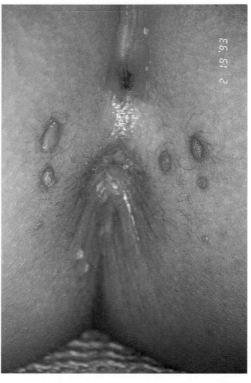

▲ 16.8, ▶ 16.9 Female aged 3 years

She was taken to the doctor by her mother for advice. Scattered perianal warts are visible extending over perineum. A friable posterior fourchette is show which bled on examination. The hymen was normal. The mother insisted that she had transmitted the warts from warts on her own hands but she had none. The mode of transmission of these warts was uncertain but was seen in association with signs consistent with intracrural intercourse.

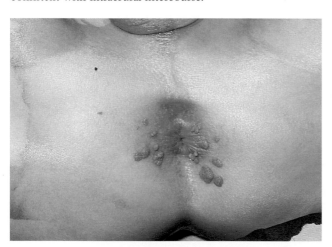

◀ 16.10, ▼ 16.11 Male twins aged 3 years

They were taken to the doctor by their mother who was concerned about their warts. The warts developed within a day or two of each other. Perianal reddening is seen with swelling of the margin and venous congestion, and perianal warts. The father admitted to having penile warts but denied any abuse.

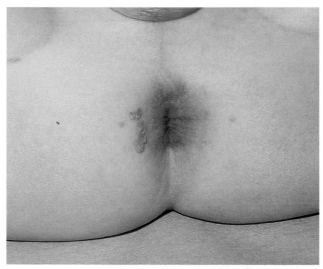

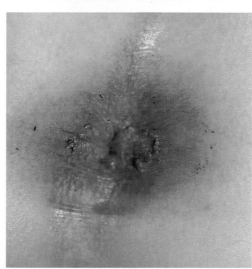

◀ 16.12 Male aged 5 years

He was taken by his mother to the doctor for advice. There are multiple anal warts and associated venous congestion. The mode of transmission of these warts was not known.

▶ **16.13 Male aged 9 years**
One of five children all of whom had been seriously sexually abused. There is perianal reddening, dilated veins and irregular folds. Microbiological investigation showed the reddening to be due to *Candida* infection.

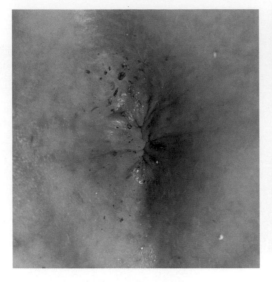

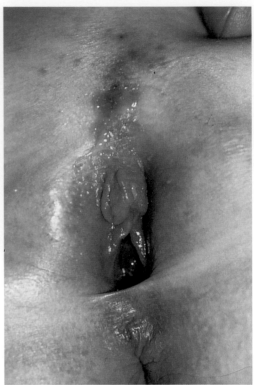

▶ **16.14 Female aged 5 years**
She was referred by her doctor because of purulent vaginal discharge. Marked vulvitis is seen with purulent discharge. Microbiological investigation was negative. Note the vascular abnormality of the perineum.

▶ **16.15, ▶ 16.16 Female aged 7 years**
She was taken to the doctor by her mother because of a painful rash in the genital area. This child and her siblings had been sexually abused by their father a year earlier, who had been convicted. Multiple vesicles are seen on Fig. 16.15. Fig. 16.16 was taken 3 days later and shows healing but persisting discharge and gaping attenuated hymen. Microbiological investigation showed a herpes type I infection.

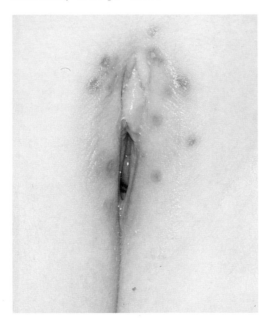

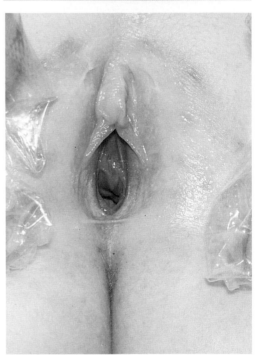

◀ **16.17 Female aged 3 years**
The child was referred to the paediatric department with an allegation of sexual abuse and was complaining of sore genitalia. Pubic lice are seen adherent to the eyelashes.

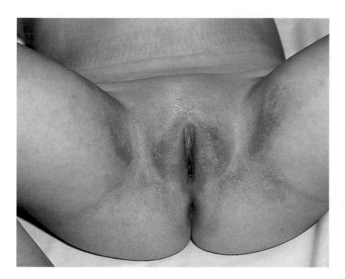

▶ **16.19 Female aged 14 years**

She went to her doctor complaining of soreness. There is a markedly inflamed vulva with satellite lesions. Microbiological investigation confirmed a candidal infection. This girl was sexually active and candidal infection is common in this group of teenagers.

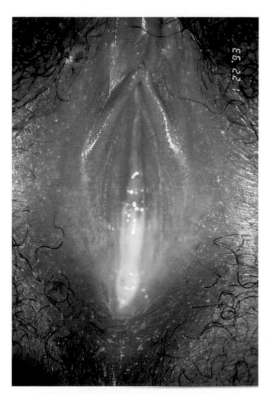

▲ **16.20 Female aged 11 years**

The child was taken by her grandmother to the doctor because of purulent vaginal discharge which had persisted over several months. Vulvitis is seen with creamy coloured discharge. There is a single small abraded area at 11 o'clock. Grossly abnormal anal findings were also seen (see Fig 15.42). Microbiological investigation confirmed a *Trichomonas* infection.

◀ **16.18 Female aged 3 years**

She was taken to the doctor complaining of soreness. Reddening of inner thighs and labia are seen. There was a purulent discharge. Microbiological investigation showed gonorrhoea. The child's father had gonorrhoea of the same type and was convicted.

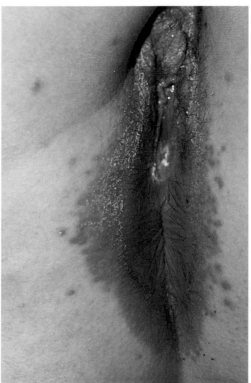

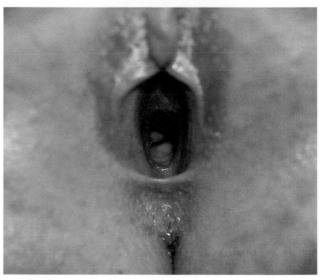

▲ **16.21 Female aged 8 years**

Social services referred the child because she was living in a household with her brother who was a convicted child abuser, and she was known to have an offensive vaginal discharge. There is marked vulvitis, and a gaping hymenal opening with attenuation of the hymen and a rolled edge. A vaginal ridge is seen at 9 o'clock. Microbiological investigation showed a bacterial vaginosis.

Chapter 17

Differential diagnosis of sexual abuse

▶ 17.1 Female aged 4 years

She was being sexually abused and developed secondary enuresis. Reddened labia are seen with satellite lesions. The signs are consistent with abuse and bed-wetting.

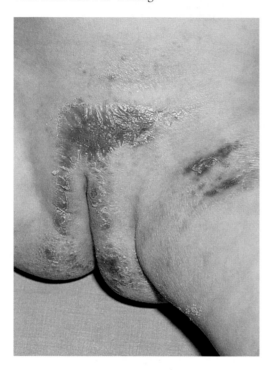

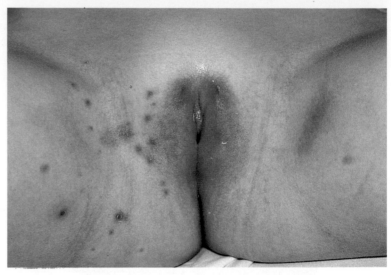

◀ 17.2 Female aged 3 years

She was referred because the social worker was anxious about the possibility of a burn or sexual abuse. Blistering nappy rash is seen.

▼ 17.3 Female aged 6 years

The child was referred because of sexualized behaviour, excessive masturbation and scratching. Thickened, dry, lichenified skin is seen across the mons pubis and labia majora, with wrinkled, flattened labia, and a scooped-out smooth posterior fourchette. Although initially it was felt that the physical signs were due to excessive scratching it is more likely that this child was being sexually abused, i.e. intracrural intercourse

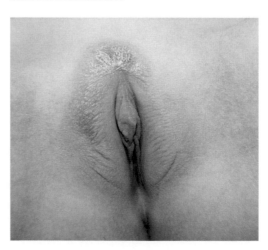

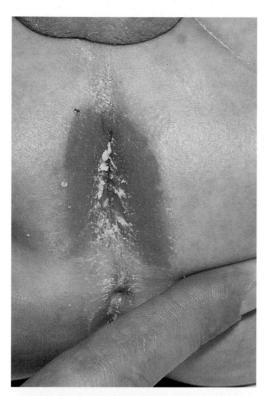

◀ 17.4 Male aged 3 months

His older sister had been sexually abused, and the referring doctor thought the baby had been abused also. There is marked perianal reddening. The diagnosis was nappy rash, which healed after being exposed for 24 hours.

▼ 17.5 Male aged 6 years

Referred by the doctor because of possible sexual abuse. Reddened swollen perianal skin is seen with superficial linear cracks. The signs are consistent with a streptococcal infection, which was proved microbiologically.

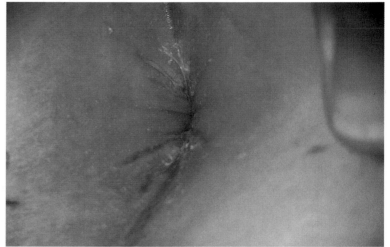

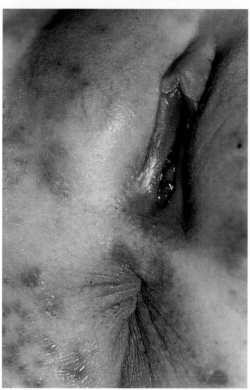

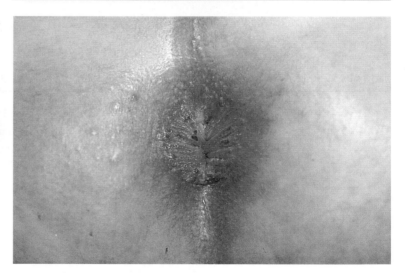

▲ 17.6 Male aged 10 months

Referred because of a sore bottom and possible fingernail scratches. Perianal reddening is seen with small areas of skin loss. The diagnosis was nappy rash associated with diarrhoea.

▲ 17.7 Female aged 18 months

She was referred because of possible sexual abuse. Marked nappy rash is seen. The child also had signs of sexual abuse: congested veins and a swollen red hymen are seen, which are not features of nappy rash.

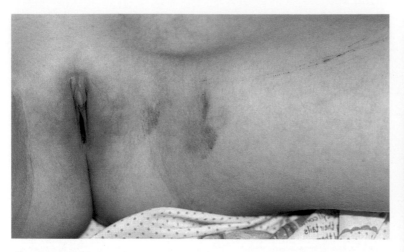

▲ 17.8 Female aged 6 years

Child was referred to hospital after the school nurse noticed bruising on her legs. The child said this was caused by an accident on a home-made see-saw. A diffuse bruise is seen on the inner aspect of the left upper thigh with superficial abrasions. There was also bruising on the outer thighs, and signs of sexual abuse (the father was later convicted). The diagnosis was accidental injury.

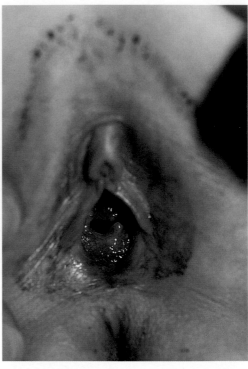

▲ 17.9 Female aged 5 years

She told her teacher she had fallen on the grass at school. She had grass marks on her dress and fresh blood in her pants. There is blood staining with a recent injury to the posterior fourchette. The hymen is red and swollen. This injury was not due to any ordinary accident. Injury of the posterior fourchette is usually specific for sexual assault or penetrating injury.

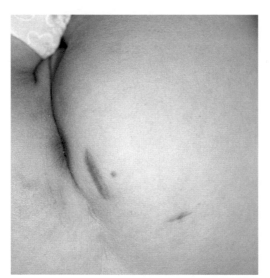

▲ 17.10 Female aged 4 years

She was referred to the paediatrician because of possible sexual abuse. The history was that the child had had recurrent perianal soreness including abscess formation. The abscess had been surgically drained. The anus is normal; there is a surgical scar. The opinion was perianal abscess. There is no known association between sexual abuse and recurrent perianal abscesses in children.

▶ 17.11 Female aged 2 years

She was referred because of possible sexual abuse, after an older sibling was found to have been abused. There is unilateral haemangioma of the labia majora, due to a congenital vascular anomaly.

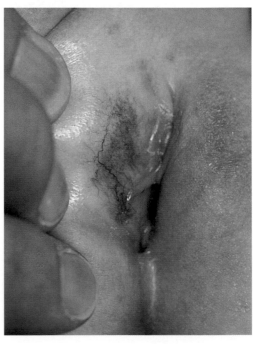

17.12–17.22 (continued overleaf)

This series of photographs show lichen sclerosus et atrophicus. Note the depigmented area round the labia, perineum and anus, and telangiectasia which may bleed on contact. There is concern that lichen sclerosus may be associated or provoked by trauma as in sexual abuse. (Note: in several of these photographs there are genital or anal abnormalities which give rise to concern, and are not clearly the result of skin lesion.) (Sexual abuse of the child in Figs 17.16 and 17.17 was confirmed) (Figs 17.19–17.21 by permission of Dr B. Priestley.)

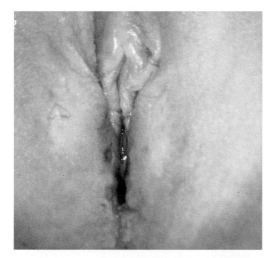
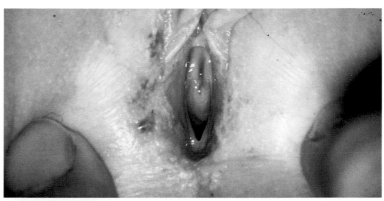
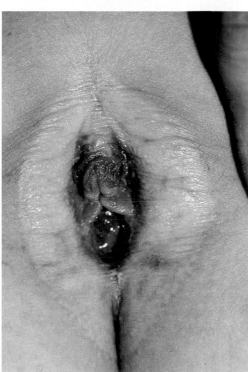
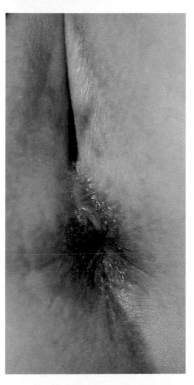
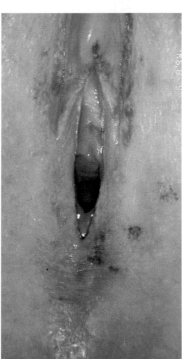
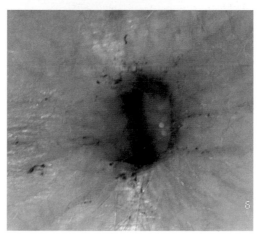

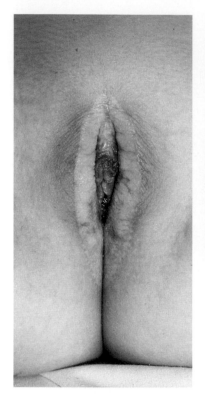

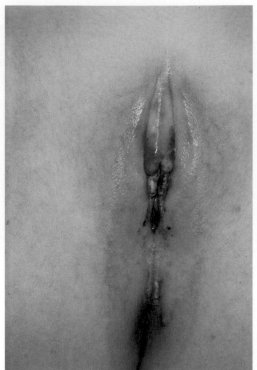

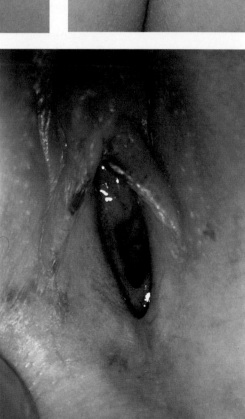

17.12–17.22 (continued)

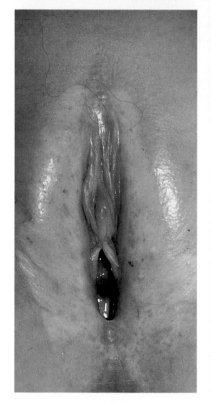

▼ 17.23, ▼ 17.24 Female infant
She was referred because of rectal bleeding. There is marked venous congestion with perianal reddening and a gaping anus with prolapsing mucosa. The signs are due to a tumour. (Note the different nature of the venous congestion here as compared with venous congestion seen in sexual abuse.) (Figs 17.23 and 17.24 by permission of Dr M. Becker.)

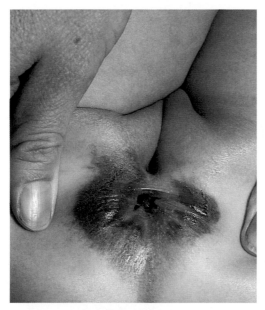

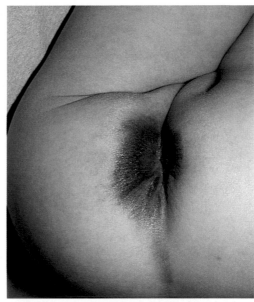

▶ 17.25 Female aged 10 years
She was referred by a gynaecologist who considered the possibility of sexual abuse. A grossly swollen left labia majorum is seen with perianal reddening and a large skin tag. The signs are consistent with Crohn's disease.

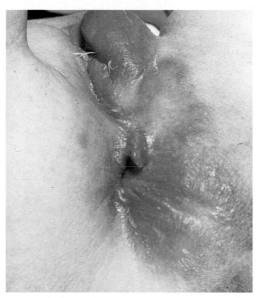

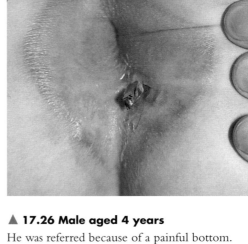

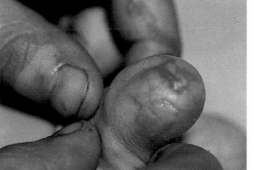

▲ 17.26 Male aged 4 years
He was referred because of a painful bottom. There was a history of falling on a milk bottle 2 years earlier. A shard of glass is seen protruding from the bottom. The diagnosis is accidental injury.

◀ 17.27 Male aged 5 years
He was referred because his sibling had disclosed sexual abuse. There is a non-retractile foreskin, scarred, atrophic skin with prominent veins, and a displaced meatus. The diagnosis was xeroderma obliterans in a sexually abused boy.